P9-DEF-693

SUUM CUIQUE: ESSAYS IN MUSIC

SUUM CUIQUE

ESSAYS IN MUSIC

. .

By

OSCAR G. SONNECK

Essay Index Reprint Series

BOOKS FOR LIBRARIES PRESS
FREEPORT, NEW YORK

STANDARD BOOK NUMBER:
8369-0031-6

LIBRARY OF CONGRESS CATALOG CARD NUMBER:
70-76916

MANUFACTURED
BY
HALLMARK LITHOGRAPHERS, INC.
IN THE U.S.A.

PREFATORY NOTE

The articles forming this book have been reprinted by courteous permission of the original publishers and practically without change. That will account for inconsistencies of opinion, if such there be. I hope that to be the case, since chronic consistency is a virtue in mummies only. At any rate, no attempt was made to adjust earlier to later views. "Paris versions" are always anachronistic, even if better.

Some readers may miss a reprint of such historical essays as that on "Early American Operas," occasionally confused with my book on "Early Opera in America." They are reserved for eventual publication in a second volume of selected assays.

To Dr. Theodore Baker my hearty thanks are due for seeing the book through the press and for his masterly atmospheric translation of the German articles.

O. G. SONNECK.

CONTENTS

SUUM CUIQUE

SUUM CUIQUE

("*Die Musik*," 1907-8, *Vol. VII, No.* 10)

Anarchy! Hypocrisy! Back to antiquity! Dash to the extreme left! Damocles' sword of beauty! Degeneration! Regeneration! Pseudo-music! Celestial super-music! Hellish discords! — What a fine thing the slogan is, forsooth! It works like effervescent lemonade tablets; one sets them foaming according to his personal taste and regales himself and others, but more especially posterity, who will wonder how it was possible to label the latest *querelle des bouffons* with the poet Henckell's saying about our "mighty age." Besides, it is really comical how that repellantly-attractive young lady Salome is all at once shouldered with the responsibility for ideas which may have worn the charm of novelty some ten years ago. One surveying this scrimmage from a distance feels tempted to provide a prelude to Master Draeseke's now so familiar dictum: *Confusion over the* "confusion in music."

In all this there is nothing mighty, save intolerance; while the angle of vision is of the narrowest. So hedged in by the bounds of the realm, that through it all one can hear the too-importunate cry "Neu-Deutschland, Deutschland über alles!" (or "Beneath criticism!" as the case may be). In a word, it would seem that in Germany itself only a few members of the Allgemeiner Deutscher Musikverein might be mentioned who, by and large, have no cause to complain of the public, the critics, and the publishers. A sufficient reason for the more tolerant attitude of the antipodean Dioscuri Strauss and Reger, as contrasted with their opponents, towards even Mendelssohn, who, after all, was not wholly without talent.

Now, what is all this hubbub about? At bottom,
merely whether the so-called immutable canons of
beauty in art permit one to write music as the laws of
his being dictate. Whereupon music-history and musical
æsthetics are forthwith brought into action — *nota bene*,
by both sides — in order to solve a problem which is
none. This prompts me to quote a paradox launched
by the poet Georg Fuchs: "There is no art; there are
only artists." For me there is far more wisdom in this
flash of wit than in dogmas on the limitations and the
true sphere of music, parading in their profundity as the
sole means of grace. The artist has a right to express
himself in tones as the spirit may move. Whoever, for
any reason, finds no pleasure in the product, has an
equal right to vent his displeasure through speech or
pen, but he must not set up to be an art-pontiff or
art-bailiff. No one man, not even a Bach, a Mozart,
Beethoven, Wagner, or Brahms, has yet possessed a
monopoly in the development of music. No more have
Richard Strauss, or Reger, and those who swell their
train for reasons intrinsic or extrinsic. Each one simply
contributes what his nature, influenced by the *Zeitgeist*,
demands of him. Whether this is done in the flush of
youthful zeal or with the cooler calculation of age, is
unimportant. Nor does it matter whether he gains
wealth and fame at a bound, or grows old hungering
before his seed brings its harvest, or even has to await
the music-historian, who in certain circles is painted as
a kind of Satan with queue *à la chinoise*.

It is equally immaterial, on what Master a composer
is based or thinks he is based; for even the wildest anarchist is demonstrably descended from one or more
masters, no matter whether he be afflicted with ill-
assimilated Wagner or ill-digested Kücken. He must
not even be forbidden to employ squeaking piglings as
orchestral color, if only he can impose the impression
on the hearer — no matter whether the latter otherwise

likes or dislikes the work — that his musico-zoölogical cult is spontaneous and sincere. He may frame quadruple fugues, or fashion a musical projection of the Leaning Tower of Pisa, should the spirit irresistibly urge him thereto. Whether genius or botcher, Jove or ox, equal rights for all. One must not even dispute an artist's right to be tasteless from the very depths of his being. Let him therefore sow whatsoe'er he will. But when he brings the fruits of his spiritual travail to market, let him, in turn, be tolerant. He must not fly into a rage when hearers and critics weigh his product with the same sincerity which constrained him to shape his note-heads thus or so. One who is confronted with a work given over to publicity, and also takes art seriously, has precisely the same right as the artist to be an anarchist or reactionary, according to his disposition; and the artist, too, has really no right to dispute *his* right to be tasteless from the very depths of his being.

Not what the composer does, but how he does it — that is the point at issue. The form, the material, the plastic or philosophical subject-matter, is the foundation from which he throws out a bridge for the valuation of his work. This foundation is the given premise, the glass, through which the composer desires his work to be surveyed, and the question is simply whether or no he has attained what he aimed at. If you approach any given work with a set of preconceived artistic beliefs, you substitute an artificial premise for the natural one, and forgo in advance the possibility of impartial receptivity. Should your premise be the same as the artist's, an overvaluation of the work usually results; but if the two are antagonistic, the work is sure to be most despitefully used. Two instances: When the composer announces a quadruple fugue, the opponent of quadruple fugues should stay at home. But, if he does venture into the lion's den, he must be prepared to meet something he dislikes. He can reasonably expect only a

quadruple fugue, and not a symphonic poem.   The
matter to be decided is solely to what extent the composer succeeded in writing a well-considered quadruple
fugue.   On the other hand, in case the composer takes it
into his head to construct a musical projection of the
Leaning Tower of Pisa, the opponents of program-music
may view this attempt with regret, but they have no
right to expect a quadruple fugue.   Contrariwise, they
are most decidedly justified in demanding a demon-
stration *ad aures* of the Leaning Tower of Pisa instead
of, say, the two leaning towers of Bologna.   Hence, let
a quadruple fugue be a quadruple fugue; let program-
music be program-music.   But both must, above all
else, be rich in musical invention!   So this Æsthetic of
the Specific requires, so to speak, homœopathic rather
than allopathic criticism.

Herewithal, war is by no means declared on either
the passionate or dispassionate, objective discussion of
æsthetic problems.   But theories have nothing in
common with an impartial estimate of a given work.
They belong in another sphere of interest, which is, in
its way, as important and necessary as artistic creation—and this by virtue of the incontrovertible consideration that everything, that exists, evidently must exist.
As far as the creative artist is concerned, historical,
æsthetic and theoretical discussions bear instruction of
chiefly technical value for him.   They are adapted, like
ball-playing for the muscles, to develop his technique
on the side of harmony, form, etc., but more particularly in the matter of taste.   It will hardly be denied
that the creative artists themselves are not invariably
persons of most refined taste; or — if this be not admitted — at least that they hold no monopoly of good
taste.   And if even this be denied, it must surely be
allowed that good taste, like any other human attribute,
can be stunted or grow to maturity.   He who by nature
has no taste — and many otherwise gifted composers

seem to suffer from this deficiency — can at least be taught to avoid glaring errors of taste, as the blind learn not to run against the wall. Now, who shall undertake the inculcation of taste? First of all, the Masters themselves, through the example of their works. True, the more magnetic their art, the more dangerous are they for composers still impressionable as wax, and many a gifted mind has become — not from lack of individuality, but on account of too early familiarity with patterns predesigned for him by Nature — a victim of the patent "process of dissimilitudinarization", by which the faithful disciples seek a further development of precisely what is perishable in the pattern, namely, the mannerisms. If only for this reason, the composers cannot claim an exclusive right to show the way to good taste through their works. Just as little can he claim this right, who has made it his lifework to excise the kernel — the representative types, as it were — from masterworks by means of investigations and comparisons in the history, technique and philosophy of art. The conclusions reached by such theoretical studies may be more or less ingenious, well grounded, shrewd and fascinating, but are not binding. At best, they merely crystallize the precipitate of personal taste into a confession of faith. They always are and must be subjective (at most, collectively subjective), and never of fundamental, universal applicability. More especially, with respect to the future. In any event, it is immaterial whether a theorist or critic (in the above sense) hits the mark with his prophecies or stultifies himself. He, too, precisely like the creative artist, can yield only what his own nature demands of him. His importance for art lies in the fact that his teachings, through the vibration of sympathetic chords in kindred souls, open the eyes of artists who yet are blind or purblind, and draw them to their predestined paths. While plotting this critical weather-report we must not be led

astray by the circumstance that the cleverest theorists
sometimes cast the gauntlet before the most prosperous
talents.   However well-intentioned, the theorist simply
can not make himself a universal guide to good taste;
all that he can do is to provide a positive stimulus for
the artist of kindred affects.   Unless we aim at inbreed-
ing, we should rejoice when all possible theoretical
colors crowd our palette.   Then each artist can select
those which he lacks for the clear emblazonment of his
artistic mission.   When once the far-reaching benefit,
for art, of such a tolerant conception is recognized in
principle, any individual may be as intolerant toward any
other as ever he pleases.   Then we should have the free
competition of contending forces instead of the em-
bittered blind-alley feuds which so deplorably distinguish us musicians from other artists.

The labyrinthine and withal narrow way from the
score to the concert-hall and the stage has the natural
effect, that we musicians cannot have the same consideration for producers of dissimilar kind as we might
willingly show, were the possibilities of "arriving" of a
less complicated sort.   Still, that is no reason for turning a necessary evil into a disgraceful outrage.   For an
outrage it is when music, in the pretended interest of
so-called progress and the thinly-veiled interests of a
"spiritual coalition," is forced into the straitjacket of
some few "tendencies," whether it be the tendency of
the trilateral fortification Berlioz-Liszt-Wagner, or yet
beyond them to Richard Strauss, or to Brahms and
through him on to Reger.   Music, now as ever, is a
realm of unlimited possibilities.   Beside her mountain-
heights she has her hill-countries; she has her steppes,
and also her forests; her rivers and her rivulets, her
sunrise and her sunset.   Such a wealth of diversified
charms has she, that every taste may find what it
seeks.   Now some one digs a couple of canals and tries
with might and main to lead taste—that is, the evolution

of music — into them, without stopping to think
that canals are artificial and gradually get choked with
mud. Many ways lead to the Beautiful; precisely so
many ways are there, as individualities. So with the
notion of "tendency" we cannot go far, for it postulates
a tablature of common characteristics, instead of finding
the chiefest charm in just those subtle divergences
which do not permit of tabulation. Now, as that
which is common must naturally form the groundfloor,
we might say that the partisan of the æsthetics of "tendency" artificially obstructs sundry wellsprings of music,
joins the union, and starts boycotting right and left.

In this chamber of horrors two Procrustean beds
occupy the place of honor; our so-called *absolute* music,
and our no less so-called *program*-music. This limitation
is masterly, but is further refined by those who consider
only the one or the other of these two species to be
admissible. Such renunciation of either species for one's
æsthetic home-consumption assuredly has a certain
charm and a certain value in educating one's taste; but
whether one does (like your humble servant) or does
not draw the line strictly between musical symbolics
and musical symbolism, and is or is not able to follow
all the contortions of certain programmists with pleasure,
not to mention the academic parade-march of certain
absolutists, no æsthetic casuistry can make away with
the fact that these two species have existed side by side
for centuries. And once again we stand face to face
with the simple consideration that whatever exists evidently must exist. The high tides in the two species do
not, however, always coincide, and our historians may
sometime accept the view which I brought forward as
long as ten years ago, which is, that a process of mutual
inoculation goes on between the two species in their
various seasons. Furthermore, since every separate
entity perishes in order to bloom again — through
regeneration or, if you prefer, through reincarnation —

in a new form, there is no reason for æsthetic anxiety.
Program-music, which for the nonce is, so to say, the
fashionable flower, will wither, will make room for the
"absolute" music which it has fructified — until the
pendulum again swings over to the other side. This
renewal of growth will repeat itself till the millennium
of music, although springing from the soil of fresh means
and modes of expression. In brief, the style changes,
the genus remains. There is, however, no metronome
for this natural, automatic process, and not even the
cleverest theorist has the slightest influence on its tempo.
Whenever the development of music depends on anything tangible, we shall generally find some external
condition, some circumstance of organization or climate,
in the environment of the creative artist: his surroundings while growing up, the composition of the orchestra,
the support of the theatre by private or public means,
the lack of concert-halls, the interest in choral singing,
the influence of war or peace on the popular readiness
to support musical enterprises, and other like matters
of a purely economic nature.

There are those who will find in these observations an
undervaluation of the idea "tendency." Perhaps we
can reach an agreement if a boundary-line be drawn
between this idea and that of the "school." What is
meant by this differentiation may be figuratively expressed as follows: Whereas, in the case of the "school,"
the development can spread by radiation, with the
"tendency" the rays are concentrated in one focus. By
following up this conception you will find that the
æsthetics of "tendency" must lead, on the one hand, to
an overvaluation of congenial spirits, and, on the other,
to pessimism with regard to one's own times. Otherwise
I, for my part, am unable to explain the oft-repeated
Jeremiads over the current poverty of invention. But
these same Jeremiads are, in turn, only the expression
of an unwholesome, chronic intolerance. He who seeks

after poverty with Diogenes' lantern, will find poverty. Whether we harbor in our midst geniuses of the incontestable greatness of Bach, Mozart, Beethoven, or Wagner, the future alone may show. However, the creative wealth of an epoch does not depend on the geniuses, but on the number of those gifted ones who possess a profile of their own. Of such there is certainly no scarcity to-day. On the contrary, our times, in that respect, are on a par with any other epoch. But we must really know our contemporaries. Of course, any one who is possessed of the tendency devil will pass by many with indifferent haste, or survey them from the wrong side, or pronounce a premature sentence on those who escape all classification and whose individuality hides behind their peculiarities as behind a hedge of thorns. Where, for example, will the æsthetics of tendency in Germany place Arnold Mendelssohn, Iwan Knorr, Anton Beer-Walbrunn? They belong to no category, and yet are striking types.

But such artists of whom too little is known should not be contrasted with or weighed over against one another, neither ought one to reproach them with the "good old" times or the "better new" times, or even boycott them because their style is not controlled by the syndicate of Strauss & Co., and because they have a mind to go their own way apart. If the creative assets of our times are to be estimated according to such criterions, then, indeed, our cavillers at the actual are right. But the outside world, at all events, need not let itself be drawn into this unprofitable quarrel. And it must be most emphatically insisted upon, that Germany has no claims whatever to a monopoly of talent at the present day. Or is it claimed that Debussy, d'Indy, Fauré, Dukas, Puccini, Martucci, Bossi, Elgar, Delius, Holbrooke, Bantock, MacDowell, Loeffler, Converse, Hadley, Chadwick, Parker, Stillman Kelley, Rimsky-Korsakow, Scriabine, Rebikoff, Rachmaninow, Balakirew,

Stenhammar, Sjögren, Sibelius, Lange-Müller, Nielson, Peterson-Berger, and many beside, who are cultivating music *after their own fashion*, are Germans, or quite unworthy of mention when a review is held of the German artists by the grace of God? In music, as in other matters, Germany is only one great power among the great powers. The other lands have allowed themselves to be fructified by the Wagner-Liszt-Brahms epoch only in so far as was artistically necessary; for the rest, they have found, either outside of Germany or at home, such inspiration for their music of the present or the future as comports with their national character. There is an inclination to poke fun at the average Italian, who, in conversation with *forestieri*, is fond of airing his next-of-kinship with Dante. Now, it is an unwelcome, unpalatable truth, which can not, of course, be appreciated to the full by the German himself, though all the better by outsiders, that for something like thirty years the average German musician has tested foreign compositions, first of all, for their German content. Should this latter be of little consequence, the whole work — for him — is apt to be thought of little consequence. Now, is the fact that the French, the Russians, etc., found it easier than the Germans to tear themselves from the arms of the giant, Wagner, any reason for getting angry with them just for doing so? Such chauvinism is the height of intolerance. Honor your German masters, but do not deny other peoples the right, when they feel the power stirring within them, to follow their own devices after a century of German tutelage.

(Translated by Theodore Baker.)

MUSIC AND PROGRESS

MUSIC AND PROGRESS

(*New Music Review*, 1908)

The popular mind believes progress to be an irresistibly steady development from good to better, but progress is rather the prompt and logical adaptation to the exigencies of changing conditions. An individual or a nation ceases to be progressive when they adhere to the methods of the past without preparing for the future. Things come and go in a kind of counterpoint, and it is not always easy to distinguish between the germ of decay and the germ of development. Nor is it at all true that the new is always really *better* than the old. It is simply different, a matter of necessity, the logical result of the modulation into new conditions; and the inventors, prophets or discoverers of any idea, political, economic, artistic, technical, are merely those who scent this change. All this seems so obvious that I almost feel ashamed of having mentioned it. Yet this cold-blooded and perhaps prosaic attitude towards progress does not appeal to those—and they are in the majority—who ultimately expect another Eden. Nor is it a Christian attitude. Still, it is just as stimulating ethically as the "progress-equal-to-better" theory, and just as sensible. Indeed, if we weigh them both in matters of art, and particularly of music, it cannot be doubtful which of the two theories is the more correct and fruitful.

Logically, the popular conception of progress would lead to the dogma that music is steadily becoming "better." In other words, sooner or later some composer without special talent would produce better music than Wagner, Beethoven, Mozart, Haydn, Bach, Monteverdi, Palestrina, simply because he had the good fortune to be born a few centuries after them. The conclusion seems inevitable, yet the absurdity is apparent. No, with all due respect for the lessons of our youth, progress is not a matter of chronology. It will be asked, Admitting that Monteverdi, for instance, was a creative genius of the first rank, that his innovations have not been surpassed in daring, that his art appealed to his contemporaries with the strongest possible force, that his insight into the esthetics of opera was amazingly keen—admitting all this, are not his operas primitive and crude as compared with those of Wagner? Is "Tristan und Isolde" really not an improvement on "Orfeo"? In many respects, unmistakably, and it would be foolish to deny a chronological improvement within a given form or species of music. But this admission immediately fixes the sphere of strength of the pet popular theory: it is relatively correct, not absolutely. And relatively correct only within narrow limits, inasmuch as, even in the field of opera, improvements do not progress chronologically in all eternity. Otherwise, again the absurd conclusion would force itself on us that some future opera composer would produce better operas than Wagner, not because he had the necessary genius, but because he came after Wagner. Or, looking into the past, are Mozart's operas really better than Gluck's, and Wagner's better than Mozart's? Some people do not hesitate to say so, but they put on the scales not only the actual musical-dramatic values, but also the *taste* of their own times, not to mention individual preferences. But changing taste is not necessarily a criterion of value. Once an art-form has passed the experimental stage, as in Monteverdi's case, and has attained maturity, as with Gluck or Mozart, the fact that a later generation, and naturally so, prefers the works of its own times, has precious little to do with the actual comparative value. Gluck's "Iphigenia in Tauris," Mozart's "Don Giovanni," Verdi's "Falstaff" and Wagner's "Tristan und Isolde" are merely different manifestations of mature genius in a mature form of art at different periods, but one is not *better* than the other.

Exactly the same arguments prevail, if we approach the field of oratorio, symphony, chamber music, song, etc. I, for one, do not concede for a moment Beethoven's symphonies or quartets to be better than certain really inspired mature works by Haydn and Mozart, or those of Brahms and César Franck to be better than those of Beethoven; though occasionally, when I feel the fascination of our times, they appeal to me more strongly than those of Beethoven, in whom, after all, a different "Zeitgeist" was at work. An experience, which many worshippers at the shrine of the classics will share with me.

Even in the matter of orchestration, it is doubtful whether the theory here attacked is sound. It would be carrying poverty to China to deny that Richard Strauss and Debussy are supreme masters of the orchestral palette, but does their orchestra really sound more beautiful than that of Mozart? Or, not to confuse the fine distinctions which alone prevent such discussions from leading us astray, does it sound more perfect? By virtue of his genius Mozart employed exactly that orchestral medium which fitted his ideas; otherwise he would not have been a genius. No later master could essentially improve on his orchestration. A re-instrumentation would produce a glaring anachronism and would destroy the perfect balance between the style and spirit of his ideas and the proper vehicle for their expression. In detail such an attempt might sound more beautiful, more opulent; but the whole, as a work of art perfect in itself, would suffer. On the other hand, an equally painful anachronism and stylistic caricature would be the result, if Mozart returned to life and re-instrumentated Strauss's "Heldenleben" in the manner of the Jupiter Symphony. Undoubtedly, Mozart's successors have expanded the orchestral possibilities, have enriched the palette, have introduced new principles of orchestral coloring and have given us a world of orchestral beauty quite beyond even a genius like Mozart. But there the comparison ceases to be fair; the fitness of things, and "progress," become incommensurable. The truth practically is, that Mozart's instrumentation fits his ideas beyond improvement, just as Wagner's instrumentation fits Wagner's ideas.

The same truth applies more or less to Mozart's contemporaries and predecessors; for instance, Gluck, Haydn, Händel, Bach. Indeed, he who once has heard Bach's orchestra sound as it should sound, that is, with a well-preserved harpsichord as backbone of the whole, the wind-instruments doubled and trebled according to the esthetic tenets of his age, and other lost traditions revived (to which the legendary lack of dynamic subtleties certainly did *not* belong), will have come to the conclusion that Johann Sebastian Bach was as great a virtuoso on his orchestra as Richard Strauss is on his. Because it sounds different and somewhat unfamiliar to us, does not imply that it is less beautiful, and if two works of art sound equally beautiful, one cannot possibly be better than the other. The trouble merely is that we so seldom have occasion to hear the old masters properly. So many conductors shut their eyes with contempt born of ignorance to the plainest historical demands of style, disregard all proper proportion between the different groups of the orchestra, play the old works without instruments called for in the score, or smother the few wind-instruments under an avalanche of strings, and then lay it at the door of the old masters if their orchestra sounds primitive, crude, unbalanced and queer.

From whatever quarter the chronological chronic-improvement theory is approached, it fails and must fail because it does not take into account that each age is confronted by different problems which the genius of the age solves at the psychological moment. Once solved, this particular problem defies further solution. Thus Palestrina created works of art which neither Bach nor Wagner nor the unborn masters of the future could duplicate in the same self-sufficient perfection; and, of course, *vice versa*.

And the lesson to be learned of this protest against a very sentimental and attractive but radically wrong theory? It leads to a coquettish, conceited over-estimation not of the present only, but, far worse, to a wilful neglect of the past, of the immediate past, even, and thereby becomes detrimental to the best interests of our art. That a sincere admiration for the beauties of the music of to-day and to-morrow may travel brotherly with a sincere admiration for the beauties of the music of yesterday, has been abundantly proved, but what is possible for a few is possible for many. Indeed, this tolerant attitude should be made the paramount issue in the development of musical taste.

In the fine arts, this catholicity of taste is recognized as a fundamental principle. There nobody, unless he be a crank, operates with the term of "better" from a shaky chronological observatory. The pictures, the statues, the palaces, themselves bear testimony too potent against any such attempt. Of course, the fine arts have this enviable advantage, that, for instance, a picture needs but a wall and a nail to speak for itself, and to be permanently before the public eye, whereas in music the ways and means for public utterance are so costly and complicated that a similar immortality becomes a physical impossibility. The nearest approach to the art museum we have is in methodically developed musical libraries, though they furnish only a very poor substitute, as the scores are but the shadows of music. Yet music possesses one advantage over the fine arts for this very reason: the bulk of the works of every age and of every art are monuments of mediocrity and not worthy of preservation. In the fine arts, thousands of these mediocrities and atrocities are dragged ruthlessly through the centuries together with the works of lasting art-value. In music, the survival of the fit and fittest is simplified by the otherwise deplorable difficulty of utterance. This granted, the question arises: Do we make the best of this advantage? Do we systematically build, as it were, dams and dikes to regulate the maelstrom of devastation and endeavor to save what should be saved? Hardly!

It is not so much a question of revival as of survival. Our musical life is as yet too poorly organized to keep somewhere and somehow, in imitation of the art museum, at least a modest selection of the representative music of all ages, nations and schools before the public and the musicians themselves. This dream of a museum of music rather than of scores may yet be realized, but until this "Stilbildungschule" becomes feasible (the problem is not at all so difficult or costly as it looks), we should attempt the next best thing. If a work composed thirty years ago, no matter whether Mendelssohn, Schumann, Wagner, Liszt or Berlioz stood sponsor, was then really a beautiful work of art, it is still beautiful to-day, regardless of changes in "taste," and it deserves to survive and to be heard. If changes in "taste" militate against the survival, then it behooves those who shape taste to force the idea of taste into the proper channel. They must consistently and unceasingly preach the doctrine that beauty is eternal and good taste not synonymous with fickle fashion or fads. Ideas (in the Platonic sense) are the real and only moving forces. Once rooted in the soil of public principle, they become irresistible and their growth projects, as it were, all the latent consequences into our daily life. Accordingly, once the principle that musical beauty of any school or style should be made to survive, underlies our art-conduct, the ways and means for this survival will present themselves automatically in spite of all obstacles. The popular chronic-improvement theory is, unfortunately, one of these obstacles. It plainly tends to impoverish rather than to enrich us. Nor does the opportunistic attitude of those who pride themselves on their practical views of life and smile at us idealists, lead to tangible reforms. If people crave for the "better," they should not seek it at the esthetic notion counter, but where improvements are possible and necessary— in the organization and development of our musical life. Let them study, unbiased by personal preferences, as easiest accessible, the piano and song literature of the past fifty years, select what is unmistakably good, and then look for the names of the composers and the titles of the pieces on the current concert programs, in the studios of the teachers, in the homes of music-lovers. They will be amazed at the starvation rations of our musical diet, and they will be compelled to admit that "wilful neglect of the past" is more than the pessimistic slogan of cranky antiquarians and critics.

NATIONAL TONE-SPEECH
VERSUS VOLAPÜK—WHICH?

NATIONAL TONE-SPEECH
VERSUS VOLAPÜK—WHICH?

("*Die Musik,*" 1903)

The irradiation of national character yields what we
are wont to call nationality in music. This is essentially
different from so-called "local color," which is often
merely a well-weighed spice and an effective device in
art, even in the hand of a foreigner; whereas the former
pervades the artist's very flesh and blood. Without
overt action on his part, it lends his individuality a
certain communistic tinge, and eludes superficial imitation. For music is no cosmopolitan growth, flourishing
beyond time and space. And the musician likewise is
rooted in Mother Earth. He is, like every individual,
the product of environment and education, the more
or less pronounced representative of his people. Moreover, between the peoples and, to go a step further,
between the races, there exist typical differences.

Of this fact our daily experience, and comparative
folklore, permit no doubt to arise. An Italian's gestures,
even at a distance, strongly contrast with those of a
German. Their temperaments, whose reflection the
gestures are, have equally distinguishable characteristics. For example, the German *Schwung* is by no means
equivalent to the Italian *slancio*, and both are distinctly
dissimilar from the *élan* of the Frenchman or the cold-
blooded dash and go of the American. The strange
veering from melancholy to fierce passion, a national
trait of the Russians, may have a pendant among other
peoples, but its full equivalent is unknown to me.

Some are fond of confuting the above considerations
by pointing out that no people has remained racially
pure, and that within the various peoples themselves

there subsist remarkable differences in character. True enough, a genuine Bavarian is not easily mistaken for a Pomeranian, and still less a genuine Irishman for an Englishman; but with such arguments one does not simplify the problem, but complicates it, together with all its inferences. It may be said that, in general, political connections, mixed marriages, common language, education and interests, leave their various impress on nations, so that dissimilarities within the political boundaries merely make the impression of dialects (if I may say so) of the folk-character. That the given folk-character may show, on analysis, a mixture of characters, makes little difference. By outsiders it is not apprehended as a mixture, but as a unity, just as green is, psychologically, a color in itself, being a mixture of yellow and blue only for the analytical mind. The total impression naturally depends on the stronger or weaker admixture of the several colors; thus the folk-character of the United States has an Anglo-Saxon stamp, for the reason that among its heterogeneous elements the Anglo-Saxon decidedly predominates.

If these things are of significance for the entire outward and inward life of the nations, they are so for music, too.

It does not do to speak of an international musical language just because the nations which come into contact with our musical life use the same instruments, the same scale-degrees—in brief, the same raw material. Painters also work with the same material everywhere, and still a Frenchman expresses himself differently from a German. The paintings of a Besnard, even without his signature, could not dissemble their French origin, and those of a Franz Stuck would infallibly bear the mark: Made in Germany. Not even similarity of technique or similarity in construction can obliterate the folk-character which pervades the artist's individuality.

Attention has been called—and not by the shallowest of our connoisseurs—to peculiar characteristics in the works of our Semitic masters. There be those who smile at this view, and would seek to trace its source to studious race-hatred. Their ridicule is ill-directed. When the sounding symbols of the inner life—melody, harmony, rhythm, and the rest—pour forth from the folk-soul of the Magyar in form-types which are seemingly controlled by psychic laws, and which affect the Teuton or the Latin as foreign, why not the same with the Semite? However environment and artistic training may have overlaid the colors, it were strange and regrettable did they not show through here and there.

The neo-Russians reproach Tschaikowsky with foreignism. They look on him, in contrast to Mussorgsky and others, as no true representative of their nation. Now, Tschaikowsky was no musical ultra-patriot, no tinker of problems; he did not seek to parade his Russianism; and, nevertheless, his predilection for the Italians and Mozart cannot disguise his Russian origin from us occidentals. We (as Riemann puts it) find in him a lyrically gifted, genuinely musical nature, but at the same time a good native Russian.

The Bohemian String-Quartet affords another instance. It has been noticed by many that these four artists give a Slavic coloring to all the works they play. While they interpret Bohemian and Russian masters with an inimitable realism and truth to nature, their reproduction of our classics has the effect of an exceedingly beautiful, charmful translation from the German into the Slavic. Under their hands, Beethoven becomes a kind of Dvořák. They themselves are probably unconscious of this. They cannot do otherwise, and any attempt at Teutonizing would be wrecked on natural laws over which they have no control. The same naturally applies to the interpretation of Italian or Russian works by Germans or Frenchmen.

Any one trying to treat this problem *in extenso*, as far as heterogeneous races may be considered, would constitute himself an Apostle of Commonplaces. The champions of an international musical speech must, therefore, confine themselves to Middle and Western Europe, if their theory (which is also their ideal) is to remain rational. This would limit us to those countries which for centuries have been continuously interchanging their musical ideas.

Now, it cannot be denied that England, the Netherlands, France, Italy, Germany, etc., have had a so nearly similar schooling and have so mutually fructified each other that their individuality has not emerged uncompromised by this manifold intermingling. But there is a vast difference betwixt a blending and an obliteration of characteristic traits. So long as peoples differ one from the other in all remaining arts, we cannot for a moment suppose that the art of music will lose its diversified physiognomy—more especially not, so long as folk-songs present such strong contrasts as they now do, and illustrate the fact that the characteristics of language help to shape directly (and in the case of instrumental music indirectly) the national characteristics of music. It seems to me that what has really become international is, at bottom, only the technique of our art-music. Beyond this, one should not surrender himself to any acoustic illusion. And how little, in certain cases, this international technique is able to bridge over the antagonisms and dissimilarities between the national souls, we can see in Mozart. The course of his development made him, in many matters, the descendant of Italian masters, for which reason overly clever persons set him down for an Italian composer. But then, how does it happen that even to this day he has never gained a firm footing in Italy, despite his Italian airs? Is it because he was unworthy a triumphal progress across the Alps? Is it because he is a true

German in Italian garb, and because the Italians penetrate his partial disguise and feel that he is not one of themselves, that he strikes chords not in consonance with their character? This last I believe to be true, and that the striking contradiction between the external and internal expression of his Italian operas, in particular, have conditioned Mozart's status in Italy.

So, twist and turn as one will, the theory of an international musical speech is not tenable. And with this disappears its qualification as an ideal aim, and thus its applicability to our future musical activities. And should any one invoke the aid of music-history, with the assertion that the branches grafted on the tree of music have borne such an abundance of good fruits during the last five centuries, that their continuance in bearing is a necessity for musical progress, he is building a castle in cloudland. For such musical grafting has done at least as much harm as good. The good (as we have pointed out) consists in the interchange of technical acquirements; the harm, in a foreignism which disintegrates what it touches.

So it came that the musical life of Germany in the eighteenth century presented a pitiable spectacle. The Italians were lords of the land. Musicians and public alike had to dance as they piped. It was the Golden Age for composers who not only learned from the Italians, but sedulously aped them. The offspring of the German Muse led the life of Cinderella. But the fairy tale came true! The former kind vanished with the fashion; while for those masters who, although acquiring the foreign technique, still stood fast-rooted in their native soil, the day of resurrection dawned slowly, but surely. And first of all for Johann Sebastian Bach! Yet even his works are not always pure in style—even he sometimes too greatly favored the fashion. However strongly his arias, for example, are imbued with his genius, they are

trimmed according to the French or Italian mode. This
robs them in good part of their vitality. They form
the—comparatively—weaker portion of his works. They
are less satisfactory in effect, because less genuine, than
the arias of many contemporary Italians, who in other
matters seem almost like dwarfs beside Bach. This
should furnish food for reflection!

Then consider the history of English music. Down
to Purcell, a flourishing period, during which the English masters, despite Italian influences, reflect the
character of their nation. Hereupon follows the Han-
delian cult; and since then England has surrendered
herself to the leading-strings of all imaginable outlandish
idols. Almost two centuries of an unexampled musical
revelry, and, at the same time, two centuries during
which the creative powers of English composers have
lain fallow. Is there no internal nexus between these
two phenomena, no mutual conformity of cause and
effect? Is it not significant, that, since an understanding
of the situation has been making headway for some
decades, the signs of a creative renaissance have plainly
been multiplying in England?

From the beginning of the nineteenth century,
Italians and Germans have been contending for the
leadership in musical affairs. For the last fifty years
the Germans have undeniably been victorious along
the whole line. So much so that Italy, already dependent
on the French, has had to bear the German yoke into
the bargain. Many Italian masters know their Wagner
and their Brahms—not to mention Bach, Beethoven,
and Schumann—with a thoroughness that might well
astonish their German colleagues. But do not think
for a moment that these musicians seek their salvation
by following in the footsteps of the Germans. Imitation,
for them, is but a means to an end. And their endeavor
is to raise Italian music from the slough of obsolete
and outworn forms of expression. Verdi's famous and

redemptive phrase, "Torniamo all' antico!" is the watchword of all clearheaded Italians. Whoever views their longing for redemption from the Teutomania due to conditions now prevailing, as an outgrowth of vanity, is sadly mistaken. They enjoin recourse to the early Italian masters in the home, school and concert-hall as to a perpetual fountain of youth. They perceive that these old masters are much closer to their native temperament than the contemporary transalpine masters. So here again it is recognized that cosmopolitanism is a source of progress for the technique only, but the bane of free expression. Their general aim is to heal music from within outward by a treatment like that of the Young-Italian School of Poetry, which, under the lead of the lofty Giosuè Carducci, is studying the poets of the trecento and quattrocento with burning zeal, in order to rid Italian literature at last of Gallicisms and other impurities. And there is no doubt that these efforts have already been crowned with success.

When one, finally, turns his eyes towards the United States, the truth of all these pronouncements will become painfully evident.

For over one hundred years the United States has been the happy hunting-ground of European musicians; not merely of those who emigrated hither, but of those who remain with us for a year or more to gather in gold and glory. English, French, Italian and German musicians have contributed more than the native artists toward the evolution, in a surprisingly short time, of an abounding musical activity; not working in succession, but side by side, except that now and then the centre of gravity of their influence was shifted. To-day they still play the principal rôle, and in most branches of musical art they have pushed their native colleagues far into the background. And first of all, the music-teachers have grafted their European *naturel* upon our music-making youth. Not only that; legions of young Americans migrate to the European music-schools, and this usually at an age when, musically at least, their typical Americanism can be (and is) eradicated. What follows? The United States, as far as musical matters go, is still in great part a European colony. So here the theory of an international musical language has been reduced to practice. Now, if such a language were the alpha and omega of the music of the future, we should have ready to hand a touchstone of its advantages, and the Americans would have every reason to be satisfied with their musical life.

But they are not at all satisfied. Our musicians, aside from those who themselves are Europeans, groan beneath the European yoke. They see with dismay what the systematic transfusion of European blood has accomplished—a stunted musical growth under a gilded exterior.

Our architects, our painters and, in particular, our sculptors, have won admiration throughout the world because their mastership is different in essentials from that of their professional brethren beyond the ocean.

Our poets, like Edgar Allan Poe, Emerson, Whittier, James Russell Lowell and Walt Whitman are typically American ornaments of universal literature, and already exercise an invigorating influence on poetry in Europe.

These artists have sent down their roots deep into the national soul, and Americans regard them as towering bulwarks of the national life. Quite otherwise with the musicians. The people do not consider them with equal respect. Music, in the popular mind, is rather an imported article of fashion than an art which, on a par with poetry, can and should ennoble, instruct and invigorate a nation.

To a European it seems fairly unbelievable that only a small minority of our singers are able to sing convincingly in the native tongue. Why, indeed, should they be able to? Most of them have been drilled to sing in Italian, or French, or German, only. The law of supply and demand so decides it. For our opera, in particular, is a cosmopolitan *omnium gatherum*. To hear and to enjoy the art of English song, one must patronize the operetta; for all attempts at an English opera have either been shipwrecked or forced down to the level of mediocrity, because the majority of our theatre-goers care less to understand what is sung than to intoxicate themselves with the charm of dearly-purchased voices.

But the worst of it is that we have no composer whom we can call genuinely and *consistently* American in point of style; not one who sets the ideals of his people to music as the poets have done in their verse. Though certain writers—like Mr. Hughes in his fascinating book "Contemporary American Composers" —may maintain the contrary, their wish is father to the thought. Our best composers do actually stand on a level with the European in technique, to be sure, but we too seldom remark, by the mode and method with which they take hold of and elaborate their themes, that they are not the bondsmen of Europe rather than Americans bearing themselves independently and naturally.[1] International reminiscences swarm in their scores, and the individuality that makes itself felt here and there often struggles in vain to break through the jungle of acquired formulas. It is not lack of talent, but the calamitous, blood-wasting inoculation of an international musical speech, which has, for the time being, made it impossible for Americans to give the world masters like Brahms, Bizet, Tschaikowsky or

[1] Is this statement substantially less true A. D. 1916 than A. D. 1903 when I wrote it? I shall accept an affirmative answer only when the younger generation of American composers produces, not as a *rara avis*, but as a matter of habit, pieces so thoroughly American in spirit as Mr. Chadwick's "A Vagrom Ballad" in his "Four Symphonic Sketches." But this gem of American musical humor, worthy of a Mark Twain, was composed in 1896, though not published until 1907! If certain of our younger composers brush aside such a piece as "old fogyish," they are welcome to this opinion as they are to their naïve preferential belief in the efficacy of French as against German measles as a musical beautifier.

Sibelius. Europeans have a right, in a way, to look down upon our composers. Eclecticism is merely a euphemism for pilfering. It is demoralizing, does not carry far, and therefore is not an element of strength, but of weakness.

Of this some of our musicians and writers on music are well aware. Their battle-cry, "Cut loose from Europe!" is of no new date. It has echoed and reëchoed for years, and is growing ever louder. Precisely as in Italy, this yearning after a music of and for the American people is no creature of national hysteria, but the outcome of serious reflection, the result of comparative musico-historical study, of a wisdom born of sad experience. Italy, however, has the better of it. She can draw fresh life from her glorious past, while the Americans, having none, are obliged to lay the foundations for a place of unquestioned power in the music of the future.

The practical application of all these considerations? It is simple and universally binding. Cultivate the good new masters of every nationality, so as not to fall hopelessly behind; also, the good old masters, so as to make timely escape from possible blind alleys; and take root in your native soil, that you may grow, and bring music so close to the hearts of your people that it shall watch over them as a mother over her child. Enjoy, compare, learn! But, of set purpose, cut the ground from under the feet of a would-be cosmopolitan art. For such art is merely the fetish of a spineless mediocrity.

(Translated by Theodore Baker)

THE MUSICAL SIDE OF OUR
FIRST PRESIDENTS

THE MUSICAL SIDE OF OUR FIRST PRESIDENTS

(New Music Review, 1907)

For generations the lives of George Washington, John
Adams and Thomas Jefferson have been described mainly
from the standpoint of men of public affairs. In reading
such biographies the conclusion is almost forced on us
that our first Presidents took interest in nothing but
politics. How absurd such a notion is appears from
the several "true" lives that have come to light in
recent years. Indeed, the lesser sides of their character,
their private life, their fancies and foibles, must be
made to frame the historical picture if we would feel
ourselves in the presence of human beings instead of
political automatons. A modest nook in the biographical
edifice should be reserved for music. To be sure, it
will not be filled with the manuscripts of concertos or
of operas written in competition with crowned composers. . The musical items to be gathered from the
writings of our first Presidents and from other historical
sources are few. Yet they are sufficient to throw interesting sidelights on our early musical history.

Of the three, John Adams seems to have been the
least artistically inclined. At least, he himself assured
Mrs. Mercy Warren (1795) that he had no pleasure or
amusement which possessed any charms for him:
"balls, assemblies, concerts, cards, horses, dogs never
engaged any part of my [his] attention . . . business
alone. . . . ;" and Peter Chardon, a young lawyer,
won his respect because "his thoughts are not employed
on songs and girls, nor his time on flutes, fiddles, concerts and card tables; he will make something." But
this was in 1758, when the Squire of Braintree had not

yet developed those aristocratic tendencies for which
the Republicans in after years, without much reason,
censured him.   The very diary in which the entry
stands belies his self-portrait as presented to Mrs.
Warren.   With an increasing fondness and appreciation
of culinary pleasures, his ears became susceptible to
the charms of music.

In 1773 (August 30) he allowed himself to be "entertained" "upon the spinet" by two young ladies, and
five years later, at Bordeaux, on his way to Paris, he
acquired his first taste of opera.   Says the future President on April 1, 1778: "Went to the opera, where the
scenery, the dancing, the music, afforded me a very
cheerful, sprightly amusement, having never seen anything of the kind before."

Again: "The music and dancing were very fine"
when he and Franklin visited the Paris Opera House
on May 19, 1778; and by the year 1782 his critical
instinct had become so keen that he expressed his
satisfaction with the "good" music upon hearing
Grétry's "Le Jugement de Midas" at The Hague.

Perhaps there was method in Adams's madness when
putting concerts and dogs into the same category of
nuisances, but leaving opera out; for of the famous
Concert Spirituel at the Royal Gardens in Paris which
he attended in 1778 he has nothing to say in his diary
except that there "was an infinite number of gentlemen and ladies walking."

Of one kind of music, John Adams was genuinely
fond—church music.   To the several quotations from
his diary to that effect which Mr. Brooks has printed
in his book on "Olden Time Music," several more
might be added, and when it was not psalmody "in
the *old way*, as we call it—all the drawling, quavering
discord in the world," as at the old Presbyterian Society
in New York, he generally used the word "sweet" to
express his satisfaction.   Two entries, not given by

Brooks, may be of interest here, one for its oddity and the other for an expression of opinion, quite extraordinary for a New Englander of Colonial times. On September 4, 1774, John Adams went to Christ Church, Philadelphia, where "the organ and a new choir of singers were very musical," and on October 9 of the same year he wrote:

"Went, in the afternoon, to the Romish Chapel. The scenery and the music are so calculated to take in mankind that I wonder the Reformation ever succeeded. . . . . The chanting is exquisitely soft and sweet."

Surely John Adams was not such a dried-up man of "business alone" as he would have Mrs. Warren believe; yet, taking him all in all, it is doubtful if John Adams really felt honored when Thomas Paine wrote his patriotic ode, "Adams and Liberty" (1798), to the tune of the English drinking-song "To Anacreon in Heaven," subsequently *shanghaied* for "The Star-Spangled Banner."

Strange, that the children of John Adams should have been so musical! The writings of John Quincy Adams abound with critical remarks on the arts in general and on music in particular, and the letters of Abigail Adams show her to have been a veritable melomaniac. Here are a few delightful lines from a letter of hers to Mrs. Cranch, dated Auteuil, February 20, 1785, and describing her impressions of the opera:

And O! the music, vocal and instrumental: It has a soft, persuasive power, and a dying sound. Conceive a highly decorated building, filled with youth, beauty, grace, ease, clad in all the most pleasing and various ornaments of dress which fancy can form; these objects singing like cherubs to the best tuned instruments most skilfully handled, the softest, tenderest strains; every attitude corresponding with the music; full of the God or Goddess whom they celebrate; the female voices accompanied by an equal number of Adonises. Think you that this city can fail of becoming a Cythera and this house the temple of Venus?

No greater contrast than between John Adams and George Washington. The "General," as his contemporaries used to call him, was, in the true sense of a much abused term, a gentleman of the world, and he cared for all those things which his successor abhorred. Some persons severely criticised him for this attitude, but, on the whole, his mode of living only served to endear him to the hearts of a people not willing to be over-ascetic or to condemn the niceties of life as temptations of Satanas.

Certainly there is an affinity between this and the fact that George Washington's praise was sung in countless songs. In fact, very few patriotic poems of those days did not wind up with the glorification of his beloved personality. The musicians, too, contributed their share of worship, and the literature of pieces written in his honor is not a small one, comparatively speaking. I allude, for instance, to the numerous Washington marches, one of which, the "President's March," was immortalised by furnishing the tune to Joseph Hopkinson's "Hail Columbia." Then again our first operatic effort on allegorical-political lines, Francis Hopkinson's "Temple of Minerva" (1781), was practically a panegyric on Washington. But in this connection the first cyclus of songs, written and composed by a native American, is of particular interest. I mean the "Seven Songs for the Harpsichord or Forte Piano" (Philadelphia, 1788), by Francis Hopkinson, the first American composer. They were dedicated to George Washington, and in his graceful letter of acknowledgment, dated Mount Vernon, February 5, 1789 —by the way, one of the very few documents in which he shows a humoristic vein—our first President writes:

> I can neither sing one of the songs, nor raise a single note on any instrument to convince the unbelieving.
> But I have, however, one argument which will prevail with persons of true taste (at least, in America): I can tell them that it is the production of Mr. Hopkinson.

This statement destroys once for ever the legend that Washington knew how to "raise" the tones of the flute and violin. If we find in his earliest account books the entry: "To cash pd. yᵉ Musick Master for my Entrance, 3.9." this probably refers, to use the words of Paul Leicester Ford, to the singing-master whom the boys and girls of that day made the excuse for evening frolics. But the statement interferes not with the fact that George Washington was fond of dancing and music. We know from George Washington Park Custis's "Recollections," edited by Mr. Lossing, that the "General" was conspicuous for his graceful and elegant dancing of the minuet. He was admired for the last time in this capacity at a ball given at Fredericksburg in 1781 in honor of the French and American officers on their return from the triumphs of Yorktown.

There is a natural connection between the love of dancing and the love of music, and an unmusical person would never have been sincerely admired for the elegant dancing of the minuet. But we possess more direct evidence to prove our point.

Mr. Custis also recollects that Washington used to visit the theatre five or six times a season, if circumstances allowed it. This statement finds more than a corroboration in Washington's ledger and diary which he kept from time to time. Mr. Paul Leicester Ford made copious use of these sources, important not only for the study of the "true" George Washington, but also for the history of the drama in Virginia and Maryland, in his masterly monograph on "Washington and the Theatre," published in 1899 by the Dunlap Society. From this book we may glean that the General, especially in his younger days, would purchase "Play tickets" three, four, and five times a month. Certainly a convincing proof of his fondness of the theatre. Now, we must remember the peculiar character of the American stage of that period. The actors would take a part in a drama of Shakespeare or Sheridan to-night and would

sing in the fashionable ballad-operas the next, or even
the same, evening, if they were given as "after-pieces."
In addition, hardly a performance passed without some
Thespian's singing popular songs or arias between the
acts, and instrumental music was played at the theatres
very much as it is to-day.   Consequently, nobody
with ears to hear could escape music if he ventured
into a theatre.   Had George Washington been indifferent
to the charms of music, he certainly would not have
cared to listen to operas.   This, however, he did and
continued to do until two years before his death.   By
combining the theatrical entries in his diary with the
dates of performances at New York, Philadelphia and
elsewhere, we learn that he was familiar with such
ballad-operas as "The Poor Soldier," "Cymon and
Sylvia," "Maid of the Mill," "The Romp," "The Far-
mer," "Rosina."   His favorite opera seems to have
been William Shield's "Poor Soldier," first performed
at London in 1783 and two years later introduced into
the United States.   At least, Charles Durang, in his
"History of the Philadelphia Stage" (partly compiled
from the papers of his father John, a ballet dancer in
Washington's days), says so, and he adds that the
"Poor Soldier" was often acted at the President's desire
when he visited the theatre.

We also know from Dunlap's "History of the American
Theatre" that he witnessed the first performance of
"Darby's Return" on November 24 (or December 9),
1789, at New York.   This ballad-interlude, written by
Dunlap as a sequel to the "Poor Soldier," in which
Darby after various adventures in Europe and in the
United States returns to Ireland and recounts the
sights he had seen, was for years very popular.   Of the
first performance the author tells us this amusing story:

"The remembrance of this performance is rendered
pleasing from the recollection of the pleasure evinced
by the first President of the United States, the immortal

Washington. The eyes of the audience were frequently bent on his countenance, and to watch the emotions produced by any particular passage on him was the simultaneous employment of all. When Wignell, as Darby, recounts what had befallen him in America, in New York, at the adoption of the Federal Constitution, and the inauguration of the President, the interest expressed by the audience in the looks and the changes of countenance of this great man became intense. He smiled at these lines alluding to the change in government:

> " 'There, too, I saw some mighty pretty shows;
> A revolution, without blood or blows;
> For, as I understood, the cunning elves,
> The people, all revolted from themselves.'

"But at the lines:

> " 'A man who fought to free the land from woe,
> *Like me*, had left his farm, a soldiering to go,
> But, having gain'd his point, he had, *like me*,
> Return'd his own potato ground to see.
> But there he could not rest. With one accord
> He's called to be a kind of—not a lord——
> I don't know what. He's not a great man, sure,
> For poor men love him just as he were poor.
> They love him like a father, or a brother,
>   *Dermot*
> As we poor Irishmen love one another.'

"the President looked serious. And when Kathleen asked:

> " 'How looked he, Darby? Was he short or tall?'

"his countenance showed embarrassment, from the expectation of one of those eulogiums which he had been obliged to hear on many occasions, and which must doubtless have been a severe trial to his feelings; but Darby's answer that he had not seen him, because he had mistaken a man 'all lace and glitter, botherum and shine,' for him, until the show had passed, relieved the hero from apprehension of further personality, and he indulged in that what was with him extremely rare, a hearty laugh."

It is a peculiar coincidence that of the two allusions to opera to be found in Washington's diary, one should again deal with a sequel to the "Poor Soldier." During the Federal Convention at Philadelphia in 1787 he made the following entry on July 10:

"Attended Convention, dined at Mr. Morris's, drank Tea at Mr. Bingham's and went to the play."

By investigating the newspapers, we are enabled to add to this meagre statement:

"*Spectaculum Vitae:* At the Opera House in Southwark This evening the 10th July, will be performed a Concert in the first Part of which will be introduced an entertainment, called the Detective, or, the Servants' Hall in an Uproar. To which will be added a Comic Opera in two acts, called Love in a Camp, or, Patrick in Prussia. . . . "

A curious advertisement, but familiar to the students of early Philadelphia papers. Its explanation is simple enough. The Quakers did their best to suppress all the theatrical entertainments after the war and would stop short of concerts only. The managers were forced to find a way out of the dilemma, and they evaded the law by giving performances under all sorts of disguises like the above. The most ingenious was that of "Hamlet" as "a moral and instructive tale" as "exemplified in the history of the Prince of Denmark."

George Washington is stated to have opposed the narrow-minded restrictions against drama, and this is given somewhere as the main reason why he "went to the play" three times in rapid succession during the Federal Convention. At any rate, he went, and if he was brought into contact with the modern English

music of his day on July 10, he was carried back to
the classical period on July 14. The "Spectaculum
Vitae"—in the innocent disguise of a concert—presented
on that day
"An opera called the Tempest, or, the Enchanted
Island (Altered from Shakespeare by Dryden). To
conclude with a Grand Masque of Neptune and Amphi-
trite: With entire new Scenery, Machinery, etc. The
Music composed by Dr. Purcell."
But George Washington not only attended such sham
concerts. We know from various historical sources
that he also went to regular concerts. Again, it is his
ledger that furnishes the most valuable clues in this
direction. *Anno* 1757 we find the entry: "March 17th
—By Mr. Palmas Tickets, 52. 6." Mr. Ford remarks:

" . . . presumably an expenditure made in Philadelphia during the officer's visit there to meet Lord
Loudon; but whether the tickets were for the theatre
or for a lottery cannot be discovered. The second entry
is more specific, being to the effect: 'April 27—By
Tickets to the Concert, 16.3.' "

Information may here be added, overlooked by our
eminent historian. In the first place, it appears from
the *Pennsylvania Gazette* that said Mr. Palma was a
musician, his Christian name being given as John,
probably the anglicised form of the Italian "Giovanni."
This John Palma gave a concert in Philadelphia at the
Assembly Room in Lodge Alley on January 25, 1757.
I find no further allusion to him, but it presumably
was he who advertised in the *Pennsylvania Journal* on
March 24, 1757:

"By Particular Desire. To Morrow Evening, in the
Assembly Room precisely at 7 o'clock, will be a Concert
of Music.

"Tickets to be had at the Coffee-House at one Dollar each."

Is it too farfetched to argue that George Washington purchased 52s. 6d. worth of tickets in advance for this concert? If not, then this concert would be the earliest on record as attended by the future father of our country. Otherwise it would be the one for which he purchased tickets on April 27, but to which I found no further allusion.

A few years later we find these entries for expenditures made at Williamsburg, Va.:

> 1765—"Apr. 2, By my Exps. to hear the Armonica, 3.9."
> 1767—"Apr. 10, Ticket for the Concert, 5s."

Of course, the Armonica was not the wretched instrument boys and sailors maltreat nowadays, but "the musical glasses without water, framed into a complete instrument capable of thoroughbass and never out of tune," as Philip Vicker Fithian (in 1774) called the then world-famous invention of a no less illustrious person than Benjamin Franklin. Whom George Washington heard perform on the Armonica, we know not, as it seems impossible to trace the two concerts mentioned.

During the War for Independence the Commander-in-Chief had but scarce opportunity for attending plays, concerts and the like. Still, a few occasions are on record. For instance, he was the guest of honor when Luzerne, the Minister of France, celebrated the birthday of the Dauphin in July, 1782, with a concert, fire-works, a ball and a supper. But the entertainment given by the Minister in December, 1781, is by far more interesting to the students of "Americana." Under date of December 19, 1781, the *Freeman's Journal*, Philadelphia, reported:

"On Friday evening of the 11th inst. his excellency the minister of France, who embraces every opportunity to manifest his respect to the worthies of America, and politeness to its inhabitants, entertained his excellency general Washington and his lady; the lady of general Greene, and a very polite circle of the gentlemen and ladies, with an elegant Concert, in which an Oratorio, composed & set to music by a gentleman whose taste in the polite arts is well known, was introduced and afforded the most sensible pleasure."

Mr. Ford certainly would have added in his charming style a few appropriate remarks had he known that this so-called "Oratorio" was identical with Francis Hopkinson's allegorical operatic sketch, celebrating the Franco-American alliance and entitled "The Temple of Minerva." I discovered their identity when studying certain manuscripts of our revolutionary poet, and I have described "The Temple of Minerva" at some length in my book on the musical career of Francis Hopkinson.

In a similar manner George Washington may be traced as a concert-goer until the year 1797, from Charleston, S. C., up to Boston. There, in October, 1789, while on his inaugural tour, he was treated to a so-called "oratorio" under circumstances described in my book on "Early Concerts in America," and Jacob Hilzheimer narrates in his diary that he was present "with his lady" at a concert in the Lutheran Church at Philadelphia on January 8, 1791. At Philadelphia it also was where the President entered in his own diary under date of May 29, 1787:

"Accompanied by Mrs. Morris to the benefit concert of a Mr. Juhan"—not Julian, as Mr. Ford erroneously gives the name.

At Charleston, S. C., in May, 1791, the President entered:

". . . . Went to a Concert at the Exchange at wch. there were at least 400 ladies the number & appearance of wch. exceeded anything of the kind I had ever seen."

And on June 1, 1791, at Salem, N. C., a Moravian settlement:

"Invited six of their principle people to dine with me—and in the evening went to hear them sing & perform on a variety of instruments Church music."

And February 28, 1797, *Claypoole's American Daily Advertiser*, Philadelphia, announced that

"The President and his family honor the Ladies' Concert with their presence this evening."

In order to give an idea of the kind of music our first President would hear on such occasions, I quote from the *Pennsylvania Packet*, June 4, 1787, the remarkable program of Alexander Reinagle's concert, which Washington, according to his diary, attended on June 12.

ACT I.

Overture...Bach
    (Of course the "London" Bach, not Joh. Seb.)
Concerto Violoncelle.................................Capron
Song..Sarti

ACT II.

Overture..André
Concerto Violon....................................Fiorillo
Concerto Flute.....................................Brown

ACT III.

Overture (La Buona Figliuola)........................Piccini
Sonata Pianoforte..................................Reinagle
A new Overture (in which is introduced a Scotch Strathspey)
                               Reinagle

It is highly probable that Alexander Reinagle, like Capron and Brown, excellent European musicians settled at Philadelphia, was engaged to give Nelly Custis harpsichord lessons. George Washington had presented to his adopted daughter a fine instrument at the cost of a thousand dollars—it is now at Mount Vernon in the drawing-room—and it was one of his great pleasures to have Nelly sing and play to him such songs as "The Wayworn Traveller," with which he kept her constantly supplied. To poor Nelly, however, the instrument became one of torture, for her grandmother made her practice upon it four and five hours a day, as her brother tells us in his "Recollections."

Few as these glimpses are into George Washington's private life, they will have sufficed to show that he was not indifferent to music, and that he by no means "appears more as a patron or an escort to the ladies than as a lover of music," as Mr. Tower has it in his "Excerpts from Account Books of Washington."

Turning to Thomas Jefferson, we gain *terra firma*, and are no longer obliged to rely upon circumstantial evidence. In fact, music was a passion with him. His own words and numerous anecdotes go to prove this. Especially his skillful violin playing has become traditional. But grandmothers in Virginia, who heard the truth from the preceding generation, quote an early authority as saying that Patrick Henry was the worst fiddler in the colony with the exception of Thomas Jefferson. So Mr. Curtis informs us in his delightful book on the "true" Thomas Jefferson. The truth probably lies between the two traditions.

At any rate, Jefferson acquired in early youth a certain proficiency on the violin. It was his constant companion; it helped to mitigate the exactions of his public duties, and even as President he would continue to practice. He used to play duets with Patrick Henry, John Tyler and other friends, and widow Martha Skelton's fondness of music surely was one of the attractions that finally, in 1772, led to her marriage with Jefferson. There is even a romance connected with his favorite instrument. If ever the history of the Cremonese violins in America should be written, it will be well not to forget the name of Jefferson, for it is possible that he owned one of the earliest Cremonese instruments brought to our country. At least, it is

certain that John Randolph, the son of the King's Attor-
ney-General, had bought a costly violin in Italy. Once
Thomas Jefferson laid his eyes on his friend's coveted
treasure and listened to its tones, it became the ambition
of his life to possess it. He rested not until the owner
agreed to part with it under certain conditions. The
contract—for it was a contract, duly signed, sealed,
witnessed and recorded in the general court of Williamsburg—reads:

"It is agreed between John Randolph and Thomas
Jefferson, that in case the said John shall survive the
said Thomas, the executors of the said Thomas shall
deliver to the said John the value of Eighty Pounds
Sterling of the books of the said Thomas, the same to
be chosen by the said John, and in case the said Thomas
shall survive the said John, the executors of the said
John shall deliver to the said Thomas the violin which
the said John brought with him into Virginia, together
with all his music composed for the violin."

If the others considered this agreement a joke, not
so Thomas Jefferson. Indeed, Mr. Curtis assures us
that he added a codicil to his will, which he wrote as
soon as he became of age, providing for the fulfilment
of the compact by the executors. But the Revolutionary
War interfered with the stipulations of the contract
and will. Said John returned to England in 1775 and
sold his precious instrument to said Thomas for the
paltry sum of thirteen pounds.

That Jefferson was not proficient on the harpsichord,
he plainly states in a letter to Francis Hopkinson in
1785; but it also appears from his correspondence that he
was constantly on the lookout for a keyed instrument
which would satisfy his tastes. For instance, he begs
Thomas Adams under date of Monticello, February
20, 1771:

" . . . to hasten particularly the Clavichord which I have directed to be purchased in Hamburg, because they are better made there and much cheaper."

A highly interesting remark, if it be remembered that not the German, but the English instruments, especially those of Kirkman in London, were then generally considered the best. If Thomas Adams hastened to comply with Jefferson's request, he must have felt embarrassed upon receiving this second letter, dated June 1, 1771:

" . . . I wrote . . for a Clavichord. I have since seen a Fortepiano and am charmed with it. Send me this instrument, then, instead of the Clavichord. Let the case be of fine mahogany, solid, not veneered, the compass from Double G to F in alt., a plenty of spare strings; and the workmanship of the whole very handsome and worthy of the acceptance of a lady for whom I intend it. [Martha Skelton?] . . . By this change of the Clavichord into a Fortepiano and addition of other things, I shall be brought into debt to you to discharge which I will ship you of the first tobacco I get to the warehouse in the fall . . as soon as you receive this . . and particularly the Fortepiano for which I shall be very impatient."

It is but natural that a man whose love of music was so pronounced should have laid stress upon a musical education for his children. This side of their proverbially excellent education seems to have been a matter of grave concern to him. Words like "Do not neglect your music. It will be a companion which will sweeten many hours of your life," run like a motto through the letters to his daughters, letters written with such paternal affection that they cannot fail to move whoever reads them. He constantly urged Mary and Patsy, as he called his daughter Martha, to keep him well informed of their musical progress, and when the young ladies preferred to neglect this wish they were sure to receive a mild scolding. Jefferson was most exacting in such matters. Though he detested professional soldiery, he certainly was a strict disciplinarian in family life. At times he would go to extremes and become almost pedantic. Of this, a letter written to his "dear Patsy" from Annapolis on November 28, 1783, when on his way to Paris, is a characteristic example:

" . . . With respect to the distribution of your time, the following is what I should approve:

"From 8 to 10 practice music.

"From 10 to 1 dance one day and draw another.

"From 1 to 2 draw on the day you dance and write a letter next day.

"From 3 to 4 read French.

"From 4 to 5 exercise yourself in music.

"From 5 till bedtime read English, write, etc.

"I expect you to write me by every post. Inform me what books you read, what tunes you learn and enclose me your best copy in every lesson of drawing. . . . "

Poor Patsy! Her father was actually starving her to death, as this wonderfully systematic distribution of time did not provide for meals. Not lacking in the sense of humor like her father, Patsy probably smiled when receiving the letter and amended the plan to give proportionate rights to body and soul.

During his long residence at Paris, Thomas Jefferson, of course, had ample opportunity for gratifying his love of music. It is but necessary to peruse his voluminous correspondence as preserved in autograph at the Library of Congress to prove this. That he was personally acquainted with such men as Piccinni we know from his letters to Francis Hopkinson, and these letters —extracts from them are to be found in my book on

Hopkinson—also prove that Jefferson took a lively and intelligent interest in his friend's "improved method of quilling a harpsichord" not only, but in his exciting project to apply a keyboard to the Armonica or Musical Glasses. Indeed, improvements of musical instruments seem to have attracted his attention whenever he heard of such. For instance, one of Jefferson's letters contains a detailed description with a careful diagram of Krumpholtz's "Foot-bass," *alias* Pedalharp, and in another letter he suggested to Hopkinson how to improve "the staccado with glass bars instead of wooden ones, and with keys applied to it," which "pretty little instrument" Franklin, as Jefferson adds, was in the habit of carrying with him.

As a specimen of the kind of musical letter that would pass between the two friends I quote here a letter from Francis Hopkinson to Thomas Jefferson under date of Philadelphia, October 23, 1788. Though preserved at the Library of Congress, I discovered it too late for publication in my book on "Francis Hopkinson and James Lyon." "The compositions alluded to are, of course, Hopkinson's "Seven Songs," that exasperatingly scarce publication of his dedicated to George Washington, the father of our country, by him who in the dedicatory preface claimed "the Credit of being the first Native of the United States who has produced a Musical Composition." I wonder if the millennium will record as *last* American composer a Member of Congress, as was the *first*.

"I have amused myself with composing six easy and simple Songs for the Harpsichord—Words and Music all my own. The Music is now engraving, when finish'd I will do myself the Pleasure of sending a Copy to Miss Jefferson. The best of them is that they are so easy that any Person who can play at all, may perform them without much Trouble, and I have endeavoured to

make the Melodies pleasing to the untutor'd Ear. My
new Method of quilling or rather tonguing the Harpsichord has had the Test of Time and answers perfectly
well in every Respect—both my Daughters play, one of
them very well. The Harpsichord is forever in Exercise
and yet my Tongues stand unimpaired, and my Harps^{d}
is always in Order, in that Respect."

The contrast in matters musical between here and
abroad would naturally impress itself forcibly upon
Jefferson's mind, especially after his return from Paris.
To be sure, our musical life made great progress after
the war, and by far greater than our historians have
been in the habit of describing it, yet it remained very
provincial and crude if compared with that at Paris.
During the war it was crushed almost entirely. Certainly no music-lover deplored this more than Jefferson,
but he was not willing to quietly submit to the logic of
conditions. Music he must have, and that after the
fashion of the *grand seigneur* of Europe. Only a Vir-
ginian Cavalier—and they all loved music—would have
dreamed in those dark days of formulating plans such
as Jefferson did in a letter addressed to an anonymous
friend, probably a Parisian, from Williamsburg on June
8, 1778. It is to be found in Paul Leicester Ford's
edition of Jefferson's writings, published by Putnam's
Sons, and it reads in part thus:

"   .   .   .   If there is a gratification which I envy
any people in this world, it is to your country its music.
This is the favorite passion of my soul & fortune has
cast my lot in a country where it is in a state of deplorable
barbarism. I shall ask your assistance in procuring a
substitute, who may be proficient in singing & on the
Harpsichord. I should be contented to receive such a
one two or three years hence when it is hoped he may
come more safely and find here a greater plenty of
those useful things which commerce alone can furnish.

The bounds of an American fortune will not admit the indulgence of a domestic band of musicians, yet I have thought that a passion for music might be reconciled with that economy which we are obliged to observe. I retain, for instance, among my domestic servants a gardener (Ortolano), a weaver (Tessitore di lino e lin), a cabinet maker (Stipeltaio) and a stone cutter (Scalpetino laborante in piano) to which I would add a vigneron. In a country where like yours music is cultivated and practised by every class I suppose there might be found persons of those trades who could perform on the French horn, clarinet or hautboy & bassoon, so that one might have a band of two French horns, two clarinets & hautboys & a bassoon, without enlarging their domestic expenses. A certainty of employment for a half dozen years, and at the end of that time to find them if they choose a conveyance to their own country might induce them to come here on reasonable wages. Without meaning to give you trouble, perhaps it might be practicable for you in [your] ordinary intercourse with your people to find out such men disposed to come to America. Sobriety and good nature would be desirable parts of their character. If you think such a plan practicable and will be so kind as to inform me what will be necessary to be done on my part, I will take care that it shall be done. . . . . "

Whether the plan was carried out, I do not know. Probably this combination of the useful and pleasing was found to be impracticable. Had the bounds of an American fortune of those days permitted the indulgence in a domestic band, who knows but that Monticello would have become the American Eisenstadt? *En miniature*, of course, and with this slight difference: that Thomas Jefferson probably would not have had, like Prince Esterhazy, a Joseph Haydn as musical factotum.

BENJAMIN FRANKLIN'S MUSICAL SIDE

BENJAMIN FRANKLIN'S MUSICAL SIDE

(Paper read in 1903 *and based on my article in "Music,"* 1900)

Benjamin Franklin's polyhistoric erudition was not merely of a receptive kind. Like Leonardo da Vinci, our "patriot and sage," as Franklin was called in eulogies, never received without giving. He suggested inventions and improvements whenever he became interested in a subject, whether in electricity, book-printing, flying machines—the latter in the modern sense of the term, not fast stage-coaches, as in the terminology of the eighteenth century—optics, chemistry, submarine boats, stoves, eye-glasses, street-cleaning, and so forth.

Strangely enough, the invention of the musical glasses, generally attributed to Franklin, was not absolutely his. He only suggested some improvements, so important and radical, however, that the instrument appeared to be original. As a matter of fact [*see* Grove],

the power of producing musical sounds from basins or drinking glasses by the application of the moistened finger, and of tuning them so as to obtain concords from two at once, was known as early as the middle of the 17th century, since it is alluded to in Harsdörffer's "Mathematische und philosophische Erquickungen" (Nuremberg, 1677, II, 147).

And long before Franklin paid any attention to the improvement of the musical glasses, they were known and heard in public. No less a composer than Gluck performed on them in London in 1746, as appears from the following oft-quoted advertisement in the *General Advertiser* for March 31, 1746:

At Mr. Hickford's Great Room in Brewer's-street, on Monday, April 14, Signor Gluck, Composer of the Operas, will exhibit a Concert of Musick. He will play a Concert upon Twenty-six Drinking Glasses, tuned with Spring water, accompanied with the whole Band, being a new Instrument of his own Invention, upon

which he performs whatever may be done on a Violin or Harpsi-
chord; and therefore hopes to satisfy the Curious, as well as the
Lovers of Musick. To begin at Half an hour after Six. Tickets
Half a guinea each.

Maybe Gluck really did invent a practicable instrument made of drinking glasses filled with water, but
Franklin certainly did not base his experiments on
Gluck. His part in the history of the now obsolete
instrument seems to have been well known in Philadelphia, for I found in a "History of the Life and
Character of Benjamin Franklin," published in the
form of a eulogy in the *Columbian Magazine* for January,
1791, pp. 55-56, this passage:

The tone produced by rubbing the brim of a drinking glass
with a wet finger had been generally known. A Mr. Puckeridge,
an Irishman, by placing on a table a number of glasses of different
sizes, and tuning them by partly filling them with water, endeavoured
to form an instrument, capable of playing tunes. He was prevented
by an untimely end, from bringing his invention to any degree of
perfection. After his death, some improvements were made upon
his plan. The sweetness of the tones induced Dr. Franklin to
make a Variety of experiments; and he at length formed that elegant
instrument, which he has called the ARMÓNICA.

These statements coincide with a detailed description
of the instrument given by Franklin himself to John
Baptist Beccaria of Turin, under date of London,
July 13, 1762:

You have doubtless heard the sweet tone that is drawn from a
drinking glass by passing a wet finger round its brim. One Mr.
Puckeridge, a gentleman from Ireland, was the first who thought
of playing tunes, formed of these tones. He collected a number
of glasses of different sizes, fixed them near each other on a table,
and tuned them by putting into them water more or less as each
note required. The tones were brought out by passing his fingers
round their brims. He was unfortunately burned here, with his
instrument, in a fire which consumed the house he lived in. Mr.
E. Delaval, a most ingenious member of our Royal Society, made
one in imitation of it, with a better choice and form of glasses,
which was the first I saw or heard. Being charmed by the sweetness of its tones, and the music he produced from it, I wished
only to see the glasses disposed in a more convenient form, and
brought together in a narrower compass, so as to admit of a greater
number of tones, and all within reach of hand to a person sitting
before the instrument, which I accomplished, after various trials
and less commodious forms, both of glasses and construction, in
the following manner.

The glasses are blown as near as possible in the form of hemispheres, having each an open neck or socket in the middle. (See Plate II, Figure 1.) The thickness of the glass near the brim about a tenth of an inch, or hardly quite so much, but thicker as it comes nearer the neck, which in the largest glasses is about an inch deep and an inch and a half wide within, these dimensions lessening, as the glasses themselves diminish in size, except that the neck of the smallest ought not to be shorter than half an inch. The largest glass is nine inches in diameter, and the smallest three inches. Between these two are twenty-three different sizes, differing from each other a quarter of an inch in diameter. To make a single instrument there should be at least six glasses blown of each size; and out of this number one may probably pick thirty-seven glasses (which are sufficient for three octaves with all the semitones) that will be each either the note one wants or a little sharper than that note, and all fitting so well into each other as to taper pretty regularly from the largest to the smallest. It is true there are not thirty-seven sizes, but it often happens that two of the same size differ a note or half note in tone, by reason of a difference in thickness, and these may be placed one in the other without sensibly hurting the regularity of the taper form.

The glasses being chosen, and every one marked with a diamond the note you intend it for, they are to be tuned by diminishing the thickness of those that are too sharp. This is done by grinding them round from the neck towards the brim, the breadth of one or two inches, as may be required; often trying the glass by a well tuned harpsichord, comparing the tone drawn from the glass by your finger with the note you want, as sounded by that string of the harpsichord. When you come nearer the matter, be careful to wipe the glass clean and dry before each trial, because the tone is something flatter when the glass is wet than it will be when dry; and grinding a very little between each trial, you will thereby tune to great exactness. The more care is necessary in this, because, if you go below your required tone, there is no sharpening it again but by grinding somewhat off the brim, which will afterwards require polishing, and thus increase the trouble.

The glasses thus tuned, you are to be provided with a case for them, and a spindle on which they are to be fixed. (See Plate II., Figure 2.) My case is about three feet long, eleven inches every way wide within at the biggest end, and five inches at the smallest end; for it tapers all the way, to adapt it better to the conical figure of the set of glasses. This case opens in the middle of its height, and the upper part turns up by hinges fixed behind. The spindle, which is of hard iron, lies horizontally from end to end of the box within, exactly in the middle, and is made to turn on brass gudgeons at each end. It is round, an inch in diameter at the thickest end, and tapering to a quarter of an inch at the smallest. A square shank comes from its thickest end through the box, on which shank a wheel is fixed by a screw. This wheel serves as a fly to make the motion equable, when the spindle, with the glasses, is turned by the foot like a spinning-wheel. My wheel is of mahogany, eighteen inches in diameter, and pretty thick, so as to conceal near its circumference about twenty-five pounds of lead. An ivory pin is fixed in the face of this wheel, and about four inches from the axis. Over the neck of this pin is put the loop of the string that comes up from the movable step to give it motion. The case stands on a neat frame with four legs.

To fix the glasses on the spindle, a cork is first to be fitted in each neck pretty tight, and projecting a little without the neck, that the neck of one may not touch the inside of another when put together, for that would make a jarring. These corks are to be perforated with holes of different diameters, so as to suit that part of the spindle on which they are to be fixed. When a glass is put on, by holding it stiffly between both hands, while another turns the spindle, it may be gradually brought to its place.

But care must be taken that the hole be not too small, lest, in forcing it up, the neck should be split; nor too large, lest the glass, not being firmly fixed, should turn or move on the spindle, so as to touch and jar against its neighbouring glass. The glasses thus are placed one in another, the largest on the biggest end of the spindle, which is to the left hand; the neck of this glass is towards the wheel, and the next goes into it in the same position, only about an inch of its brim appearing beyond the brim of the first; thus proceeding, every glass when fixed shows about an inch of its brim (or three quarters of an inch, or half an inch, as they grow smaller) beyond the brim of the glass that contains it; and it is from these exposed parts of each glass that the tone is drawn, by laying a finger upon one of them as the spindle and glasses turn round.

My largest glass is G, a little below the reach of a common voice, and my highest G, including three complete octaves. To distinguish the glasses the more readily to the eye, I have painted the apparent parts of the glasses within side, every semitone white, and the other notes of the octave with the seven prismatic colors, *viz.*, C, red; D, orange; E, yellow; F, green; G, blue; A, indigo; B, purple, and C, red again; so that glasses of the same color (the white excepted) are always octaves to each other.

This instrument is played upon, by sitting before the middle of the set of glasses as before the keys of a harpsichord, turning them with the foot, and wetting them now and then with a spunge and clean water. The fingers should be first a little soaked in water, and quite free from all greasiness; a little fine chalk upon them is sometimes useful, to make them catch the glass and bring out the tone more readily. Both hands are used, by which means different parts are played together. Observe, that the tones are best drawn out when the glasses turn *from* the ends of the fingers, not when they turn *to* them.

The advantages of this instrument are, that its tones are incomparably sweet beyond those of any other; that they are swelled and softened at pleasure by stronger or weaker pressures of the finger, and continued to any length, and that the instrument, being once well tuned, never again wants tuning.

In honor of your musical language, I have borrowed from it the name of this instrument, calling it the Armonica.

With great esteem and respect, I am, &c.,   B. FRANKLIN.*

*See Bigelow, "The Complete Works of Benjamin Franklin. . . Vol. III, pp. 198-204. G. P. Putnam's Sons, 1887. In 1769 an Italian version of this letter was published in pamphlet form (8 leaves, 12 mo.) The title reads: "L'Armonica. Lettera del Signor Beniamino Franklin al padre Giambattista Beccaria regio professore di fisica nell'Università di Torino dall'Inglese recata nell'Italiano. Nella reale stamperia di Torino." A copy of this extremely scarce pamphlet is in the Liceo Musicale of Bologna. *Is there a copy in America, and is the publication known to American Franklin bibliographers?*

Our knowledge of Franklin's share in the development of the Armonica rests on this letter and one dated London, December 8, 1772, answering the queries of M. Dubourg concerning the best method of playing the instrument.

As the outlines of Franklin's autobiography included a descriptive history of the Armonica, it is to be regretted that the book remained a torso.

The ingenious instrument soon aroused widespread interest. The *Hannoversche Magazin* and the *Leipziger Wöchentliche Nachrichten die Musik betreffend* both contained descriptions of it as early as 1766. The *Musikalischer Almanach für Deutschland auf das Jahr 1782* said:

Of all musical inventions, the one of Mr. Franklin has created perhaps the greatest excitement. Concerning the way of producing tones, it is an entirely new kind of instrument.

By that time the Armonica had become fashionable. We remember the delightful passage in the Vicar of Wakefield:

They would talk of nothing but high life, and high-lived company; with other fashionable topics, such as pictures, taste, Shakespeare and the musical glasses.

Goldsmith's masterwork was published in 1761; it might be asked why I bring his words into connection with *Franklin's* musical glasses. Certain chronological reasons will offer an explanation.

The musical glasses were not played in private circles only, but in concerts, and the names of several Armonica virtuosos have come down to posterity.

Miss Marianne Davies, the daughter of a relative of Franklin, must have been the first virtuoso on the instrument, as she evidently used the first instrument built by Franklin. This fact appears from a communication printed under date of "London, Jan. 12, 1762" in the *Bristol Journal* and reprinted in the *Magazine of American History* (1883). We find advertised:

> The celebrated Glassy-Chord, invented by Mr. Franklin of Philadelphia; who has greatly improved the Musical Glasses, and formed them into a compleat Instrument to accompany the Voice; capable of a thorough Bass, and never out of Tune.
> Miss Davies, from London, was to perform in the Month of January, several favourite Airs, English, Scotch and Italian, on the Glassychord (being the only one of the kind that has yet been produced) accompanied occasionally with the Voice and German Flute. *Vivat Rex & Regina.*

This advertisement helps us in two directions. In the first place, it shows that the original name of the instrument was Glassy-Chord, and not Armonica. This, of course, interferes in no way with Franklin's statement to Padre Beccaria that he named it Armonica in honor of the musical Italian language.

In the second place, the advertisement proves that Franklin must have built his first instrument prior to 1762 and after 1757, as otherwise he would have mentioned the fact in his autobiography. Now, Miss Davies certainly did not appear in public as a performer on the Glassy-Chord without being proficient on it. Proficiency requires practice and practice requires time. Furthermore, the Glassy-Chord is already spoken of as a celebrated instrument. It could not very well become celebrated over night. Therefore, we might approximately fix the date of Franklin's invention as not later than 1761; and thus it appears why I brought Goldsmith's words into connection with Franklin's Musical Glasses.

After creating quite a sensation in England, Miss Davies went to the Continent with her sister Cecilia, a vocalist of some fame. The performances of the two sisters took the Continental public by storm. Especially in Vienna they were received with the utmost approbation. Metastasio, the court poet, in a letter dated Jan. 16, 1772, described the beautiful tone of the instrument and the admirable manner in which Cecilia

assimilated her voice to it, so as to render it difficult
to distinguish the one from the other (*see* Grove).
Mr. Jared Sparks informs us in his life of Franklin
(1840, p. 264) that the two sisters performed an *Ode*,
written by Metastasio and composed by the not less
famous Hasse, in the presence of the Imperial Court of
Vienna at the celebration of the nuptials of the Duke of
Parma and the Arch-Duchess of Austria, and he printed
the Ode from a manuscript copy found among Franklin's
papers.

POESIA

Per L'Occasione Delle Nozze Del Real Infante Duca Di Parma
Con L'Archiduchessa D'Austria, Cantata In Vienna Dalla Cecilia
Davies, Detta L'Inglesina, Sorella Dell'Eccellente Sonatrice Del
Nuovo Istrumento L'Armonica, Inventato Dal Celebre Dottore
Franklin.

Ah perchè col canto mio,
Dolce all' alma ordir catena
Pe chè mai non posso anch'io,
Filomena, al par di te?

S'oggi all'aure un labbro spande
Rozzi accenti, e troppo audace;
Ma, se tace in dì si grande,
Men colpevole non è.

Ardir, germana; a tuoi sonori adatta
Volubili cristalli
L'esperta mano; e ne risveglia il raro
Concento seduttor. Col canto anch' io
Tenterò d'imitarne
L'amoroso tenor. D'applausi e voti
Or che la Parma e l'Istro
D'Amalia e di Fernando
Agli augusti imenei tutto risuona,
Saria fallo il tacer. Ne te del nuovo
Armonica strumento
Renda dubbiosa il lento,
Il tenue, il flebil suono. Abbiasi Marte
I suoi d'ire ministri
Strepitosi oricalchi; una soave
Armonia, non di sdegni
Ma di teneri affetti eccitatrice,
Più conviene ad amor; meglio accompagna
Quel che dall' alma bella
Si trasfonde sul volto
Alla Sposa Real placido lume,
Il benigno costume,
La dolce maestà. Benchè sommesso

Lo stil de' nostri accenti
A Lei grato sarà; che l'umil suono
Non è colpo o difetto;
E sempre in suono umil parla il rispetto.

Alla stagion de' fiori
E de' novelli amori
E grato il molle fiato
D'un zeffiro leggier.

O gema tra le fronde,
O lento increspi l'onde;
Zeffiro in ogni lato
Compagno è del piacer.

Questa cantata fu scritta dal Abate Pietro Metastasio, e messa in musica da Giovanni Adolfo Hasse, detto il Sassone.

Gradually Marianne's nerves became so seriously affected by her performance on the Armonica (so frequent a result of continued performance on the instrument as to have occasioned official prohibition of its use in many Continental towns), that she was compelled to retire from her profession. She died in 1792.

It is quite in keeping with the sensation created by the Armonica that Miss Davies did not remain without rivals. The *Almanach für Deutschland auf das Jahr 1782* mentions among "Clever instrumental artists in Germany" who performed on the Armonica one Fricke, Court Organist of the Markgraf von Baden-Baden, and a certain Röllig and Marianna Kirchgaessner, a blind musician born 1770 in Waldhäusel near Bruchsal, who seems to have been hardly less popular than Miss Marianne Davies.

Of course, the Armonica was not unknown in our country. Though I do not know how the Northern Colonies took to it before the war, I have at least evidence that it was looked upon with favor and interest in the Middle and Southern Colonies. Naturally we turn to gay old Virginia if we desire to find the latest English fads and fashions imported to the Colonies. We look into Glenn's charming work on Colonial

Mansions, and read on every page that the Cavaliers of Virginia, their dames and damsels, laid much stress upon being as little provincial as possible; and in the description of Councillor Robert Carter's mansion *Nomini Hall* we find a passage in Mr. Carter's notebook where he graphically describes one of the wonderful new instruments, invented by

Mr. B. Franklin of Philadelphia an Armonica, being the musical glasses without water, framed into a complete instrument capable of thorough bass and never out of tune.

That the Councillor was proficient on "the musical glasses without water," and loved them, we know from an equally delightful book, Philip Vickers Fithian's "Journal and Letters."

Fithian was tutor at Nomini Hall from 1773 to 1774, and his Journal abounds in musical items showing that if there ever lived a sincere lover of music it was the Councillor.

"He has a good ear for Music, "says Fithian, "a vastly delicate Taste and keeps good Instruments; he has here at Home a Harpsichord, Forte Piano, Harmonica, Guitar & German Flute, & at Williamsburg has a good Organ, he himself also is indefatigable in the Practice."

In the person of Mr. Stadley he seems to have had, we might say, a court musician of no mean ability, he too being a skilled performer on the Armonica. That the two gentlemen, whether playing solos or duets, had an attentive and enthusiastic listener in Fithian, his journal proves on more than one page, and the Musical Glasses especially seem to have impressed him deeply. I cannot refrain from quoting his naïve opinion of the same, as it is a proof that Franklin's instrument found fervent admirers in our country as well as abroad:

Wednesday, 22 Dec. (1773) . . . Evening. Mr. Carter spent in playing on the Harmonica; It is the first time I have heard the Instrument. The Music is charming! The notes are clear and inexpressibly soft, they swell, and are inexpressibly grand; and either it is because the sounds are new, and therefore pleased me, or it is the most captivating Instrument I have ever heard. The sounds very much resemble the human voice, and in my opinion they far exceed even the swelling Organ.

But, about ten years prior to Fithian's enthusiastic criticism, the music-lovers of Philadelphia had occasion to thank Benjamin Franklin personally for the pleasure his instrument afforded them. I copied from the *Pennsylvania Gazette,* ·Philadelphia, Dec. 27, 1764, the following advertisement:

> For the Benefit of Mr. Forage, and other Assistant Performers at the Subscription Concert in this city, on Monday, the 31st. of this instant December, at the Assembly Room in Lodge Alley, will be performed A CONCERT OF MUSIC: consisting of a Variety of the most celebrated Pieces now in Taste, in which also will be introduced the famous Armonica, or Musical Glasses, so much admired for the great Sweetness and Delicacy of its Tone. Tickets at 7s. 6d. each.

Mr. Forage seems to have been the first musician to introduce the Armonica in our country, and it is quite possible that we owe to him George Washington's entry for April 2, 1765, at Williamsburg, Va., "By my Exps. to hear the Armonica, 3. 9." In 1774 a Signora Castella appeared in concert on the instrument at Charleston, S. C. About the same time, and later, George James L' Argeau made a specialty of it for many years. He taught at his "Musical Room" in Baltimore

Violencello, Bassoon, Harpsichord, Pianoforte, German Flute, Oboe, Clarionet, French Horn, and Guitar.

—a really formidable array of instruments—besides dancing and fencing; and he advertised in the *Maryland Gazette* (Annapolis, October 6, 1774) his intention of performing on the Musical Glasses

> That harmonic instrument every day, between the hours of 3 and 6 in the afternoon, next door to Mr. Aikman's circulating library. . . half a dollar each.

And as late as 1790 he ends an advertisement in the *Maryland Journal*, Baltimore, July 23, by saying:

> The Musical Glasses are performed to any Number of Ladies and Gentlemen, by giving timely Notice.

A few years later, the versatile P. A. Van Hagen played at a concert at New York in March, 1794, his own "Concerto (by particular desire) on the *Carillion*, or Musical Glasses," the "or" being a little puzzling since *carillons* are not exactly made of glass, but perhaps the added *i* made all the difference in the world between a *carillon* and a *carrillion*. Then there was also Mr. John Christopher Moller, who, with Messrs. Capron, Carr, Gillingham and Reinagle, played a prominent part in the musical life of Philadelphia, advertised in Dunlap's *American Daily Advertiser*, 1795, May 4th, for the following day a "Miscellaneous Concert. . . under the direction of Mr. Moller at which will be introduced the Harmonica." The interesting program reads:

ACT I.

Overture...Haydn
Song arranged for Harmonica by......................Moller
Quintetto..Pleyel
Concerto Violin..................................Gillingham
Full Piece...Pleyel

ACT II.

Overture...Pleyel
Quartetto, Harmonica, Two Tenors and Violincello by....Moller
Concerto Violincello.........................Manell [Menel]
Fantasia Pianoforte................................Moller
Finale...Haydn

Mr. Forage's instrument certainly was a copy of Franklin's, and Mr. Moller's instrument might already have shown some of the improvements attempted by the Abbé Mazzuchi on account of "the many and great inconveniences in the Harmonica of the celebrated Dr. Franklin," for Moller adds to his remarks quoted from the *Phila. Gazette*, April 3, 1795,

This instrument since so much improved in Europe, by the first artists, is, in point of tone and sweet harmony, second to none, and in performance of modulation from which it derives its name not excelled by any other.

That Mons. Jacobus Pick used one of Mazzuchi's instruments for his performances on the Musical Glasses at Boston and elsewhere, from 1792 on, appears probable from his playing a "Sonata on the Italian Harmonica with several known airs" at Petersburg, Va., June 25, 1795.

One of the principal modifications, according to Forkel's *Mus. Krit. Bibliothek* (1779), was to produce the tones with a fiddle-bow instead of using the fingers. Mazzuchi also made experiments with wooden boxes, which are said to have produced tones similar to those of the flute. Equally ingenious was the above-mentioned Fricke's project (1769) to apply a keyboard to the instrument. That the same idea occurred in 1786, independently, to Francis Hopkinson, I have demonstrated in my book on him. The arch-democrat Thomas Jefferson was so pleased with his project that in his opinion (expressed in a letter from Paris, December 23, 1786) its success would be "the greatest present which has been made to the musical world this century, not excepting the pianoforte." Hopkinson claimed a few months later, in his letters to Jefferson, that he had successfully "applied Keys to the Glasses, furnished with artificial Fingers"; but he also admitted partial failure because "it required too much Address in the manner of wetting the Cushions for Common Use." Whether or no he resumed his experiments after Jefferson (in his letter from Paris, May, 8, 1788) told him of having seen "a very simple improvement" in the matter of wetting the glasses ("by a piece of woolen cloth pasted on the edge of the case in front and touching the glasses"), I do not know.

All this, and the fact that the Armonica formed part of the Court Orchestra at Darmstadt, that C. F. Pohl was engaged there exclusively for the instrument as late as 1818, that Johann Gottlieb Naumann, a famous composer of the eighteenth century, played it and wrote six sonatas for it, that Mozart composed— probably in 1780—an Adagio for Harmonica in C

major, and, on May 23d, 1791, for Marianna Kirchgaessner, an unpublished "Adagio und Rondo für Harmonica, Flöte, Oboe, Viola und Violoncello" which his
biographer Otto Jahn calls remarkable for the blending
of the instruments,—I mention all this, and that even
Beethoven composed a little melodramatic piece for
the Armonica for the "Leonora Prohaska" of his friend
Duncker in 1814 or 1815, published for the first time
in Grove's Dictionary, because these facts show the
remarkable influence Franklin and his Armonica once
had on the lovers of musical curiosities.

Those interested in further particulars concerning the
history of the instrument, obsolete for the past eighty
years, will find them in the "History of the Harmonica"
published by Karl Ferdinand Pohl, (the son of the
virtuoso) in 1862, though he is silent on Hopkinson's
ingenious experiments.

Undoubtedly, Franklin himself was proficient on his
instrument. But if the Armonica ruined the nerves of
other performers—and this probably was the main
reason for its short life of only sixty years—Franklin
seems not to have suffered from these bad effects. The
late Paul Leicester Ford, devoting four pages in his
book on the Many-Sided Franklin to the musical side,
wrote:

He himself took great pleasure in playing upon it, and an amusing
glimpse is obtained of him during his last years through a paragraph
in one of his letters, in which he says: "Mr. Pagin did me the honor
of visiting me yesterday. He is assuredly one of the best men
possible, for he had the patience to listen to me playing an air on
the Armonica, and to hear it to the end."

Again, Mme. Brillon, seeking to tempt him to her home, promises
that "Father Pagin will play the *God of Love* on the violin, I the
march on the piano, you *Little Birds* on the harmonica"; and the
same writer, in describing their future life in heaven, prophesies
that "Mr. Mesmer will be contented with playing on the harmonica without boring us with electric fluid."

Finally, while Mr. Sparks informed us that Metastasio
was officially called upon to write an ode in honor of
Marianne Davies, I am able to furnish an ode written

in praise of Franklin's own performances on the Armonica—and not *par ordre de Mufti*. It might not
be interesting as a poetical effort, but is interesting in
this connection and as a poetical effusion of one of our
earliest American poets. It is to be found in Nathaniel
Evans' "Poems on Several Occasions—Philadelphia,
Printed by John Dunlap, in Market Street, 1772";
and reads:

TO BENJAMIN FRANKLIN, ESQ., LL.D.

Occasioned by hearing him playing on the *Harmonica*.

In grateful wonder lost, long had we view'd
Each gen'rous act thy patriot soul pursu'd;
Our little State resounds thy just applause,
And, pleas'd, from thee new fame and honour draws;
In thee those various virtues are combin'd,
That form the true preëminence of mind.

What wonder struck us when we did survey
The lambent lightnings innocently play,
And down thy rods beheld the dreaded fire
In a swift flame descend—and then expire;
While the red thunders, roaring loud around,
Burst the black clouds, and harmless smite the ground.

Blest use of art! apply'd to serve mankind,
The noble province of the sapient mind!
For this the soul's best faculties were giv'n,
To trace great nature's laws from earth to heav'n!

Yet not these themes alone thy thoughts command,
Each softer SCIENCE owns thy fostering hand;
Aided by thee, Urania's heav'nly art,
With finer raptures charms the feeling heart;
Th' HARMONICA shall join the sacred choir,
Fresh transports kindle, and new joys inspire.

Hark! the soft warblings, sounding smooth and clear,
Strike with celestial ravishment the ear,
Conveying inward, as they sweetly roll,
A tide of melting music to the soul;
And sure, if aught of mortal-moving strain
Can touch with joy the high angelic train,
'Tis this enchanting instrument of thine,
Which speaks in accents more than half divine!

The Armonica, however, was not the only instrument Franklin enjoyed and knew how to play. Mr.

Ford claims that previous to the development of the Armonica he also knew how to play on the harp, the guitar, and the violin; and Mr. Parton adds to these instruments the violoncello. I have been unable to verify Franklin's proficiency on the violoncello and violin, but he may have been a harpist, for in France a friend wrote him that he had "searched for harps everywhere without being able to find any." Certainly, Franklin, like most gentlemen of his time, knew how to play on the guitar. "I shall never touch the strings of the British lyre without remembering my British friends, and particularly the kind giver of the instrument," he wrote from Philadelphia (Dec. 7, 1762) to Mr. Whiteford, who congratulated him upon the marriage of his son William. He even offered his services as a guitar-teacher to Leigh Hunt's mother, but she was too bashful to become his pupil—so her son informs us in his autobiography.

So much on Benjamin Franklin as the "inventor" of the Armonica and as a "virtuoso." But what did he mean in his letter to Padre Beccaria by "Italian music —of the soft and plaintive kind"? As this letter was written in 1762, his knowledge of Italian music naturally was restricted to what was known of it in the colonies, and especially in Philadelphia.

The opinion has prevailed that the musical life of America was exceedingly primitive during the eighteenth century, but a few degrees less so in sacred music than in secular. To be sure, our early musical life had a rather provincial aspect if compared with that of London, Paris, Vienna or Rome, but it was by no means so primitive as historians usually picture it. As a rule, they make the great mistake of observing things through a New England church window instead of studying more than superficially the secular music of "ye olden time" in the Middle and Southern Colonies. Their treatment of the subject did more harm than good.

Our early musical life was provincial, but not so primitive as to deserve to be ridiculed. And if it is to be called primitive and crude, our early sacred music deserves this verdict more than the secular.

We had more or less regular operatic seasons in New York, Philadelphia, Baltimore, Annapolis, Charleston, the répertoire consisting, of course, mostly of English ballad-operas and, later, a few French and Italian operas translated into English, for instance Pergolesi's "La Serva Padrona." We had regular orchestral subscription or amateur concerts; we had musical societies; we did not neglect chamber music, and music played a prominent part at all College Commencements. The German flute, the guitar, the harpsichord—the fashionable instruments of the time—the pianoforte, the violin, the bass-viol, were not missing in well-to-do families of Colonial times. Not even the strolling Italian and French virtuosos were wanting, nor the blessed "Wunderkinder."

About 1760 the musical life of Philadelphia depended more or less on such "imported" musicians as Albert, Bremner, Fyring, John Schneider, Forage and Gualdo, and native amateur musicians like Governor Penn and Francis Hopkinson, the first American composer. It is easy to ridicule their talent and ability, but it is difficult to deny the fact that under their guidance the music of Leo, Galuppi, Pergolesi, Corelli, Geminiani, not to mention minor lights, or of the then fashionable British composers, or of the German masters Gluck, Hasse, Händel, was sold, taught, played and enjoyed in America.

These facts throw some light upon Franklin's seemingly odd words. At least they go to show what kind of music he might have known and enjoyed, if really interested in music. If his share in a musical invention alone renders his interest undeniable, it can be traced through all his writings.

While at Bethlehem in 1757, studying the institutions of the Moravians, he evidently took an interest in their highly developed musical life. He says in his autobiography:

I was at their church, where I was entertained with good musick, the organ being accompanied with violins, hautboys, flutes, clarinets, etc.

From a household letter, written to his wife, June 22, 1767, in London, we know that even his house was not without relations to music. He gives her instructions about the "blue room," telling her to "let the papier mache musical figures be tacked to the middle of the ceiling." If his various instruments were located in this "blue room," as we may suppose, it must have had quite a musical atmosphere, especially when crowded with friends who came to hear him perform on the musical glasses.

That Franklin attended concerts and operatic performances while abroad is certain, and it seems as if he saw Händel conduct *The Messiah* for the last time, eight days before his death, on the sixth of April, 1759. At least, I reach this conclusion from the following remarks in Mr. James Parton's biography of Franklin (I, pp. 260-262, 397):

Franklin was just in time to see the sublime old man, one of the sturdiest characters of modern times, led to the organ for the last time, and conduct one of his own works. He heard Handel's oratorios and his now forgotten operas, always with admiration, but not with blind admiration.

The same historian lays some stress upon the fact that Franklin was fond of social gatherings and always ready to do his part with jest, anecdote and song, and that he was especially fond of Scotch songs.

Three songs that he used to sing are known to us. One was the "The Old Man's Wish," which he says he sang "a thousand times in his singing days."

Another of his songs was "My Plain Country Joan," a long ditty, written by himself in praise of his own wife.

> Of their Chloes and Phyllises poets may prate,
>   I sing my plain country Joan,
> These twelve years my wife, still the joy of my life,
>   Blest day that I made her my own. (*etc.*)

Another song, written by Franklin in the Junto days, and often sung by him at the Junto rooms, the entire club joining in the chorus, is in a different strain.

Franklin, when seventy years of age, mentioned this third song in a letter to the Abbé de la Roche:

"I have," he writes, "run over, my dear friend, the little book of poetry by M. Helvetius, with which you presented me. The poem on 'Happiness' pleased me much, and brought to my recollection a little drinking song which I wrote forty years ago, upon the same subject, and which is nearly on the same plan, with many of the same thoughts, but very concisely expressed. It is as follows:

> SINGER: Fair Venus calls; Her voice obey.
>   In beauty's arms spend night and day.
>   The joys of love all joys excell
>   And loving's certainly doing well.
>
> CHORUS: Oh! No!
>   Not so!
>   For honest souls know
>   Friends and a bottle still bear. the bell."

And so on between singer and chorus. I do not know whether Franklin himself or one of our early composers ever tried to compose this jolly drinking song, or, following the custom of the time, tried to adapt some popular tune to it. I believe the latter, and doubt very much that Franklin ever tried his hand at composition, as Mr. Ford was inclined to believe on the strength of a letter written by Mme. Brillon, in which she acknowledges the receipt of "your music engraved in America."

Mr. Ford adds "that it has not been possible to identify the piece." I fancy that our eminent historian was discovering too many sides in Franklin and that, even if the piece should be identified, the discovery would not reveal Franklin as a composer. Probably Mme. Brillon's words refer either to some music belonging to Franklin and engraved in America, or to some music engraved by Franklin himself. Perhaps some of the works mentioned as printed by Franklin in Mr. James Warrington's "Short Titles of Books relating to or illustrating the History and Practice of Psalmody in the United States, 1620-1820 (1898, Philadelphia)" contained music engraved in his office. At any rate, it would not surprise me to find Franklin an engraver of music. He might have had some knowledge of the trade, having been a journeyman at the office of John Watts of Lincoln's Inn Fields, a British music-publisher who printed a "Musical Miscellany" in six volumes between 1729 and 1731, that is, during Franklin's employment as his journeyman.

It would have been easy enough for Franklin to find a composer, as he took a lively and encouraging interest in the beginnings of our artistic life, and as he, from some letters, appears to have been personally acquainted with our early painters, poets and musicians. An extract from his letters to Mary Stevenson, Philadelphia, March 25, 1763, may prove this. He writes:

After the first cares of the necessaries of life are over, we shall come to think of the embellishments. Already some of our young geniuses begin to lisp attempts at painting, poetry and music. The manuscript piece is by a young friend of mine, and was occasioned by the loss of one of his friends, who lately made a voyage to Antigua to settle some affairs previous to an intended marriage with an amiable young lady here, and unfortunately died there. I send it to you because the author is a great admirer of Mr. Stanley's musical compositions, and has adapted this piece to an air in the sixth concerto of that gentleman, the sweet solemn movement of which he is quite enraptured with. He has attempted to compose a recitative for it, but not being able to satisfy himself in the bass, wishes I could get it supplied. If Mr. Stanley would condescend to do that for him, he would esteem it as one of the highest honors, and it would make him excessively happy. You will say that a recitative can be but a poor specimen of our music. It is the best and all I have at present, but you may see better hereafter.

Inasmuch as James Lyon and Francis Hopkinson, both in Philadelphia in 1763, had already won some reputation in America as composers and compilers, it may seem strange that Franklin does not mention them, though he, as a printer, must have noticed the publication of Lyon's "Urania" in 1762 and Hopkinson's "An Exercise" in 1761. Perhaps he did not think it worth while to mention their crude efforts when talking of a fashionable European composer like John Stanley, to whom the great Händel bequeathed part of his library.

I have dwelt upon all these minor details in order to show that Benjamin Franklin possessed a keen interest for music and a certain knowledge of its literature. But so far, with exception of his traditional invention of the musical glasses, he did not surpass the many other lovers of music in colonial America. The two following documents, however, place him high above the average amateur, not only of his own country and time, but of Europe and to-day.

The first letter was addressed from London, June 2, 1765, to the philosopher and *bel esprit* Lord Kames of Edinborough. It is, in my opinion, a surprisingly original and important document. Here the American sage appears as an ardent admirer of a folk-lore pure and simple, not embellished or overloaded with modern "Verschlimmbesserungen," long before our historians brought similar theories into practice. Moreover, Franklin expresses ideas on melody, usually considered of newest date, and which it took the psychologists of music more than a century to explain, prove and develop. When this extremely interesting letter was first reprinted in Dwight's *Journal of Music* and other reviews from Spark's edition of Franklin's works in 1856, if I remember the year correctly, it was done with a benevolent smile. The letter was spoken of as an antediluvian curiosity and as a *corpus delicti* of Franklin's musical illiteracy. How surprised would these writers be to hear that similar theories, though in a clearer and more elaborate form and without certain deviations from the correct path, have been formulated by such eminent scientists as Karl Stumpf and Hugo Riemann! Benjamin Franklin wrote, one hundred and thirty-five years ago:

> In my passage to America I read your excellent work, "The Elements of Criticism," in which I found great entertainment. I only wish that you had examined more carefully the subject of music, and demonstrated that the pleasure artists feel in hearing much of that composed in the modern taste is not the natural pleasure arising from melody or harmony of sounds, but of the same kind with the pleasure we feel on seeing the surprising feats of tumblers and rope-dancers, who execute difficult things. For my part, I take this really to be the case, and suppose it to be the reason why those who are unpracticed in music, and therefore unacquainted with those difficulties, have little or no pleasure in hearing this music. I have sometimes, at a concert, attended by a common audience, placed myself so as to see all their faces, and observed no signs of pleasure in them during the performance of a great part that was admired by the performers themselves; while a plain old Scotch tune, which they disdained, and could scarcely be prevailed on to play, gave manifest and general delight.
>
> Give me leave, on this occasion, to extend a little the sense of your position, that "melody and harmony are separately agreeable and in union delightful," and to give it as my opinion that the reason why the Scotch tunes have lived so long, and will probably live forever (if they escape being stifled in modern affected ornament), is merely this, that they are really compositions of melody and harmony united, or rather that their melody is harmony. I mean the simple tunes sung by a single voice. As this will appear paradoxical, I must explain my meaning.
>
> In common acceptation, indeed, only an agreeable *succession* of sounds is called *melody*, and only the *coexistence* of agreeable sounds *harmony*. But, since the memory is capable of retaining for some moments a perfect idea of the pitch of a past sound, so as to compare with it the pitch of a succeeding sound, and judge truly of their agreement or disagreement, there may and does arise from thence a sense of harmony between the present and past sounds equally pleasing with that between two present sounds.
>
> Now, the construction of the old Scotch tunes is this, that almost every succeeding emphatical note is a third, a fifth, an octave, or, in short, some note that is in concord with the preceding note. Thirds are chiefly used, which are very pleasing concords. I use the word *emphatical* to distinguish those notes which have a stress laid on them in singing the tune, from the lighter connecting notes that serve merely, like grammar articles in common speech, to tack the whole thing together.
>
> That we have a most perfect idea of sound just passed, I might appeal to all acquainted with music, who know how easy it is

to repeat a sound in the same pitch with one just heard. In tuning an instrument, a good ear can as easily determine that two strings are in unison by sounding them separately as by sounding them together; their disagreement is also as easily, I believe I may say more easily and better, distinguished, when sounded separately, for when sounded together, though you know by the beating that one is higher than the other, you cannot tell which it is. I have ascribed to memory the ability of comparing the pitch of a present tone with that of one past. But if there should be, as possibly there may be, something in the ear, similar to what we find in the eye, that ability would not be entirely owing to memory. Possibly the vibrations given to the auditory nerves by a particular sound may actually continue some time after the cause of those vibrations is past, and the agreement or disagreement of a subsequent sound becomes by comparison with them more discernible.

[Franklin for a moment leaves the musical subject and explains similar optical phenomena, stating that it is easier to retain the impression of lines than of colors.]

Farther, when we consider by whom these ancient tunes were composed and how they were first performed, we shall see that such harmonical successions of sounds were natural, and even necessary, in their construction. They were composed by the minstrels of those days to be played on the harp, accompanied by the voice. The harp was strung with wire, which gives a sound of long continuance, and had no contrivance like that in the modern harpsichord, by which the sound of the preceding could be stopped the moment a succeeding note began. To avoid actual discord it was therefore necessary that the succeeding emphatical note should be a chord with the preceding, as their sounds must exist at the same time. Hence arose that beauty in those tunes that has so long pleased, and will please forever, though men scarce know why. That they were originally composed for the harp, and of the most simple kind, I mean a harp without any half notes but those in the natural scale and with no more than two octaves of strings, from C to C, I conjecture from another circumstance, which is, that not one of those tunes, really ancient, has a single artificial half note in it, and that in tunes where it was most convenient for the voice to use the middle notes of the harp and place the key in F, then the B, which, if used, should be a B flat, is always omitted by passing over it with a third. The connoisseurs in modern music will say I have no taste, but I cannot help adding that I believe our ancestors, in hearing a good song, distinctly articulated, sung to one of those tunes and accompanied by the harp, felt more real pleasure than is communicated by the generality of modern operas, exclusive of that arising from the scenery and dancing. Most tunes of late composition, not having this natural harmony united with their melody, have recourse to the artificial harmony of a bass and other accompanying parts. This support, in my opinion, the old tunes do not need, and are rather confused than aided by it. Whoever has heard James Oswald play these on his violoncello will be less inclined to dispute this with me. I have more than once seen tears of pleasure in the eyes of his auditors; and yet, I think, even *his* playing those tunes would please more, if he gave them less modern ornament.

It goes without saying that Franklin's excursion into the history of music was not very lucky and that his philippics against the *artificial harmony* in operas must not be taken too literally; but his closing remarks certainly prove that he possessed an uncommonly clear idea of the true character of folk-songs and of the best way of performing them. This same critical faculty appears in a letter addressed to Peter Franklin of Newport. It is without date, but Bigelow rightly published it among the London letters of 1765. It was first published in the *Massachusetts Magazine* for July, 1790 (p. 412-414), under the title "Criticism on Musick." As a "Criticism on Modern Musick. . ." it appeared in the *Universal Asylum and Columbian Magazine* for August, 1790 (p. 97-99). It reads as follows:

Dear Brother: I like your ballad, and think it well adapted for your purpose of discountenancing expensive foppery and encouraging industry and frugality. If you can get it generally sung in your country, it may probably have a good deal of the effect you hope and expect from it. But as you aimed at making it general, I wonder you chose so uncommon a measure in poetry that none of the tunes in common use will suit it. Had you fitted it to an old one, well known, it must have spread much faster than I doubt it will do from the best new tune we can get composed for it. I think, too, that if you had given it to some country girl in the heart of Massachusetts, who has never heard any other than psalm tunes or "Chevy Chase," the "Children in the Woods," the "Spanish Lady," and such old, simple ditties, but has naturally a good ear, she might more probably have made a pleasing popular tune for you than any of our masters here, and more proper to the purpose, which would best be answered if every word could, as it is sung, be understood by all that hear it, and if the emphasis you intend for particular words could be given by the singer as well as by the reader; much of the force and impression of the song depending on those circumstances. I will, however, get it as well done for you as I can.

Do not imagine that I mean to depreciate the skill of our composers of music here; they are admirable at pleasing practiced ears and know how to delight one another, but in composing for songs the reigning taste seems to be quite out of nature, or rather the reverse of nature, and yet, like a torrent, hurries them all away with it; one or two, perhaps, only excepted.

You, in the spirit of some ancient legislators, would influence the manners of your country by the united powers of poetry and music. By what I can learn of their songs, the music was simple, conformed itself to the usual pronunciation of words, as to measure, cadence or emphasis, etc., never disguised and confounded the language by making a long syllable short, or a short one long, when sung; their singing was only a more pleasing because a melodious manner of speaking, it was capable of all the graces of prose oratory, while it added the pleasure of harmony. A modern song, on the contrary, neglects all the proprieties and beauties of common speech, and in their place introduces its *defects* and *absurdities* as so many graces. I am afraid you will hardly take my word for this, and therefore I must endeavour to support it by proof. Here is the first song I lay my hand on. It happens to be a composition of one of our greatest masters, the ever famous Handel. It is not one of his juvenile performances, before his taste could be improved and formed; it appeared when his reputation was at the highest, is greatly admired by all his admirers, and is really excellent in its kind. It is called, "The additional favorite Song in Judas Maccabeus." Now I reckon among the defects and improprieties of common speech the following, viz.:

1. *Wrong placing the accent or emphasis* by laying it on words of no importance or on wrong syllables.

2. *Drawling;* or extending the sound of words or syllables beyond their natural length.

3. *Stuttering;* or making many syllables of one.

4. *Unintelligibleness;* the result of the three foregoing united.

5. *Tautology;* and

6. *Screaming* without cause.

For the wrong placing of the accent or emphasis, see it on the word *their* instead of being on the word *vain,*

with their____   vain,__ mys - te - rious__ art ____

And from the word *from*, and the wrong syllable *like,*

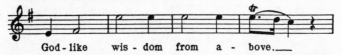

God - like   wis - dom   from   a - bove.__

For the drawling, see the last syllable of the word *wounded.*

Nor__   can   heal__ the   wound-ed__   heart.

And in the syllable *wis*, and the word *from* and the syllable *bove:*

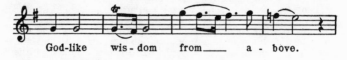

God-like   wis - dom   from____   a - bove.

For the stuttering, see the words *ne'er relieve* in:

mag-ic____   charms can   ne'er___ re - lieve you

Here are four syllables made of one, and eight of three; but
this is moderate. I have seen in another song, that I cannot now
find, seventeen syllables made of three, and sixteen of one. The
latter, I remember, was the word *charms*, viz., cha-a-a-a-a-a-a-a-
a-a-a-a-a-a-arms. Stammering with a witness! For the unintelligibleness, give this whole song to any taught singer, and let
her sing it to any company that have never heard it. You shall
find they will not understand three words in ten. It is, therefore,
that at the oratorios and operas one sees with books in their hands
all those who desire to understand what they hear sung by even
our best performers.

For the tautology, you have, *with their vain, mysterious art*,
twice repeated; *magic charms can ne'er relieve you*, three times;
Nor can the wounded heart, three times; *God-like wisdom from above*,
twice, and *this alone can ne'er deceive you*, twice or three times.
But this is reasonable when compared with the *Monster Polypheme*,
the *Monster Polypheme*, a hundred times over and over in his
admired "Acis and Galatea."

As to the screaming, perhaps I cannot find a fair instance in
this song; but whoever has frequented our operas will remember
many. And yet there, methinks, the words *no* and *e'er*, when
sung to these notes, have a little of the air of *screaming*, and would
actually be screamed by some singers.

I send you enclosed the song with its music at length. Read
the words without the repetitions. Observe how few they are, and
what shower of notes attend them; you will then, perhaps, be
inclined to think with me that, though the words might be the
principal part of an ancient song, they are of small importance in
a modern one. They are, in short, only a *pretence for singing*.

I am, as ever, your affectionate brother,

BENJAMIN FRANKLIN.

P. S.—I might have mentioned *inarticulation* among the defects
in common speech that are assumed as beauties in modern singing.
But as that seems more the fault of the singer than of the composer, I omitted it in what related merely to the composition.
The fine singer, in the present mode, stifles all the hard consonants
and polishes away all the rougher parts of words that serve to
distinguish them one from another; so that you can hear nothing
but an admirable pipe, and understand no more of the song than
you would from its tune played on any other instrument. If ever
it was the ambition of musicians to make instruments that should
imitate the human voice, that ambition seems now reversed, the
voice aiming to be like an instrument. Thus wigs were first made
to imitate a good natural head of hair; but when they became
fashionable, though in unnatural forms, we have seen natural hair
dressed to look like wigs.

No doubt, Franklin shows a remarkably pure taste in this polemical essay. Very few critics and professional musicians had or have equally independent esthetical reasoning powers, and probably contemporaneous artists, when "talking shop" with Franklin, haughtily sneered at his provincial ideas. The modern historian, however, will side with Franklin and agree with the lexicographers Gerber, Fétis, and Grove, who report that he possessed a deep insight into musical acoustics and esthetics. But this insight certainly was not due only to the improvisatory genius and instinct of a many-sided man. It is clear that Franklin must have given much critical thought to problems in music. We therefore regret that his writings contain comparatively so little on this art and that his discussions of musical matters with friends musical and unmusical have not been preserved. Probably his remarks on other subjects besides folk-songs and the harmonic structure of melodies were not less original. Perhaps he foresaw the music of the future in more than one respect, for to-day it is generally admitted that Händel's musical declamation was indeed often faulty, like that of many of his contemporaries. If the composers of the nineteenth century, especially the song-composers of the last thirty years, have improved upon the masters of the eighteenth century, it is not because they possess greater creative powers, but, in part, because they pay more attention to the artistic intermarriage of poetry and music, that is, because they seek to avoid the defects and improprieties of musical speech so ably pointed out, in the music of his time, by Benjamin Franklin.

MACDOWELL VERSUS MACDOWELL

MACDOWELL VERSUS MACDOWELL

A STUDY IN FIRST EDITIONS AND REVISIONS

(Proceedings of the Music Teachers' National Association for 1911)

Remembering that as yet no library possesses a complete file of the first editions of our classics, Haydn, Mozart, Beethoven, etc., I conceived the plan, some years ago, of assembling in the Library of Congress, as a precautionary measure at least, a complete file of the first editions of Edward MacDowell, the foremost American composer. No serious obstacles were anticipated at the time, but the simple statement that we have not yet reached the goal permits the inference that the task cannot be so easy as it looked at first.

Surely an amazing statement, in view of the fact that MacDowell's earliest published work, the First Modern Suite, op. 10, appeared in 1883, and his last, the New England Idyls, op. 62, in 1902. The succeeding years, until his pitifully tragic end in 1908, saw the inception of several new works, but not the completion of any. Op. 1-9 (an overture for orchestra, pieces for violin and piano, etc.), were suppressed. A waltz for piano was advertised as op. 8 in 1894 and 1895, but not published, and the "Two Old Songs," published as op. 9, were really composed about ten years after op. 10. Add to the pieces published with opus-numbers the seven published under the pseudonym of Edgar Thorn, seven works under MacDowell's own name, without opus-numbers, some twenty part-songs, and about forty piano pieces arranged or edited by him, and the output is still far from voluminous. Under normal circumstances it would be a fairly easy matter to collect the first editions of about one hundred works of any composer, published, as it were, under our own eyes, ad-

vertised in musical magazines, duly listed in the bibliographic tools of the music-dealer and musician, and
many deposited in the Library of Congress for purposes
of copyright.

Under the fascinating influence of MacDowell's interpretation of his own works—a revelation to any one
who might have had his doubts as to MacDowell's
genius as a composer—I took up what, at its worst,
looked like the task of a few months. Hardly had I
commenced compiling a preliminary list of MacDowell's
works when the puzzles began to crowd each other. In
my despair, I took the shortest way imaginable out of
the difficulties, and in 1904 submitted the list to Mr.
MacDowell for suggestions, corrections, and additions.
Ever ready to help and to encourage others, MacDowell,
tired—indeed, tired to death—as he was, complied with
my request. It was after the receipt of *his* marginal
notes that I first fully realized the hornet's nest of
annoying, trivial, evasive problems which I had approached too closely. Neither MacDowell himself, nor
the music-dealers and publishers to whom we subsequently gave purchasing orders, quite understood our
object. With remarks like "new edition will soon
appear," "will be revised by me," "only new edition is
valuable," "all these are now A. P. Schmidt" (to whom
P. L. Jung's copyright had been assigned in 1899),
"these belong to me," "no copyright for the U. S. A.,"
"*nicht eingetragen*," "no copyright in America at that
time," he brushed aside (with the best of intentions,
of course) the very things which I desired to know.
But MacDowell's marginal notes also showed that there
really was occasion for a by no means dry piece of
bibliographic research-work which might also have a
practical value beyond the merely bibliographic sphere
of interest.

Here is a concrete example. The Library of Congress
had ordered the first edition of MacDowell's "Erste

moderne Suite," op. 10, published by Breitkopf & Härtel of Leipsic in 1883 with the publishers' plate number 16205. The date of publication, in pursuance of the old and often-deplored policy of music-publishers, does not appear on the title-page. Our agent therefore insisted that the copy sent us was of the desired first edition because it contained the original plate-number 16205. He overlooked the fact that the opening page of the suite's "Praeludium" contained the claim "Copyright by E. A. MacDowell, 1891." This is the copyright-date of the "Neue Ausgabe" of the "Praeludium" published *separately* in that year. Yet this particular copy of the Suite, though it included the "Neue Ausgabe" of the "Praeludium," could not have been published even in 1891, much less, of course, in 1883. And this for another reason overlooked by our usually very careful agent. The title-page, one of the collective title-pages so popular with music-publishers, refers to E. R. Kroeger's Suite, op. 33, which was not copyrighted until the year 1896. Consequently, this particular issue of MacDowell's first suite, though printed from the plates of the first edition of 1883, was not struck off until 1896 at the earliest. Now, in 1891 there appeared, also separately, the "Intermezzo" from the suite, op. 10, but in a "Neue, vom Componisten umgearbeitete Ausgabe." This revised edition, augmented from 86 to 132 bars, was *not* included in the (*circa*) 1896 issue of the complete suite, but it *was* included in the edition copyrighted in 1906. The other movements, too, now contained numerous revisions and alterations. The fact of revision is not mentioned on the title-page, which is exactly the same as the title-page of the (*circa*) 1896 issue, and it appears only in the following rather confusing—because partly impossible—marginal claim on the opening page of the "Praeludium": "Revised by Edward MacDowell, 1906. Copyright by Edward Mac-Dowell, 1891. Copyright, 1906, by Breitkopf & Härtel."

Wherein the revisions consist, only he can tell who happens to compare the three editions, bar for bar, which is not likely to occur outside of the innermost circle of MacDowell specialists. Yet such a comparison bears directly on the interpretation of MacDowell's suite. The following, not at all far-fetched, hypothetical case may serve to illustrate this. Supposing pianist A, one of the older generation, has studied the suite in the first edition of 1883, and plays it thus publicly. In his audience sits pianist B, who has studied the suite in the issue of 1896, and the critic C, who knows the suite in the version of 1906. Would it not be entirely human for B and C to accuse A of having taken extraordinary, inexcusable liberties with MacDowell's composition? On exchanging, in detail, their views on A's vandalism or lack of memory, would not B and C begin to form some rather decided opinions of each other's ignorance, until they found out that the dissension was due only to the pardonable ignorance of A, B, and C of the complicated history of MacDowell's suite?

For just such pitfalls as these, the bibliography of MacDowell's works is perhaps the most complicated of recent times. At any rate, an example for the truth that modern music, too, is replete with bibliographic puzzles, and of a kind quite foreign to older music. In MacDowell's case, "Copyright" and "Revised editions" are the principal instruments which, singly or in combination, have twisted his musical output into such a confusing mass of conflicting details.

MacDowell was one of those composers who retain a fatherly interest in their works even after publication. Eminently of a self-critical turn of mind, he would detect flaws in his published compositions and found no rest until he had given them that finish of detail which is so characteristic of his art at its best. This desire for improvement, this (one might almost say) mania for revision, in itself does not usually help to complicate matters. Such revisions, as a rule, remain hidden in the composer's private copies and do not reach the public. In the first place, comparatively few compositions sell well enough to warrant new editions; in the second place, publishers, unless moved by strong commercial reasons, dread the expense of printed revised editions. Ordinarily they prefer simply to strike off a fresh supply of copies from the unchanged plates, adding only a new title-page for the purposes of more effective advertisement.

Perhaps the steadily growing popularity of MacDowell's works in the smaller forms would have furnished a sufficient commercial incentive to his publishers to deviate from the rule, and to risk the expense of printing new editions with all those revisions and improvements which MacDowell's maturing mind wished to embody in his earlier compositions. However, the same result was effected by considerations of a more practical nature. These were considerations of copyright.

Until our copyright-agreements with certain foreign governments went into effect on July 1, 1891, music by foreign composers published in foreign countries could not be protected in our country by copyright. This provision of the law was clear, at least by inference. Nevertheless, it was not always properly understood. Hence, if, for instance, as far back as 1846, Schumann's "Vierzig Clavierstücke für die Jugend," published abroad, contain a "New York Southern District" copyright-claim in the name of Schuberth & Co. of New York, this claim is nothing more or less than a copyright curiosity, and quite naturally no entry will be found in the records of our Copyright Office. Entirely different was the situation with composers who were citizens of the United States. The law did not stipulate that their compositions must have been published in the United States in order to be amenable to United States copyright. If the composer was an American citizen, his works could be copyrighted in our country, no matter where they were published, provided only that certain formalities of registration had been observed, and that the copyright was taken out, not in the name of the foreign publisher, but in that of the American composer or in the name of any other American citizen to whom the composer assigned the copyright. Therefore, while it was impossible for a foreign publisher to claim a United States copyright on his publications of American compositions, it was entirely possible for the American composer himself or an American publisher acting as his copyright assignee to do so.

If this liberality of the copyright law as in force before July 1, 1891, had been properly understood by all the different foreign publishers of MacDowell's early works, there would have been no necessity later to rush to cover, and it would not be a fact that Mac-Dowell was powerless to prevent reprints by the wholesale of certain of his early works, simply because the European publishers did not avail themselves of Mac-Dowell's rights as an American citizen. Some of his publishers abroad, however, realized their and his danger, and availed themselves of the law's opportunities. This explains why they printed title-pages with dated United States copyright-claims in the name of G. Schirmer of New York below their own imprint. Although MacDowell, in his marginal notes mentioned above, says of his "Idyllen," op. 28, "*nicht eingetragen*" (not registered), it is nevertheless a fact that the original edition bears Schirmer's copyright-claim of 1887, that the work was duly registered, that the "Vier Stücke," op. 24, were copyrighted in the same year, "Hamlet-Ophelia," op. 22, in 1885; and that a copyright-claim in MacDowell's own name appears on the title-page of the Pianoforte Solostimme of the Second Concerto, op. 23 (1888), and of op. 25, "Lancelot and Elaine" (1888), etc.

Then came the far-reaching and in some respects totally different copyright law of 1891. At last it became possible for those European publishers who had not availed themselves of their previous opportunities, to protect their MacDowell publications against possible reprint in the United States. Not the original editions, nor mere new issues from the unchanged plates—that, too, remained impossible—but editions with new matter of any and every description, whether in the music, in the text, in the interpretation-marks, or what not—in brief, *revised* editions. Thus the exigencies of the copyright situation afforded an opportunity to print copyrightable new editions (which presumably would have a preferential sale over the old editions), with the revisions already contemplated by the composer. Not only this, but the very nature of the situation must have prompted the publishers to impress the advisability of revisions of the more popular pieces on Mac-Dowell, in his interest, in theirs, and in that of the public. The result was threefold—first, a complication of the purely bibliographical history of MacDowell's music, second, an intensely interesting development of the music itself, and third, the puzzles growing out of the combination of these two elements.

I have prepared a bibliography of first editions of MacDowell for publication by the Library of Congress. To digest the results in the form of a lecture would perhaps be possible, but to do so without going into a mass of details in themselves uninteresting, and without endless explanation of technical terminology, would be impossible—at any rate, for me. Therefore, dispensing here with the publisher's side of the matter, I shall limit myself to "MacDowell *versus* MacDowell," and that, again, without attempting an exhaustive treatment of the theme. The idea is merely to cast a glance into MacDowell's workshop and to contrast some of the more conspicuously "revised" editions with the originals.

Such revisions as are for the eye only, and not for
the ear, may properly be disregarded; that is, mere
revisions of orthography. They are not infrequent.
For instance, MacDowell in the 1895 edition of the
"Drei Lieder," op. 11, changed an A-sharp leading to
the A in a D-major chord to B-flat, or in the 1901
edition of the "Idyls," op. 28, No. 3, rewrote a chro-
matic chord-passage of several bars in stricter obedience
to enharmonic rules; the grammarian, when reading
the pieces, will be delighted, but the listener is none
the wiser. To a similar category belong the instances
where MacDowell has redistributed passages or even
chords for the hands, and has added, canceled, or changed
the fingering. More significant, though still negligible
for the present purpose, is the greater care he bestowed
in later years on interpretative symbols, and sometimes
the revisions consist merely in such things. For instance,
the 1896 ed. of op. 28, No. 5, is musically absolutely
the same as in the original edition, except that a few
marcato-signs have been added.

Decidedly important, though still "visual," revisions
are those of the interpretative headings. In his earlier
days, MacDowell followed the international custom of
using the Italian *Andante, Largo, Presto*, etc. Gradually
it became a principle with him to supplant them by
English equivalents, or at least to add these to the
Italian. (As a curiosity, I may mention that in the
"Sonata Eroica" he gives English and German headings,
but not Italian.) Here a question of principle was
involved, and, as we all know, there still exists considerable difference of opinion as to the comparative
merits of the two systems. MacDowell became quite
radical in this matter. Thus, in the 1901 ed. of the
"Goethe Idyls," op. 28, *Allegretto* is replaced by "Lightly,
almost jauntily," *Andante con indolenza* by "Slowly,
swayingly," and, instead of the rather restricted number
of current (and I may add, often vaguely and indifferently

used) Italian indications, we get in MacDowell's later years a profusion of such clear-cut English substitutes as "slightly marked," "sadly," "placidly," "murmuringly," "very faintly," "despondently," etc. (op. 28, 1901).

And now, before we proceed—with Mr. Albert Lockwood's kind assistance—from opus to opus, so far as selected for the present purpose, just a few words on a matter which MacDowell took very much to heart. It is the matter of the texts which he so often selected as mottoes for his pieces. In the marginal notes added to my list of his works, he makes this characteristic remark about op. 31, the "Sechs Gedichte nach Heine": "Translated by me. The only really authorized ed. is pub. by Schmidt"—"only new edition is valuable." He means the edition of 1901, published as "Six Poems after Heine," and he adds, in my manuscript: "The English transl. are hideous." Quite so, as you will agree if you compare Heine's original with the translation which the publisher, Hainauer, used for a "new edition" of op. 31 in 1898, the newness of which consisted merely in the addition of the "hideous" English translation. One of the original German poems reads:

> Fern an schottischer Felsenküste,
> Wo das graue Schlösslein hinausragt
> Ueber die brandende See,
> Dort, am hochgewölbten Fenster,
> Steht eine schöne, kranke Frau,
> Zart durchsichtig und marmorblau,
> Und sie spielt die Harfe und singt,
> Und der Wind durchwühlt ihre langen Locken,
> Und trägt ihr dunkles Lied
> Ueber das weite, stürmende Meer.

Here is the translation which Hainauer "with permission of the publishers, Messrs. G. Bell & Sons, London," added, and which aroused MacDowell's ire:

> Far away, on the rock-coast of Scotland,
> Where the old grey castle projecteth
> Over the wild raging sea,
> There at the lofty and archy window

Standeth a woman, beauteous, but ill,
Softly transparent and marble-pale,
And she's playing her harp and she's singing,
And the wind through her long locks forceth its way,
And beareth her gloomy song
Over the white and tempest-toss'd sea.

And here is MacDowell's own translation in the *really*
new edition of 1901, from which the German poems
have been dropped entirely, and to which characteristic
English titles were added. This piece in particular, a
flash of genius, is familiar to all of us under its title:

SCOTCH POEM

Far on Scotland's craggy shore
An old gray castle stands,
Braving the fierce North Sea;
And from a rugged casement
There peers a lovely face,
A woman's, white with woe.
She sweeps the harp-strings sadly,
And sings a mournful strain;
The wind plays through her tresses,
And carries the song amain.

I have selected the "Scotch Poem" as a fair example
of MacDowell's translations. Literal they surely are
not, and sometimes they seem to take on a different
flavor from the originals, but at least they are not
"hideous." They read like real poems, not like the
rhymed exercises of foreign school-boys in the English
language. And what is true of op. 31 applies also to
op. 28, which was treated similarly in 1901 under the
title of "Six Idyls after Goethe."

The fact is significant that MacDowell concentrated
his labors of revision chiefly on the poetic mottoes of
op. 28. With the music itself, as first published in
1887, he must have felt fairly satisfied even as late as
1901, since the changes are few and far between. No.
2, for instance, he did not alter at all. The music of
No. 5 he left untouched as it had appeared in the
P. L. Jung edition of 1896; No. 4 remained as in Jung's
edition of 1894; and No. 5 was retouched in 1896 only

to the extent of a few *marcato*-signs. In No. 1, too, the revisions are negligible, and in No. 6 he merely added an organ-point, doubled the bass in one place, spread a chord differently in another, but otherwise left the piece as it stood originally. No. 3, now known as "To the Moonlight," though in the edition of 1901 only slightly different from the edition of 1887, nevertheless illustrates the two chief points of interest in MacDowell's revisions beyond matters of orthography, etc., already discussed. The two points here are that (1) he rarely changes his melodies, (2) he changes them, if at all, generally for the purpose of a more typically MacDowellian harmonic zest and lucidity.

[Illustrations at the piano by Mr. Albert Lockwood, of the University School of Music, Ann Arbor.]

Just as remarkably different are the last thirteen or fourteen bars of the "Revery," op. 19, No. 3, in the original version of 1884, from the version of 1894, though the thematic material remained the same, as comparison proves.

There is one matter to which MacDowell paid more attention in his later than in his earlier years. It is an interestingly fluent motion of the middle voices. As a neat little illustration for this one may contrast the last four bars of op. 31, No. 3, now known as "From Long Ago," in the 1887 edition with the same bars in the 1901 edition. Beyond such slight yet significant improvements, the "Six Poems after Heine," as op. 31 is now known, remained practically untouched except the middle section of No. 4, which in 1901 was thoroughly overhauled under the title "The Post-Wagon."

Comparison so far, it will be agreed, proves that MacDowell's mania for revision produced, as a rule, improvement. I say, as a rule, because there are a few, though exceedingly few, exceptions. At any rate, I believe that MacDowell did not show a lucky hand in the only noteworthy change in the "Vier kleine Poesien," op. 32. It occurs in the "Eagle." Every one remembers the lines in the motto:

> The wrinkled sea beneath him crawls;
> He watches from his mountain walls,
> And like a thunderbolt he falls.

How realistically, yet beautifully, MacDowell's music illustrates these lines! But contrast the first edition of 1894 with the corresponding bars in the revised edition of 1906, and it is quite obvious, at least to me, that the "thunderbolt" has become much tamer.

Haydn is supposed to have suggested "wenn Einem nichts einfällt, macht man eine Pause," or words to that effect, and we all know from personal experience how wonderfully our professors improved our early efforts in composition by killing notes wholesale and letting, as it were, light and air into our stuffy juvenile masterpieces. MacDowell, too, when revising his early works, repeatedly heeded Haydn's witty and wise counsel. Take, for instance, the "quasi trillo" bars in the Presto (p. 13) of the First Modern Suite, as originally published; they sound rather clumsy and poverty-stricken. But notice the remarkable improvement in the 1906 edition, brought about in the simplest manner possible by a few rests and the tip-toeing bass.

To enumerate all the revisions of detail in the later editions of MacDowell's works would be tiresome. One would have to speak of the more massive opening of the First Concerto, of the condensation from twelve to eight bars in the 1895 edition of the fugue in op. 11, of how the at first optional octaves have now become obligatory, and of many other such alterations that attract the attention of him who happens to have the different editions handy for comparison. However, enough of these minor examples have been adduced, I believe, to show that the work of revision was one of love and labor combined, and that MacDowell had at least this in common with genius, that he took infinite pains.

Before proceeding to those revisions which one might almost call recompositions, just a few words on the humorous side of the subject. It is known how Mac-Dowell came to hate his "Witches' Dance," to hate it for a popularity so out of proportion to the merits of the piece. Well, MacDowell either hated the very sight of the piece or he considered it lost beyond redemption. At any rate, except for the interpolation of a full-rest bar with hold before the *staccatiss. leggiero* passage, he handed it back to a loving public with practically no improvements whatsoever. And, let me illustrate just what a funnily subtle thing the copyright law is by the "Schattentanz" from the "Twelve Études," op. 39, published in 1890. The piece was detached in 1892 with four other études as "Fünf Stücke" with next to no changes, and no claim of revision was made until 1898, when Schmidt published it in an "augmented edition." I assure you that, except for the addition of two bars at the beginning (where everybody must see them), the "augmented" edition is absolutely identical with the original edition.

Passing on to those pieces in which revision went far beyond the readjustment of details and assumed the character of recomposition, I select the first "Sere-nata," op. 16, published in 1883. The very fact that in the revised edition of 1895 the piece fills only five (instead of seven) pages shows that some radical surgical operation must have taken place. The "Andante con moto" has remained the same, but then, after eight bars of the "Un poco animato," the two versions remain totally different until the end. The "Barcarolle," op. 18, No. 1, originally published in 1884, shows a similar process of condensation in the 1894 edition, the Tempo I° section (with a varied repetition of part A) having been reduced from forty-six bars to twenty-six. But not alone this; MacDowell unhesitatingly dropped the virtuoso bars at the top of p. 5. This is typical of a fact well worth studying by his biographers, who so far have not paid much attention to such evolutional matters. The fact is, that MacDowell learned the difficult art of subduing the virtuoso in the composer. In his later years he blue-penciled with unerring judgment brilliant virtuoso passages that, as in this Serenata, were utterly out of place. Most pianist-composers, I fancy, would have revised the piece by making it still more acrobatic. The "Revery," op. 19, no. 3, was mentioned as a good example of how MacDowell would revise a piece without, if at all possible, affecting its thematic curve. The "Dance of the Dryads" in the same opus is a more extended and even more instructive example of this kind of revision. In the edition of 1894 he did not deviate from the thematic material of 1884, or rather he recurred to it every few bars; yet (as under the circumstances only a full comparative quotation can prove) it has become an altogether different piece, more lucid and much more interestingly varied in the arabesque.

In my introduction I spoke of the puzzles in the bibliographical history of MacDowell's First Modern Suite, op. 10. Of course, musically, no puzzles remain to be solved, once the different editions are spread before us for comparison. Unfortunately, I have not been able to procure a copy of the real first edition of 1883,[1] and I therefore do not know wherein it differs from the edition published *circa* 1896, in which the "Neue Ausgabe" of 1891 of the "Praeludium," but not of the "Intermezzo," was included. The latter, however, forms part of the revised edition of 1906 of the entire suite, and therefore a comparison of these two editions, at least, was easy. The "Praeludium" of 1906, for

[1] I am now in a position to state that it does not differ at all, and that there is nothing *new* about the 1891 issue of the Praeludium except an added few staccato marks, and the like.

instance, starts out "Largamente con energia—with energy and breadth," instead of "Ad libitum—Lento," as originally. Seeing how the initial octaves are doubled and the brilliant "accelerando" passage is rearranged, one begins to anticipate a rather complete revision, but after the introduction the piece settles down again without any substantial changes, except that (on p. 6) several bars are moved an octave lower. In the "Presto" the changes have become more numerous. They are sprinkled throughout the piece, smoothing out wrinkles and picking up flaws, and one of the most characteristic revisions has already been quoted. Similar improvements have been chiseled out of the "Presto con bravura," now headed "Più allegro e risoluto." While, therefore, this calls for no further comment, much less the preceding "Fugue," which has remained the same, a very radical departure from the 1896 edition appears in the other movements. Thus the "Andantino" and "Allegretto," with the motto "Per amica silentiae luna," while practically the same on p. 16-17, has become, from p. 18 to the end, totally different (fully twenty bars shorter) and in MacDowell's best vein.

While this movement is an instructive example of condensation, the "Intermezzo," on the contrary, is an example of expansion. As the 1896 edition did not include the "Neue, umgearbeitete Ausgabe" of 1891, we, of course, have in the 1896 edition the piece in its original form. As such it totaled eighty-six bars. In the "Neue, umgearbeitete Ausgabe" of 1891, subsequently embodied without changes in the 1906 edition of the whole suite, it has grown to 132 bars! Clearly, these two versions would be admitted in court as strikingly different, even without oral proof. Finally, the Rhapsodie, too, with the motto "Lasciate ogni speranza voi ch' entrate," though of practically the same length and of the same material in both editions, was so thoroughly overhauled as often to sound like

a new piece. However, as the illustration of this fact
would require a complete rendition in order to be convincing, I prefer to proceed to the *finale* of this study,
namely, the classic example of MacDowell's art of
revising.

I mean the amazing contrast between the original
edition of 1888 of the "Marionettes," op. 38, and the
revised edition of 1901—published by Schmidt. I now
quote what I said of this contrast in a lecture-recital on
MacDowell at Washington in 1905:

> Candidly, MacDowell's attempt to portray a clown, a witch,
> a villain, etc., in the "Marionetten" was a failure. One point
> strongly favors this opinion. MacDowell himself seems to have
> felt dissatisfied with the Marionetten as originally published in
> 1888. Though he retouched most of his earlier works in recent
> issues, none were overhauled to such an extent as these miniatures.
> These finishing touches and skillful changes show, more than
> anything else, the extraordinary progress MacDowell made as a
> composer. Compare, for instance, the beautiful filigree-work of
> the additional "Prologue" and "Epilogue" with the rather hasty
> workmanship of the first edition of the Marionettes. Then observe
> how strikingly the short run in the "Villain," where he seems to
> be ready to seize his victim and then of a sudden sinks back, has
> improved this gentleman of doubtful character. The "Clown,"
> too, in his new garb appeals very much more to our sense of humor,
> merely on account of a few subtle rhythmic and harmonic modi-
> fications. But the most astonishing changes occur in "Sweetheart."
> Formerly as "Lady-Love" almost commonplace and decidedly the
> weakest of the Marionettes, she is now dressed to such advantage
> as to be easily the best. In fact, as "Sweetheart" she is now so
> full of tenderness and passion as to present one of MacDowell's
> most artistic genre-pictures. And how was this incredible improve-
> ment accomplished? Without practically any changes in the melody,
> but with an exquisite polyphonic filigree of which only a past-
> master of the art of harmonization knows the secret.

You see, I put a construction on the motive underlying
the revision of the "Marionettes," totally different from
that suggested by Mr. Edward Burlingame Hill in an
analytical article, "MacDowell's Marionettes," in the
Musician, 1910. I do not underestimate the value of
his careful analysis in the least—Mr. Hill can always
be depended on to write with knowledge of his subject,
and interestingly—but I do believe that he was sorely
mistaken in attributing the revision of the "Marionettes"

largely to a desire to facilitate and simplify the pieces for the ultimate consumer. I believe that MacDowell's motive was strictly esthetic, and technical only from his advanced standpoint as composer. As the proof of the pudding lies in the eating, I would invite oral comparison of "Lady-Love," vintage of 1888, with "Sweetheart," vintage of 1901.

A NATIONAL CONSERVATORY

A NATIONAL CONSERVATORY

SOME PROS AND CONS

(*Musical America*, 1909)

Is a National Conservatory of Music in our country desirable or necessary? The question may be traced back for more than sixty years through newspapers and magazines. It has also been brought to the attention of Congress, but the few bills proposed have shared the fate of many thousand other bills—that is, they have been pigeonholed. Nor is there any likelihood that a new bill will have a better fate in the near future.

It appears to be generally agreed that our Federal Constitution has not provided for such an institution. However, once Congress in its wisdom looks upon the idea of a National Conservatory with favor, there may be found in our Constitution, so others believe, a paragraph elastic enough for the purpose in the same manner as our copyright laws include things that a strictly literal construction of the paragraph on copyright in the Constitution would exclude.

Others seem to think that, even if the establishment of a National Conservatory should be unconstitutional, the individual States might be allowed by their respective constitutions to found State Conservatories either as departments of State universities or independently. The governing principles would, of course, be the same in both cases. But I am not concerned here with State Conservatories.

As regards constitutional barriers, the problem of a National Conservatory may be deemed purely academic, yet it is a live problem, and as such should never be allowed to become comatose. The question merely is, Why is a National Conservatory desirable, or perhaps necessary, for the healthy development of our musical life? The necessity has often been denied; first, because the private conservatories and the musical departments of our colleges are held to provide sufficiently and efficiently for our national needs; second, because of a fear of stagnation of methods and ideals in a National— that is to say, Government—Conservatory.

Neither argument, the one positive, the other negative, is wholly logical. The danger of stagnation is imaginary. Because such criticism has been directed with more or less ground against the institutions at Paris and Berlin is no reason why such a danger could not be avoided here. Indeed, since we should know the mistakes made elsewhere, we could profit by the experience of others and thus easily prevent stagnation.

But is such a danger really latent in national, in government institutions more than in private? The truth probably is that errors of management are more perceptible in government institutions, for the simple reason that they are public institutions, subject to public scrutiny and depending more or less on the confidence of the taxpayer. If the searchlight of public criticism, maybe even for political reasons, is turned on them, the weak spots in the management appear sooner or later, whereas private institutions may lead a shadowy and shady existence sublimely indifferent to public opinion. With them good and progressive management is a matter of business, and if the director of a private conservatory should see fit to mismanage it, nothing will prevent him except eventually the alarm of the trustees or stockholders, if such there be, at the truth of Lincoln's famous dictum.

This is, of course, an extreme hypothetical case, but it serves its purpose of showing how the fact that a private conservatory is fundamentally a business undertaking does not *a priori* guarantee progressive or sensible management. The director of a National Conservatory, too, must obviously be a man of business—that is, of executive and administrative ability, and in the last analysis it is always the personality, properly placed, that counts. Yet there is this difference:

A public official who does not give, or is supposed not to give, satisfaction, may be removed, whereas the director of a private conservatory is a relatively permanent fixture. Undisturbed by an official probe and by the press, he may advertise his institution quite out of proportion to its merits, and he may surround himself with a mediocre faculty whose chief virtue is colossal bluff. His institution, as long as he can fool the parents of his pupils, may remain a dispensary of poor music and still poorer methods of instruction.

The possibility of unceremonious removal of an inefficient public official, whether in form of discharge or of forced resignation, is a strong argument in favor of a government conservatory, and the recent history of the Paris Conservatory proves that this drastic remedy is adopted if sufficient pressure be exercised. On the other hand, the danger is that an efficient public official may be removed for purely political reasons or before he has had time to prove that his seemingly questionable management really would ultimately benefit the institution.

Nobody in his right senses denies that private conservatories may and have efficiently upheld high and progressive standards of systematic instruction, and thereby merited not only the gratitude of those immediately concerned, but also of the public at large. Nor can it be denied that some have done so not only efficiently but sufficiently, yet they are of necessity exceptions. It requires more than a clear and ambitious vision, more than executive ability and tenacious energy of high-minded purpose, to build up a great conservatory with all the branches of musical study; it requires the *nervus rerum*, namely, capital.

Though artistic in its aims, the best and most fully equipped private institutions must of necessity be based on commercial considerations. The greater the financial risk, the vaster the financial problems will be, and the easier the temptation to sacrifice the science of teaching to the science of meeting bills. Especially in our country, where evil influences have been at work to undermine the distinction between music as a profession and music as a commercial pursuit, this temptation is bound to lead many astray. Unless generously endowed or safely beyond the experimental stage, the private conservatory will be an institution of compromises, not perhaps because the director or the faculty favor compromises, but simply because "business" demands them. In fact, such an institution is only too often merely an organized competitor of the independent private music-teacher.

To deny the right of existence to private conservatories would be idiotic. On the other hand, if it is sometimes claimed that a government institution would unfairly compete with private enterprise—the great bugbear in American public opinion—the history of musical education proves the fallacy of such an argument.

Can it be asserted that the Schola Cantorum is less flourishing, because a National Conservatory exists at Paris?

Have the municipal and government institutions in Berlin and elsewhere interfered with private enterprise?

The answer is a most emphatic denial. An institution like the New England Conservatory would suffer very little because a National Conservatory existed at Washington.

On the other hand, a National Conservatory would add strength to smaller private conservatories because they would, as they have done everywhere, take their cue from the government institution, would be forced to keener competition, and would therefore for sound business reasons have to keep their standards as high as their finances warranted. The public would gain by this competition, and, after all, public usefulness is the keynote and crucial test of every educational institution. It may fairly be asked whether part of the opposition to government competition is not a mere cloak for brutally selfish interests.

Any attempt to demolish such opposition by arguments would be useless. It is a conflict between principles, and the stronger principle is bound to win in the long run. Experience proves that in all such contests the negative interests dominate the situation at first, because the supposed danger of their "business" forces them into an early organized resistance.

To organize the affirmative interests is a very much more difficult task, and almost impossible in this matter, as it concerns musical folk, by nature easy-going and by training sublimely indifferent to questions of public policy. Yet it is about time for those who firmly believe in the desirability of a National Conservatory to reach a concerted plan of action. On what fundamental principles do they base their belief—not negative principles as criticised above, but positive principles, since such alone are at the bottom of every new movement?

They take it for granted that the noblest and most important duties of a nation, and consequently of the government representing the nation, are centered in public education. They further take it for granted that art ever has been and ever will be a powerful, uplifting factor of civilization. They wish to see our own civilization at least on a par with that of other nations, particularly that phase of our national life which emanates from our musical instincts. Individual effort alone cannot accomplish this. Concerted action is necessary, and government is but another word for national coöperation. Logically, they claim it to be the duty of our government to help to provide the proper opportunities for developing and perfecting the musical talent that slumbers in the maturing generation, on which in every respect the future welfare of our nation depends. This goal, they are convinced, can be reached only with the assistance of a generously endowed National Conservatory.

Is it not humiliating for the American musician, they ask, that of all nations the United States alone should have failed to recognize officially in the art of music an essential factor of national culture, a recognition that everywhere else has found its outward public expression in national conservatories, not to mention government subvention of a National Opera and the like? Doctrines of State socialism and paternalism! Exactly, and for this reason, if for no other, the negative private interests will be supported by the average member of Congress until he feels convinced that the average American desires to be represented on these "socialistic" grounds in matters of national art and music.

The opponents of a National Conservatory would probably tell Congress this: Such doctrines are public-spirited enough, but they are visionary, impracticable and lead to wanton extravagance. The National Conservatory of the United States should be a model institution. This implies that every instrument in the modern orchestra should be taught by the best masters obtainable. The same should be true of voice-culture classes, classes in musical history, esthetics, sight-singing, liturgy, choral singing, chamber music playing, orchestra training, harmony, counterpoint, composition, conducting, concert and operatic interpretation and the thousand and one other things that make for proficiency in musical art, not to mention general culture, languages, etc. This is our ideal, too, as set forth in our catalogues

and circulars, but we do not quite live up to our adver-
tisements, on account of business obstacles. Such an
ideal institution would call for a very large faculty of
picked men and women. Since in private life such
teachers could earn a comfortable income, since our
government does not offset the disadvantage of small
salaries by the advantage of a civil service pension,
you would have to offer substantial salaries to attract
the masters and mistresses in their particular field of
activity. This would involve a yearly expenditure of
about half a million dollars in teachers' salaries, for
the clerical and administrative force, for a suitable
conservatory library supplementing the collections in
the Library of Congress, not to mention such prosaic
things as gas and coal bills. Nor is this all.

This whole pedagogic machinery would have to be
housed. Since no power on earth can prevent the
American people through their chosen representatives
from doing things on a magnificent and munificent
scale once they decide to do them at all, this building
would be not only serviceable, but monumental, a
stimulus to the national eye from without, as it would
be intended as a stimulus to the national ear from
within. And serviceable such a building could be only
if in addition to the many classrooms it included a
small hall for chamber music, etc., a large hall for orchestral and choral concerts and a fully equipped
modern operatic stage and auditorium.

Though probably you could economize by relying on
the ingenuity of the architects to combine satisfactorily
the large concert auditorium and the operatic stage,
this proposed National Conservatory would cost the
nation about three million dollars. You may think
that the tuition fees exacted from a thousand students or
more will yield a sufficient income to pay for the interest
on the building, for its maintenance, the teaching faculty,
etc., but this is not at all the plan of our friends yonder.

Far from it; they want the nation first to build a National Conservatory and then to administer to the needs of our musical youth absolutely free of charge. Do you feel justified in carrying your sentimental and patriotic sympathy with music in America so far as to levy an initial impost of several million dollars and an additional yearly tax of about five hundred thousand dollars on the American taxpayer?

If these arguments did not permit of rebuttal, undoubtedly it would be the duty of our Solons to vote the propsition into the abyss of Congressional pigeon-holes. Should, on the other hand, the champions of a National Conservatory succeed in proving that, even at such extravagant figures, the cost of a National Conservatory would not be out of proportion to the profits derived from it in some tangible form by a perceptible percentage of the population, the proposition would have some chance of serious consideration.   Once convinced that it would be a *sound national business investment,* Congress would probably concur in the view that a National Conservatory should not be subjected in its management to those commercial risks, drawbacks and compromises which cannot be avoided by private institutions based on the principle of to buy and to sell.   In other words, Congress would probably not see fit to discriminate between this and other national institutions of an educational type by levying in addition to the indirect national tax a direct tax on the students of their parents, who already would be contributing their share to the indirect tax.

Possibly, though won over to the main principle of a free National Conservatory, Congress might at first contend that the institution should be thrown open to whoever cared to enter it, with no entrance examination at all or only a sham examination; but they probably would soon realize the folly of such a policy.

Better no National Conservatory at all than an official incubator of a musical proletariat.   It should be the gift of the nation to the musical, not to the unmusical, carrying with it the premise of musical talent, obligations of strictest discipline and serious effort to become worthy of the gift.

On the other hand, the National Conservatory should have this feature in common with all other conservatories, that it would aim not so much to discover, breed and perfect geniuses as to send back among the people an army of well-trained musicians and music-teachers of at least average musical gifts.

If they included, as has been so conspicuously the case at Paris, men and women of extraordinary talent, so much the better; but the healthy development of our national musical life depends not so much upon the brilliant deeds of a few as on the solid missionary work of the many.

Since the American people cherish an ultra-democratic respect for the average mortal, since they are avowed devotees to numerical majority, and since they are not yet given to fostering officially unconventional genius, the standpoint just analyzed, and presumably no other, would appeal to Congress after Congress has commenced to look with favor on a National Conservatory as a national business proposition.

But would a National Conservatory be a profitable investment of national funds? To wax eloquent over the waste of public funds in erecting a monumental building for this purpose is, of course, absurd, because the funds would flow back into the pockets of the bricklayer, the mason, the architect, the manufacturer, the marble or granite companies, and so forth. Therefore the question really is, Would the specified use of the building be profitable for the nation?

One might say that it makes little difference whether music-students pay for their instruction indirectly through the Treasury Department as trustee of national funds or directly to private music-teachers. The fallacy of this argument is obvious, because the burden, be it ever so infinitesimal, would really be thrown on many millions of tax-payers instead of on a few thousand whose children alone would derive an immediate educational profit.

Not much sounder is the argument that, while access to the classes of the conservatory would be free under adequate rules of examination and other restrictions, access to the concerts and operatic performances would not, and that these entertainments would therefore contribute to the maintenance of the institution. The trouble with this argument is, that the American people are conspicuously and splendidly opposed to charging admission fees, etc., to any of their national institutions. Nor would this source of income, even if based on optimistic estimates, be considerable enough to influence Congress one way or the other in its decisions.

Quite different is the argument that a National Conservatory would gradually help to stop millions of American dollars from being poured into the coffers of European conservatories, European music-teachers, European boarding-house keepers, European merchants, European this and that.

Furthermore, a National Conservatory would gradually help to undermine the fad, so far as it is a fad, of importing European "stars" and celebrities who then export millions of American dollars to Europe.

The business of playing in American orchestras, of conducting American orchestras, of impersonating heroes and heroines on the American operatic stage, etc., would gradually become, within reasonable limits and *without chauvinism*, a homespun business exactly as it is in every European country, with the partial exception of England.

If the champions of a National Conservatory thus convince Congress that *music in America largely rests on a fundamentally wrong economic basis*, that a National

Conservatory will help to rectify this basis, and therefore that it will be a profitable investment from a
broad national business standpoint, their case is practically won.

We shall then have a National Conservatory, and
within a few years the results will force the people to
wonder why its establishment was so long delayed.

Not merely this, but the strength of arguments
of a certain type would soon be felt which, by reason
of their "sentimental" character, cannot be expected to
appeal to a legislative body of men of affairs as they do
to us musicians and music-lovers, and which it might
be a tactical blunder to press into service too soon.

I mean this. A National Conservatory would signify
the official recognition by the American people of music
as an essential factor of national culture.

Dignity would be added to the musical profession,
the cause of reputable and meritorious private competitors would be strengthened, and that of unsound
institutions would be weakened.

A still more important result for the musical welfare
of our country would be, that an outlet for the thousands
of talented home-trained instrumentalists and vocalists
would become imperative.

Good symphony orchestras and chamber music organizations would spring up everywhere by sheer force
of economic necessity. For obvious reasons their
financial problems would be less difficult than those of
the now comparatively few permanent local orchestras
in America. While they would naturally interfere
with the activity of the traveling orchestras, they
would give what these, with all due respect and gratitude for their splendid pioneer and missionary work,
cannot give to the communities on their circuit, namely,
a healthy musical backbone.

Furthermore, the frightfully provincial performances
of the great oratorios, etc., with a screeching organ, or

"two" pianos or a fragmentary orchestra, would gradually become a thing of the past.

I also firmly believe, for the economic reasons stated above, that the establishment of a National Conservatory would help considerably in dotting the country with permanent homes for the operatic repertory sung in English by skilled American vocalists for an adequate but not exorbitant compensation. Then, and not until then, will our country have what we lack, in spite of contrary opinion that does not look beyond the horizon of a few musical centres, namely, a musical atmosphere.

In Europe this mysterious yet omnipresent musical atmosphere is but the love, desire and respect for musical art permeating in proportionate degrees all strata of society through the medium of local choral societies, local orchestras, local chamber music, local opera.

If competition between a National Conservatory and the great private conservatories will help to generate and to spread this precious musical atmosphere, by all means let us have a National Conservatory.

A SURVEY OF MUSIC IN AMERICA

A SURVEY OF MUSIC IN AMERICA

(Read before the "Schola Cantorum" at New York City, April 11, 1913, and privately printed in the same year.)

An American fairly conversant with the musical life of Europe will find it by far easier to survey acceptably music in Germany, France, Italy, than music in his own country. Indeed, I defy anybody to survey the musical life of America with accuracy. At least, in the form of a lecture. Yet here I am, committed to exactly that task. The only way out of my predicament will be to restrict myself to the cursory discussion of a few phases of our musical life.

For instance, there is the problem of municipal, state or federal subvention of music. Perhaps not as yet a really acute problem in our country, but one that will call for solution some day and one to which several lectures might profitably be devoted. As you know, our musical life is based practically on what I have elsewhere called "Privatbetrieb," a term not fully covered by the translation "(under) private management." We belong with England and Italy to the small group of countries standing apart from other civilized countries, where the musical life depends on a coöperation between private enterprise and the government's paternalistic interest and support. I had planned to convince you, if possible, that this mixed system is by far the better of the two and of necessity will produce the better results, but time forbids making propaganda here for my pet theories.

Not so many years ago the idea of governmental subvention of music would have met with the same shallow argument still hurled in our country at every progressive economic proposition tinged with so-called

socialism, namely, that it is un-American. Well, a
thing is un-American until it becomes American. I am
glad to see the idea of governmental support of musical
talent and interest in music—national assets just as
much as are potash deposits—spreading its roots
throughout our country. The city of New York, for
instance, is now spending considerable sums in that
direction, and it would be a regrettable retrograde step
if these sums were decreased instead of increased in
the future. The time will yet come when our progressive
municipalities will either own and manage their own
opera houses or will exempt bona-fide grand opera
houses from taxation (as has been proposed in Boston),
or in some other form will subvention opera not from
mere sentimentality, but from the standpoint of civic
business. And if more and more of our state universities find it necessary or desirable to include musical
departments, I really can not see why the idea of a
National Conservatory of Music should meet with
opposition. Of course, such one-sided and half-baked
schemes as have been outlined recently will never do,
especially no scheme which proposes to build up a
National Conservatory on private donations. The
raison d'être of a National Conservatory is the official
recognition by a people of the higher professional
training in music as a national asset, with all the educational, artistic and economic advantages to be derived
therefrom. The most generously endowed private institution with a national name would be a rather poor
substitute for the real thing. If such substitutes are
offered simply because of fear of the possibilities of
"graft" in a governmental institution, then the promoters
should be reminded, on the one hand, of the fact that
"graft" is not quite unknown to private business; on
the other, of the fact that our Federal Government is
as clean as that of any other nation. Once the pressure
behind Congress attains such an impetus as to put a

National Conservatory within reach of our people, you may rest assured that it will be made an institution worthy of the name, provided the musical profession undermines the lobbying proclivities of petty schemers and sees to it that Congress entrusts the plans to a competent commission of experts. Such experts we have in plenty, and once the heads of our great private conservatories appreciate the certainty that the dignified competition of a National Conservatory will strengthen rather than weaken them in the pursuit of their educational ideals, our Government will find them ready to coöperate in removing the main difficulty: to put a National Conservatory speedily on the same level of efficiency with these great private institutions.[1]

Time forbids me to go into details concerning these and other aspects of musical education in America. For obvious reasons, it is the musical education of the young on which the future appreciation and cultivation of music in America depends. Roughly classifying it, this education proceeds from four main sources: Musical instruction in the home, in the public schools, in the colleges, and in professional music schools; and all four depend for positive results, of course, on the efficiency of the teachers. It can not be maintained that we have passed the period of experimentation entirely— perhaps still most noticeable in our public school music —but on the whole we are pushing ahead rapidly and intelligently. Leaving fakers and parasites out of the question, of whom every country has its share—and our country, by reason of its peculiar history, more than its legitimate share—I believe that we have now reached the stage when our music-teachers, a host of them with a thorough European training, compare

[1] Those interested in my views on a National Conservatory, I may add here, will find them in an article of mine in "Musical America," September 4, 1909. It is, by the way, the only article ever contributed or sold by me to "Musical America," and does not occupy itself at all with the Music Division of the Library of Congress, regarding which I never contributed or sold an article to "Musical America " (But compare "Musical America," April 19 and 26, 1913.)

quite favorably with the music-teachers abroad. Not only this, but we have reached the stage where we shall have to depend primarily on our own crop of teachers, not on a further influx of foreigners; though this does not preclude the desirability of incorporating into our educational system preëminently able foreign musicians. Indeed, America can only congratulate herself if uncommonly gifted artists and educators in the broad sense— such as courtesy forbids me to mention here by name —continue to settle in America and to take a visible and unprejudiced part in shaping our musical destiny.

One has but to watch the growth, for instance, of the American Guild of Organists, with its high ideals and pretty stiff tests of efficiency, or to study the "Proceedings of the Music Teachers' National Association," to be impressed with the vigor, the knowledge, the methodical thoughtfulness of the new generation of the American musician and educator, who, though professedly in music as a business, is nevertheless an idealist. Not a dreamer, but a man who has visions of his peculiar country's peculiar needs and strives after these ideals with good old-fashioned practical common horse-sense. Uplifting forces are rumbling below the surface which the uninitiated barely suspect, and the occasional eruption of premature fantastic bubbles merely demonstrates that the weakness of these powerful educational tendencies is an excess of individualism and a lack of coördinated organization. In this movement I consider myself only an interested bystander, just as I should not presume to pass judgment on the rather confusing status of music in our colleges and universities. We may view with serene patience the controversy of professors over questions of administration, standardization, credits, and what not. The main point is, that the art of music has invaded the American college and will not be driven out again. I even consider the mere injection of music-schools into the academic body a matter of secondary importance. The potential possibilities of the movement, I think, lie less in the direction of technique than of culture. On the one hand, the musician trained at college will, or at least should, get a college education, and thus learn some things quite as vital to an artist as the happy faculty of grammatically harmonizing "Yankee Doodle." On the other hand, the student-body at large will learn to see in the art of music something quite as respectable as chemistry or law, and those students whose musical instinct and interest have been aroused at college by the opportunities there offered to hear and appreciate the art of music, will carry this cultural asset with them through life. In proportion as the number of college-bred men increases in America, the number of American men who do not consider it an effeminate pastime and below their dignity to attend concerts will increase. In fact, I believe that the future of musical culture in America now depends more on the intelligent support of the men than on that of the women. What we now need is not less femininity in our musical life, but more masculinity. The American woman has done her share and more than her share, and she still continues to do so. Moreover, she can point to one achievement which is unique in every way in the annals of music. She has crystallized her interest in music into a vast and flourishing organization: I mean the National Federation of Musical Clubs. Granted that now and then individual clubs move erratically along the border lines of amateurish piffle, yet, on the whole, the ladies seem to know pretty well what is best for them. However, one thing is absolutely certain: Within its limited sphere of opportunities the National Federation of Music Clubs has done more for the American composer and the American musician than any other agency.

The temptation to survey church-music in America I can resist with ease. Abstinence from churchly

habits unfits me for intelligent utterance on the subject.
That there is room for reforms is clear, otherwise pens
and typewriters would not be kept busy demanding
and suggesting reforms.   Whether or not the church is
still often looked upon by many church-goers as a kind
of concert-hall with liturgy, sermons, prayers, etc.,
thrown in, where one can hear music excellently performed and practically for nothing, I am not prepared
to say.   If that still be the case, those engaged in sub-
ordinating the charms of music to the dignity of Divine
Service have my heartfelt sympathy.   My impression
is that things are not nearly so bad as they used to be.
The pendulum seems to be swinging from mere music
in churches to more churchly music.   With this impression uppermost in my mind, I prefer to look on
such a program as I happen to have on my desk at
home as a mere freakish curiosity.   The program is
that of a musical evening service in a fashionable
church, and one-half of it consists of anthems by one
Richard Wagner—yes, anthems by Richard Wagner, or
rather selections from his operas designated as anthems
after the substitution of sacred English words for the
original secular German.   Add to that "processional
marches" arranged for the organ from his operas, and
you will know my reason for not going to church on
that occasion, at least.

Why is it practically impossible briefly, yet accurately,
to survey music in America?

By America, I hasten to add, I do not mean the
Island of Manhattan, nor even greater New York with
the cities of Boston, Philadelphia and Chicago generously
thrown in, but the three million square miles that
stretch from the Pacific to the Atlantic and are populated
by ninety-two million inhabitants; a mere handful, if
contrasted, for instance, with Germany's 208,000 square
miles and sixty-five millions inhabitants.   Now, the
cultivation of art is practically a city-bred function of

the human mind. Hence, the rural population is and always has been a negligible quantity, in Europe as well as in America. This statement means that of our ninety-two million inhabitants forty-nine rural millions do not count for purposes of an art-survey, if we accept the definition by the Census Bureau of a rural population as of people residing in cities of less than 2,500 inhabitants. But, as a matter of fact, in America as in Europe, cities of even 10,000 inhabitants may, with very few exceptions, safely be classed as musically rural in the above sense. And (at least in a comparatively new country like ours) a noteworthy musical life may be said to be restricted to cities of 25,000 inhabitants or more. Of such cities we had in 1910 only 229 with a total population of 28 millions. If we take it for granted, though of course with notable exceptions, that the opportunities for a well-regulated, wholesome musical life increase with the size of cities, then it is instructive to bear in mind that this country of 92 million inhabitants has only fifty cities with 100,000 or more inhabitants against Germany's 47. Furthermore, the majority of these fifty cities will be found in that relatively small section of the United States north of the Potomac and Ohio and east of the Mississippi, with not less than forty per cent. of our total population. This section comprises, with the exception of Virginia, the Carolinas and Louisiana, all States whose principal cities look back to prerevolutionary times for the beginning of a well-regulated musical life. On the other hand, there are in the newer Middle-Western States and, of course, still more so in the Far Western States a number of musically flourishing cities which, fifty or even less than fifty years ago, had not outstripped the rural stage, while some Far Eastern cities of now less musical importance were enjoying the then best in music. Finally, attention should be called to the fact that the total population of the United States, in 1910 ninety-two millions, in 1880 was only fifty and in 1850 only twenty-three millions.

All these figures have simply been adduced here as statistical food for the thought that it is absurd to compare in the same breath the musical life of a country like Germany with that of the United States. On the whole our country does not yet and can not yet possess a well-developed musical life. Those gentlemen who assiduously spread the rumor that we Americans move in a musical atmosphere just as do the Germans, simply, with patriotic pens dipped in Metropolitan ink, cross out the most elementary premises of musical "Länderkunde" that stand as barriers between fancy and fact. Moreover, population statistics demonstrate inexorably that music in America must be unbalanced and very unevenly distributed, as indeed it is. Therewith we have the fundamental difference between a here thickly and there very thinly settled country like ours and an evenly and thickly settled country like Germany. In Germany, therefore, a fairly even distribution of musical interest and activity would be the logical result, even without centuries of decentralization of culture and other significant phases of her cultural history. I do not believe for one moment that the desire for culture in Germany is more sincere or deeper than it is in our country, in those strata of society that really count; but no amount of sophistry can remove Germany's immense advantage that she is, in population and in musical culture, settled to her fullest capacity. This insures the further advantage of stability of musical contours; so, with the assistance of an abundance of reliable literature in the form of general and local musical histories, a surveyor of modern musical Germany has a fairly easy task of triangulation.

The surveyor of music in America faces an entirely different problem. If the contours in our country, by force of circumstances as yet musically unsettled, were stationary, the very fact of this unsettled condition might simplify his task. Unfortunately for him, but fortunately for us, this is not the case. To borrow a happy phrase from Prof. Stanley of Ann Arbor, our country musically, as in so many other respects, is "im Bau begriffen," that is, in course of construction. Not even here, in the old and settled East, have the contours as yet become fixed. Taking our country as a whole, they are constantly and visibly changing. Snapshots of our country's musical landscape, therefore, can possess only a momentary value. A fairly accurate picture taken in the year 1913 is bound to have become inaccurate, because antiquated, by the year 1923. Furthermore, the vastness of our country simply forbids a comprehensive tour of inspection and research by any one individual. Of necessity, then, the surveyor will have to fall back on what has been written by others on music in America.

I have touched a rather sore spot. The plain truth of the matter is, that the literature on music in America is woefully inadequate both in quantity and quality. Most of this literature was written and continues to be written with the connivance of editors and publishers by persons to whom the term "historian" applies only by courtesy. The compilation of facts, or near-facts, or supposed facts, in an entertaining form is a fascinating pastime, but the mere compilation of facts is not history. Register accurately all the facts of a city's or country's musical activity, be it even in strict chronological order, and yet you have not history. It is the logical and dis-criminating interpretation of facts from the evolutional bird's-eye view that makes for history and the happy faculty to lay bare the influences that, so to speak, forced the musical tree to take on its own characteristic shape and no other.

To wax eloquent over the relatively tremendous ex-pansion of our musical activities during the last fifty years is very well and good, but such retrospective reminiscences, comparisons, estimates, etc., do not necessarily produce even sound local history, unless informed by the proper historical perspective. This quality they too often lack, with the result that the American eagle struts about in these pictures, more than life-size. We have a right to feel proud of our accomplishments during the past fifty years, but it would not detract in the least from the full measure of credit due this and the last generation, if previous generations received more generous and more enlightened credit for their pioneer work, since it is historical nonsense to suppose that music in this country suddenly sprouted from the soil about 1860 like mushrooms after a rain. Until the gap between the Colonial period and the second half of the nineteenth century has been bridged by a sound bit of historical reasoning, we shall not be in a position to understand even our current musical history with scientific intelligence. Moreover, too often the fact is lost sight of that the expansion and dissemination of musical activity during the last fifty years —what one might call the consumption of music, with a proportionate increase in the sums spent on music— has been a world-movement, and not at all restricted to America.

Supposing for a moment that the existing literature were methodologically above criticism, does it enable anybody to survey music in America with a fair degree of accuracy? By no means, since it is so poverty-stricken in quantity as to be a disgrace to a nation of ninety-two million inhabitants. There is not a city in this country that can point to a comprehensive, authoritative, scientific history of its musical life. Valuable, even splendid books on certain phases exist— yes, and New Yorkers should feel under obligations to a certain much abused gentleman for just such books— but comprehensive histories of every phase of a city's musical life do not exist. As to general histories of music in America, they plainly suffer from a dearth of local or otherwise specialized literature. A statement which finds its corroboration in even the best of existing histories of music in America, since the book hails from Boston in New England to such an extent that even New York and Philadelphia, not to mention Chicago, seem to disappear in the fog.

That mythical region which we Easterners call the West and about which we Easterners in politics and sundry other respects have such hazy notions, is practically *terra incognita*, so far as the historian of musical America is involved. Yet the musical winning of the West is, in the last analysis, the most interesting phase of recent musical history. Indeed, for a somewhat *blasé* historian, it is the only really interesting phase. That the older, more settled and culturally riper East should expand musically, is a mere matter of evolutional logic, not at all surprising, and a development for which we Easterners do not deserve special credit. On the other hand, that so many western cities, barely out of the backwoods stage of civilization, should be pushing forward musically with such rapidity and energy that they have already outstripped many eastern cities and have completely changed the map of musical America in a few years, is without precedent or parallel in musical history. Any book that in the future fails to do justice to the irresistible musical expansion of the West and to emphasize the fact that this expansion is really the only characteristically American contribution to the world's musical life at large, should be condemned unmercifully by the critics. However, the powers of original research in any one human being are necessarily limited, and since a general historian must lean heavily on specialists, the West will have to produce its own chroniclers before it can expect intelligent consideration at the hands of Eastern historians. And, taking a still broader view of this whole matter of American musical history, we can not do ourselves justice or expect justice at the hands of foreigners until we have produced a methodologically correct and abundant literature of city and state musical histories, on a critical digest of which the general historian may safely base his survey.

From the discussion of books to the discussion of our musical news magazines from whose columns the historian, though with exceeding caution, will have to extract much of his wisdom, is a short and logical step.[1] However, I am not foolhardy enough to semi-publicly record in detail my impressions of our musical news-magazines. Granted and gladly granted that these magazines have on their staff efficient and unbiased chroniclers of current events, contributors of well-stored and brilliant minds and earnestly striving to help the cause of music in America; further granted that the editorial matter in certain of these magazines appears to be untouched by sordid commercial considerations; yet, in appearance and substance, all these news-magazines impress me in the main as being advertising organs rather than magazines. Quite true, there evidently exists an economic demand for this type of magazine and it must be supplied, but I am not deeply enough engaged in the business of music myself as teacher, virtuoso, publisher, etc., to relish as a mere reader the cancerous growth of the advertising department all over the body of a musical news-magazine.

This self-advertising pest has unfortunately also infected mainly literary and educational musical magazines. Practically all of these are issued by music-

---

[1] Caution will become imperative, I may add here, if the historian faces therein so-called statistics that are not limited to fields covered by expert specialists. The historian's scepticism will be the more pronounced, the wider the scope, the greater the pretensions and the bigger the figures of amateur statistics are, and the farther they go beyond the statistics really available at the U. S. Bureau of Education or at the U. S. Census Bureau. Amateur statistics in the form of estimates that are well meaning, even correct in principle, but in detail largely impossible of scientific verification, are too apt to remind professional statisticians of their stock *bon mot*, that the trouble with statistics is not that figures lie, but that liars figure

publishers and dealers as vehicles for the display of their particular goods. While some publishers succeed in doing this in forms subdued and not at all offensive, others parade their wares and the purveyors of their wares with blatant brass. A spirit of make-believe too often pervades such magazines—I do not mean publishers' bulletins, etc.—and their literary matter too often serves as a cloak for the real object of the publication. In the last analysis such magazines are but a more attractive modern species of the time-honored trade-catalogue. Furthermore, nearly all of our musical magazines—like our daily newspapers—suffer from the raging craze for circulation *via* bulk. To cater to the tastes of as many readers as possible, presumably pays from the business standpoint, but with such tendencies no editor can possibly maintain a uniformly high standard of contents. Hence you will observe, even in our best-known magazines, those addressed to the average teacher and student, an indiscriminate mixture of amateurish trash with wholesome, thoughtful, masterly articles well worth reading, by the best of specialists in any given field. From whatever angle one may view the problem of musical magazines in America, it is a fact that so far every attempt to produce and *permanently* maintain a musical magazine of the highest *literary* type, such as flourish in Europe, has failed in America. Either our musicians and music-lovers are not ripe for such magazines, or they do not relish them, which perhaps amounts to the same thing.

Possibly the extraordinary development of the musical column in our metropolitan dailies has been a handicap to our musical magazines, for the reason that not a few of our best critics happen to be also our best musical littérateurs, and these dailies and not the magazines usually harvest the best of their literary efforts in the form of articles that are likely to interest and instruct the musical reader of the newspapers. A weakness of

the musical column may be, that it is practically closed
to all except the accredited musical critic of the paper.
On the other hand, the dual function of critic and
littérateur indirectly lends weight to the critic's critical
utterances, since the readers learn to see in such a man
something more than an appraising reporter of current
events.   Right here I wish to say a kind word for the
much maligned music critic.

Generally speaking it is true that musical criticism in
America is still in a deplorable state of inefficiency,
chiefly, I believe, because of the consequences of the
world-wide notion that the art of music is a matter of
the heart merely and not of the brain, and that therefore any fool may write intelligently about music.
This notion is shared by the majority of newspaper
editors, with the natural result that the majority of
our musical critics are indeed fools, as their grotesque
terminological antics prove every day.   But there exists
within the critical fraternity a noticeable minority of
men who do not deserve such a slur on their activity—
men endowed by nature with the critical talent, a
talent, by the way, quite as specific as the talent for
composition, and one which many a composer or performer does not possess—men, moreover, who have
acquired that ready knowledge of the ways and means
of music which again the critic and nobody else specifically needs; men, in short, who have the moral right
to act as musical critics and who do so in a manner
to challenge comparison with the very best critics in
Europe.   Such critics are by no means to be found only
on the staffs of New York papers, or newspapers published in our largest cities, and that is a very healthy
sign of improved conditions.   Neither is it true that
such papers always have competent critics, nor is it
true that musically obscure cities are without competent
critics.   I suspect that, whenever such a critic is found
on the staff of a daily newspaper, it simply means the

managing editor's infection with the bacillus of musical culture. In fact, I believe that the whole perplexing problem of musical criticism in our country will solve itself automatically, once the average newspaper editor ceases to be musically uncultured, ceases to pride himself on his ignorance of music, and begins to realize that it is a swindle and an insult to intrust the considerable power for good and evil of the music critic to persons with perhaps no other qualification than that of turning out "good copy."

Some writers claim that the American spirit of life differs fundamentally from the European and that therefore the American aspect of art, and of music in particular, must, in course of time, become fundamentally different from the European. I confess that this thought, especially when, as often happens, couched in pseudo-philosophic language, lies beyond my horizon. Nevertheless, I respect it, because back of it moves the desire to find vital distinctions between what is characteristically American and what is characteristically European in the musical life of our time. I, too, have speculated along these lines, but my prosaic mind has not yet found that the message and mission of music is spiritually different in America from what it is in Europe. Opportunities differ, of course, and owing to the difference in conditions, music in America presents characteristically different forms of life and in certain respects our people even assume a characteristically different psychological attitude; but I maintain that music as a commodity, music as a factor of esthetic culture, music as a power for spiritual uplift, and music as a nuisance, is substantially the same here as abroad.

To illustrate, out in California the yearly "High Jinks" of the Bohemian Club of San Francisco have grown into artistic manifestations of national celebrity. I dare say many of us have sighed to witness these solemn offerings to the Muses in the giant red-wood forests under the glorious skies of California when arts and crafts and nature are combined into a "Gesamtkunstwerk" of fantastic originality. But this originality is one of form, not of idea. The "High Jinks" are, after all, only an adaptation of the "open-air theatre" idea to peculiar local conditions, and this idea has its votaries in Europe as well as here. Or again, take our rapidly increasing pageants. They represent but a revival of a never quite extinct idea, and our pageants differ from European pageants merely in the themes suggested by our own history and perhaps in external treatment. Again, take the now famous festivals at the "Music Shed" in Norfolk, Conn., founded, inspired and practically financed by Mr. Stoeckel far from the inevitable commercial atmosphere of other festivals. Nothing quite like these festivals is known to me in Europe, but the very fact that they have been dubbed the "Bayreuth of America" shows that the fundamental idea is considered neither absolutely new nor genuinely American. It is the same with the splendid "musical settlement" movement, with the equally splendid movement to organize the musical talent in factories and department stores for purposes moral, esthetic and economic. It is the same with any and every other musical movement in our country; and I maintain that the chauvinistic effort to interpret such tendencies as typically and independently American manifestations of the social mind, simply because of characteristically American details, tends to discredit our people by separating them artificially from the rest of the world. I, for one, derive much more satisfaction from the observation that nothing foreign is quite foreign to us. Not a field of musical endeavor in which our voice does not to-day command recognition abroad, and it matters little, if this recognition is accorded us only grudgingly at times. One cannot expect Europeans to adjust themselves *prestissimo con slancio* to the new order of things which consists in this, that musically America has become an exporting country and is no longer exclusively an importing country. The more evenly balanced this exchange of values becomes, the sooner deep-rooted prejudices against us will disappear.

One of these European prejudices is that against the American composer. If our European critics merely contented themselves with stating the undeniable fact that we have not yet produced masters of the first rank, we should have no ground for complaint; but it is just a little galling to be told *ad nauseam* that "commercial" America never can produce great creative musical artists, that even our best composers are but weak dilutions and imitations of an inferior European article, and that our only noteworthy contribution to music has been "rag-time." Such shortsighted nonsense is not dictated by a spirit of fair play, but by prejudice. As a matter of fact, we have composers of real merit in America, and more gratifying still, we have American composers. I mean composers whose musical idiom is permeated with a recognizable American aroma, whose works carry with them an American atmosphere because they reflect in some definite or indefinite manner the character and the temperament of the American Nation.

Some people deny to this composite nation of ours telling national characteristics, but this is another prejudice which we need not take seriously. No matter how, by looks or accent or temperament, we Americans may betray our different ancestry, yet back of these distinguishing features we possess a more or less pronounced common something in appearance, in speech, in thought, in mental attitude, which stamps us everywhere as Americans. Whether acquired by contact, one might almost say by contagion, or inherited, the American characteristics can not but make themselves felt in the utterance of the American musician as well as

of any other type of American. Nature demands that
they come to the surface, and they do. I am deliberately
refraining from mentioning names of the living in this
lecture, so I must use MacDowell's rather exceptional
case as a concrete illustration. Deduct from his art
everything that smacks of the "Made in Germany,"
deduct his indebtedness to Grieg, Raff, and others,
deduct even his own powerful individuality, and there
remains, especially in his mature works, the subtle,
yet unmistakable atmosphere of the New World. His
music could never have been composed by a European
master of equal technique and genius. Psychologically
it is in the last analysis American music. It is of us and
ours, and therewith you have the explanation, why
Europeans do not share with us that impression of
MacDowell's music which goes deeper than the mere
appeal of beauty, originality and mastery of technique.
What is true of MacDowell, is also true of lesser American composers in varying degrees. Indeed, the mode of
musical speech of certain of our most representative
composers of the "Made in Germany" or "Made in
France" era is sounding a more and more sympathetic
American undertone the more distant their early surroundings become.

   If identical art-economic conditions prevailed here
and abroad, this theory of an *inevitable* Americanism
in music would be too obvious for discussion. As a
matter of fact, however, they differ in one very important point. Nothing interferes with the ripening of a
European composer in the soil in which his nature
roots. A German composer, as a rule, is trained by
Germans in a German atmosphere, a Frenchman in
France by Frenchmen. Thus such national characteristics as add zest and sap to every artistic utterance,
permeate his music unobtrusively and without external
hindrances. It is German music made in Germany by
Germans; not necessarily good music for that reason,

of course, but at least homogeneous. Not so with the American composer. Conditions forced him to seek his musical education abroad at an age when his mind was impressionable as wax. He would be influenced not merely by the powerful personality of his teacher— let us say, for instance, by a Rheinberger—but also by Rheinberger as a German, and his innate Americanism would become atrophied. Hence, the music by American composers now in their prime so often sounds like German music made in Germany by Americans, not necessarily poor music for that reason, of course, but somewhat incongruous and heterogeneous in its funda- mental racial psychological elements. At any rate, if nothing else can be said against the music of an American composer, it is quite customary to level criticism against his German or French accent. He is condemned as an imitator, without fair consideration of the fact that he is the victim of circumstances.

Unfortunately, this outpouring into Europe of our students of composition continues unabated, though no longer necessary. I am not advocating an educational boycott of Europe—far from it; but I do believe that the American student of music and especially of compo- sition should now be sent to Europe, not at the beginning or in the middle of his training, but at the end, when his character is likely to have passed the formative period and when his horizon is likely to be widened, rather than narrowed, by a sojourn in Europe at the feet of one or more masters of different nationality. Once the present tendency of expatriation of adolescent Americans with all its unavoidable consequences stops, once the American composer has practically become a home-pro- duct, then his Americanism will inevitably assert itself. It will assert itself, moreover, spontaneously and without recourse to artificial, much less to chauvinistic, means.

This qualifying remark aims at the fallacy that the national backbone of a composer will be stiffened by a plentiful injection of folk-song virus into his system. I admit that the folk-song may serve as a powerful antidote against the loss of national identity in these days of internationalism, but I do not admit that the free administration of folk-song tonic will save composers who have already lost their national identity or never had any, and still less that folk-songs as substitutes for a composer's own thematic thoughts are sufficiently nutritious in themselves to create or build up a national musical art. Folk-songs will not even generate convincing local color or mental associations unless the composer hears in these folk-songs, as it were, an echo of the psychological keynote of his own race. If the mere masterly use of folk-songs could turn the trick, then Dvořák would have given us a genuine New World Symphony instead of a beautiful outburst of Bohemian home-sickness with Afro-American ingredients. And, more striking still, when the late Coleridge-Taylor —half African Negro as you know—edited his volume of American Negro songs, he accomplished a very musicianly piece of work, but as the musical portrait of the American Negro it is to me a weird failure. His harmonic, rhythmic, racial treatment of the songs has about as much to do with the American Negro as Beethoven's treatment of Scotch folk-songs with Scotland, and the psychological background of the volume suggests London or Leipzig rather than the regions south of the Mason and Dixon line. The volume contains many enchanting folk-songs of the American Negro, but his spirit is missing. In other words, an Afro-English composer attempted to do what only an Afro-American composer could do convincingly.

On purpose I have just used the term *folk-songs of the American Negro*, because they are exactly that and not American folk-songs of a pure type. To my way of thinking, the real and pure American folk-songs are folk-songs which the component *white* elements of the

American people brought with them to these shores and
WHICH HAVE SURVIVED THE TRANSPLANTATION, *plus*
songs of folk-song character created by these elements
on American soil.   If this definition logically denies
songs of folk-song character by, the American Negro
to be our only or even main source of folk-songs, then,
of course, I am absolutely compelled to deny that the
American Indian supplies us with *American* folk-songs[1].
I deny this most readily, at the same time confessing
that his music, be it of the ritualistic kind or not,
interests and impresses me deeply.   The folk-songs of
the Indians are American folk-songs only in a geographical sense, just as the Indian is an American only in a
geographical sense.   It would be stretching the maxim
that the spoils belong to the victor too far, if a mistaken
idea of what constitutes American folk-songs should
prompt us to appropriate the Indian's folk-songs also,
simply because they are indigenous to this soil.   The
argument, that other victorious nations or races have
included the folk-songs of the conquered in their loot,
does not hold good in our case, because the Indian's
musical system is ethnomusically too different from
our inherited European system for any such process of
absorption.   And if the Indian's folk-songs are to be
absorbed by us as folk-songs, then the champions of
this doctrine should at least limit themselves to the
Indian's *folk-songs*.   They should not reach out for
that music of his which is not of the folk-song type.
They should not overlook the fact that the Indian
shares this with every intellectually advanced "primitive" race, that his artistic instincts have led him beyond
the realm of folk-songs into the realm of—one might
almost say—*l'art pour l'art*.   To pronounce Indian
songs that are folk-songs and, Indian songs that are

---

[1] This sentence originally read: "If this definition logically excludes songs of
folk-song character by the American Negro, at any rate as our only or even
main source," etc.   This sentence was misleading.   The above represents my
views more accurately.

not folk-songs, indiscriminately as *American* FOLK-SONGS, is really pushing the anxiety to endow our people with an ample fund of folk-songs entirely too far.

Nothing in musical esthetics prevents our composers from utilizing the Indian's music to their heart's content. Let them draw from this source of inspiration with all the skill and taste at their command, provided the movement does not become a fad; but they must not delude themselves or us into the belief that they are operating with American folk-songs, or that they are *eo ipso* weaving American music out of Indian melodies. American their music will be, not because of such Indian or Afro-American ingredients, but in spite of them, if American at all.

Whatever may be the proper definition of American folk-songs, this much is clear—that the mere use of folk-songs neither lessens nor enhances the art-value of compositions. An obvious truism; but, strange to say, now and then some hyper-Indianized enthusiast would almost have us believe that the Reds are outspurting the Whites in the race for immortality because the latter do not abjure their so-called European themes in favor of the slogan of "idealization of folk-songs indigenous to the American soil." A felicitous and handy phrase; but if the American composer's imagination is so poverty-stricken that his salvation depends on mortgaging himself to Zunis, Apaches, Chippewas, etc., he might just as well stop composing, since, as I said, the mere use of folk-songs has absolutely nothing to do with the art-value of compositions. Now, I do not for a moment deny that some very enjoyable and artistically highly successful experiments have left the laboratories of the idealizers of Indian music—instead of spoiling it as some have done—but I also contend that these successful experiments constitute as yet only a relatively insignificant corner in that American musical art which is of high artistic value.[1]

[1] Under normal conditions a French composition will remain essentially French, a German essentially German, an American essentially American, quite irrespective of the geographic or ethnographic source of the thematic material. This axiom

With all due respect for the American composer's critics at home and abroad, I really can not help thinking that he has done remarkably well during the last forty years with or without the help of the Indian. Indeed, a certain type of American composer seems to be quite the vogue in Europe just now wherever and whenever the enjoyment of music is combined with exercise of the lower extremities. It is not the type of American composer—with some rather notable exceptions—of whom we feel particularly proud, but maybe this type will help to pave the way for a readier recognition abroad of other types of the American composer.

At home, the American composer has certainly come into his own in the smaller forms of music, including music for the studio, the school and the church. The publishers meet him more than halfway in this

appears to me to be so unassailable that I am at a loss to understand why some of our most successful American idealizers of Indian themes seem to resent the theory that they can not help writing music with a more or less perceptible American psychological background, whether their themes be Indian, Spanish, Chinese, Swedish or what not.

Indian themes will suggest America to the hearer, if he knows that these themes are borrowed from the North American Indian. If he does not know this, he will merely gain the impression of something exotic. He will not suspect the composition to be of American origin, unless the composer, like MacDowell in his wonderful "Indian Suite," has breathed a distinctively American spirit into his work. It is quite conceivable that a typical Frenchman may utilize Indian themes with skill and genius equal to that of MacDowell. Does it not stand to reason that nevertheless the psychological background of his composition will be essentially French? In other words, it is not the use (or abuse) of Indian themes in itself, which makes for an essentially American atmosphere, but the element of national psychology which is quite beyond the control of the composer.

By utilizing themes not his own or not of his own people and race, a composer will move, as it were, between two more or less conflicting atmospheres. His esthetic problem and difficulty will be to blend them either in favor of the one or the other. If he succeeds, he will have created an unobjectionable work of art. If he does not succeed, the result will be a hybrid, a mongrel product. The weakness of the movement here under discussion lies exactly in this danger of an unnecessary musical miscegenation, its strength in a fresh source of inspiration which may be exactly the one needed by certain men of talent in order to give us their best.

I have added these remarks to my lecture so as to make it perfectly clear that I am not criticising certain talented composers because they utilize Indian themes. The issue is one of principle, not one of inclination, talent, skill or of success, artistic and otherwise

It goes without saying, I trust, that I am not opposing the study or the students of Indian music. I have endeavored to facilitate this study by compiling a bibliography of books and articles on the music of the North American Indian and therefore may claim to have shown an active and positive interest in his music My only regret is that the music of the American Negro has not been studied with the same intense and scientific interest. Yet his music presents problems quite as interesting, complicated and suggestive as those of the Indian's music. With every year of delay, the solution of these problems will become more and more difficult. The work should either be undertaken by our Government or otherwise, before it becomes too late to discriminate scientifically between what is African, European and American in the Afro-American's music.—Mr. Krehbiel's thoughtful book on "Afro-American Folksongs" (1914) is happily a step in the right direction.

direction. He has ground for complaint only in the field of chamber music, symphonic music, oratorio and opera—opera as distinguished from so-called "comic" opera. This complaint, however, he would not be justified in addressing exclusively to any one set of men, on whose contact his chances for deserved or undeserved recognition depend, principally publishers, managers, conductors, performers. They are just as much victims of the peculiar art-economic conditions in our country as he is, and any propaganda of theirs for him must reckon with the unpardonable indifference of the American musical public to the prospects of the American composer in larger forms.

This or that publisher may take and does take a patriotic pride in furthering, for instance, orchestral music by American composers without prospects of tangible profits, but no sensible person can expect· of him to tie up his capital by the reckless publication of expensive orchestral scores without some consideration of the present demand by our orchestras for such works, a demand based on the lukewarm demand by our audiences for hearing, and what is by far more important, rehearing of American symphonic works.

Now, every lover of orchestral music, who is fairly conversant with our musical life, can mention offhand in addition to the several New York orchestras the Boston Symphony Orchestra, the Philadelphia and the Theodore Thomas Orchestras of Chicago, the orchestras in Minneapolis, St. Paul, St. Louis, New Haven, Cincinnati, Kansas City, San Francisco, Los Angeles, and one or two more American orchestras fully equipped to play complicated modern scores, but then the names begin to flow very much slower from our tongue. We realize that it is but a question of time until every self-respecting city of wealth and culture in America will have its own well-equipped orchestra, but we are forced to admit that as yet such orchestras are rather few and far between in the United States. Consequently, the American composer's opportunities for gaining a hearing would be limited even without the fact that he has to make headway against a repertoire which in America is more cosmopolitan than in other countries.

This is but logical in a country like ours, and though the majority of our imported conductors hail from Germany and Austria and therefore quite naturally show a decided tendency to give the German label of approval and taste to their programs, yet they can not let their Teutonic tendencies run so amuck as to superimpose on the American public exact replicas of Berlin or Vienna. Furthermore, our conductors see themselves obliged to restrict their choice of novelties to such works as, in their individual opinion, stand out preëminently for this or that reason from the hundreds of scores published annually abroad, and publication in itself generally means a selection of the supposedly best. Now and then our conductors may show a lack of critical discrimination in their selection of novelties, or a taste too one-sided and too partisan, but on the whole the novelties performed each season in America fairly represent the best in the current European output. Accordingly, the American composer, beyond the limited opportunities for a hearing to which he is restricted by the limited number of orchestras capable of adequately performing his music, on the one hand, and the unlimited repertoire, on the other, must face a competition, not of the average run of European composers, but of a select few. This very important point too often escapes the consideration of his critics. If they were forced to sit through a winter of novelties at Berlin, or even one of the annual festivals of the "Allgemeiner Deutscher Musikverein," with its program of novelties passed on favorably in advance by a jury, then their respect for the American composer would increase substantially. Speaking for

myself, there are at least half a dozen American composers whose new works I would much rather hear than
many foreign importations, whose main function is
merely to keep us abreast of the times.

However, personal preferences are a dangerous battle-
ground. The question resolves itself after all into this:
Does the American composer deserve to be heard, and
does he receive fair play? In answer to this, I can not
rid myself of the impression that some of our imported
conductors—but those in the East more than those in
the West—neglect the American composer unnecessarily.
If it be one of the most obvious duties of a conductor to
lend a helping hand to talent struggling for recognition,
and this with reasonable subjugation of his personal
tastes, surely this duty involves also impartial willingness
to foster the talented composer of the country which has
entrusted an important part of its musical uplift to him
in preference to many other equally capable men, and
pays him more than handsomely. Indeed, such an imported conductor would be entirely justified if he, in
the interest of our country's creative musical development, stretched his artistic conscience and if he did not
apply the same rigid test of value to native works of art
as he does, with all respect for his own by no means
infallible taste, to foreign composers. His attitude
towards American composers impresses me sometimes
as being rather passive, not the result of an active
missionary effort to encourage and stimulate American
composers and therewith to do here for us the same
missionary work that he does not hesitate to do for
the composers of his own country.

Since the temptation has been too strong to use the
much-abused term of mission, I might just as well add
that another mission of the conductor in our country is
not being realized by him as it might be.

The system prevails here to provide cities without
the means or interest for a good local orchestra with

symphony concerts given by visiting crack organizations. In this manner, such cities have learned to enjoy the best music in more or less frequent doses in renditions far superior to those in European cities of average musical culture and opportunities. The system has its disadvantages, inasmuch as this supply of the best from without is too apt to spoil the taste for the merely good supplied from within. In other words, this system of importation of crack orchestras blunts the interest in local enterprise and stunts rather than promotes the growth of a city's active musical life from within, without which in the last analysis no city can ever attain to a healthy and potential musical life of its own.

We shall have to face these conditions for some time to come. But so must also the conductors of visiting orchestras. Under the circumstances, it seems to me that their mission is to promote the musical welfare of what one might call their colonies, or even patients, not haphazard but systematically. This requires purposeful study of a city's needs, of a city's actual acquaintance with symphonic literature. It would be such a simple matter to find out with which composers the concert-goers of a particular city in the musical provinces of America are on speaking terms, and with which not, and then to widen their musical horizon by a judicious selection of known and unknown works, instead of treating them, as is the rule, to three, four, five or even more routine "circuit" programs of the mixed classic-romantic battle-horse type. To what absurd results this leads may be illustrated by a recent experience of us Washingtonians who have not yet heard a work of Delius, Bruckner, Scriabine, Sgambati, Pfitzner, and many others, but who were treated to not less than four performances, I believe, of Beethoven's Fifth Symphony in a total of about fifteen concerts by different orchestras in one season.

The same system of colonization prevails in our operatic life, only that cities with an operatic backbone of their own are still fewer. In order not to complicate matters, let me disregard New Orleans, where opera has been cultivated for so many years after the approved manner of prominent cities in the provinces of France, and that without affecting opera in other American cities to any noteworthy extent. For a similar reason, San Francisco may be disregarded, where opera is made to flourish on the typically Italian plan. We may also disregard, for the moment, the several itinerant opera stock-companies with no permanent home of their own and without permanent affiliation with any particular city.

What, then, is the situation? Our operatic life depends on probably less, but certainly not more, than four distributing centres: New York, Boston, Chicago, Philadelphia. Since the days—only half a dozen years ago—when the Metropolitan Opera House Company was the sole distributor, a net gain of three cities whose inhabitants may now boast of a regular season of opera with all the earmarks of what we provincials sometimes call the approved "New York plan of opera." On these four distributing centres the rest of us depend for the from two or three to perhaps a dozen yearly opera performances, euphemistically called "seasons," at prices, so a certain circular stated, within the reach of all, which meant six dollars in the orchestra and two in the gallery. But such is the lure of stellar opera and such the ravenous hunger of our people for hearing and seeing (through the medium of half a dozen or less famous operas) half a dozen or less box-office magnets whose unquestionable genius as artists is matched only by the genius of their press agents, that our people, with a subdued murmur of protest, but otherwise gladly, pay these prices, necessary probably on account of the great expense of "grand opera" on the road, but outrageous exactly under these circumstances. If the cultivation of the art-form of opera, of what opera may mean to a people in their craving for esthetic culture and pleasure, in short, of a wholesome operatic life, depends on such artificial conditions, then opera in America—in America, not in four or even three times four American cities—is condemned to a pitiful failure. Those who think that a chain of fifty or more uniform opera houses and the uniform dispensation of opera along this chain, will solve the complicated problem of opera in America, are very much mistaken; that is, if they erect their opera houses as merely so many more receptacles of opera devoted by way of speculation to the "New York plan of opera."

Nobody in his right senses will question the excellence of opera performances in New York or in the three cities so slavishly imitating New York. The performances by no means always bear out the boast that opera has reached a state of perfection in New York not to be found elsewhere in the world, but the average is high enough for the most fastidious taste. It is not the quality, nor the quantity of opera in New York with which I find fault, but the fundamental aspect of your—from an art-economic viewpoint—so dangerously topheavy institution. Opera in New York impresses me like an enormously expensive hot-house full of enormously expensive exotic plants of luxuriant growth. In my humble opinion, the Metropolitan Opera House Company shares this distinction with Covent Garden, its twin, that it is a huge incubator of an *antiquated system of opera*.[1] Antiquated, because all other nations have found out long ago that a healthy operatic life depends on opera in the vernacular. Does anybody suppose for a moment that Italian opera would have become ingrown into the Italian nation's daily life, if for centuries opera had stubbornly been performed in Italy in English instead of in Italian? Does any one believe

---

[1] Please note that I did not say "antiquated opera house," "antiquated operas," or other nonsense of that kind. I am criticizing the *system* of presentation of opera as antiquated.

for a moment that Wagner, and what Wagner means to the German mind, would have been possible, if the Germans had not thrown off the foreign yoke long ago? Is anybody naïve enough to fancy that French opera would be so fascinatingly French, if the clear-cut maxim pronounced by Perrin and Cambert, the founders of French opera, 1659, in the preface to their very first joint creation, that operas to be properly appreciated should be performed in the language of the audience, had not been heeded by Lully and his successors down to Debussy?

But I do not intend to shake the yellow banner of "Votes for Opera in English" at you. I have been an advocate of opera in English for so many years that I no longer allow myself to be dragged into argument on the subject. I now answer all questions of *why*, wearily with the counter-question of *why not*? In your newspapers and elsewhere the arguments for and against opera in the vernacular—which, by the way, had a very respectable artistic and even financial record in our country before it was temporarily side-tracked by the present system—have been thrashed out so often and so thoroughly that it would serve no useful purpose to add here to the number of dead and wounded. Only this I wish to say, that in my opinion every argument, except one, usually advanced against opera in the vernacular, which in our country, of course, means opera in English, deals with difficulties, but difficulties are never reasons for or against the adoption of reforms. This one exception is the argument that a performance of an opera in its original language comes nearest to esthetic perfection.

In theory, yes; in practice, not necessarily so; but, quite aside from the ludicrous inconsistencies of the champions of this argument, it is the argument of the selfish esthetic gourmet, not the argument of the man who has the best interests of opera at heart, as viewed from the standpoint of national need. An opera may or may not lose something of its esthetic significance by translation, but this eventual loss is more than offset by the gain that opera in the vernacular, from the standpoint of the auditor desirous of understanding and not only hearing and seeing opera, stops being a *pantomime with vocalises* and becomes, what it was intended for by its creators, a musical drama. Whenever this libretto bugaboo is paraded before me, I can not help thinking of Germany. There Goethe, Schiller and Shakespeare form the triumvirate of the dramatic repertoire. Not Shakespeare in English, but Shakespeare in translations that are works of art; and the love of educated Germans for Shakespeare, their appreciation of his genius, their familiarity with his works, is something wonderful to behold. This being the case, I ask the simple question: Did Shakespeare suffer or gain by his conquest of Germany through the medium of artistic translations?

The more radical opponents of opera in the vernacular sometimes deny that the texts of operas sung in English would really be so much better understood than the texts if sung in the original language. They point to some rather notable failures in this respect, when opera in English with very commendable good will was tried on our audiences. The argument has been answered in several ways, but one telling answer or explanation, it seems to me, has been neglected. It is this, that a language sung and a language spoken, sound very different. Language sung is a jargon, the understanding of which depends on an acquired taste and on practice. Supposing a Frenchman who has never been to opera hears for the first time his language sung from the stage by artists famed for their clear diction and enunciation. I guarantee that he will not understand five per cent of the words this first time, and that without the fault of the singers. But with continued practice of his ear, he will gather in a higher and higher percentage, until it may reach forty or fifty. In other words, the success of opera in the vernacular depends as much on the practice of the audience to listen to its own language in the disguise of musical speech, as on the practice of the singers to sing therein and the practice of the composer to compose therein. At any rate, it seems to me that a system of opera which *might* enable the practiced listener to understand forty per cent of the words— which means a proportionate better understanding of the subtle relations between text and music—is decidedly more sensible than a system of opera which offers him only five chances in a hundred.

In this connection I should like to draw attention to a correlated fact, usually overlooked in the discussion of the problem. The artificiality of our present system has not been so apparent here as it would be in cities abroad, because the population of New York is so cosmopolitan. Especially the German language has no terrors for a considerable percentage of your opera-goers, for the very simple reason that they are German-Americans and understand German. But the German emigrants to the United States now amount to only about 15,000 persons a year; moreover, it is a well-known fact that the second and surely the third native generation of German-Americans loses its command of the German language completely. The more the consequences of such facts spread to our art-economics, the more apparent, even to New Yorkers, the artificiality of their operatic system will become.

That opera in English will be a panacea for all the evils in our operatic life, or that opera in English *per se* will produce great American opera-composers, is not my contention, but this much I predict without hesitation: Unless the system is again reversed *preponderantly*— I do not say exclusively—in favor of opera in the vernacular, we shall not have a healthy operatic life in this country. Nor do I fear for the ultimate outcome. The readjustment will be difficult and will require extraordinary executive ability and bull-dog tenacity, but it will come sooner or later. Then, not the type of art-speculator who dabbles in more or less shrewd experiments with public taste, will stand out in our operatic history as the moving force, but those men who have been for years the practical pioneers in this movement for opera in the vernacular and whose faith in the common sense of our people will yet be vindicated. Their itinerant companies often leave much to be desired from the purely artistic standpoint, but nevertheless they are doing more for a proper dissemination of opera as an intelligible form of art in *America at large* than the Metropolitan Opera House Company and all its imitators put together. And should luck so favor the English-speaking nations as to give us in the near future opera-composers of the victorious sweep of a Gounod or Puccini, not to mention giants like Wagner and Verdi, the doom of the present system will be sealed irresistibly and rapidly.[1] To harp on the deserved or undeserved failure of a few American operas by composers without previous individual or collective experience as opera-composers as proof that English-speaking people can not produce real opera-composers, is eminently silly. If English-speaking people could produce a musico-dramatic genius like Henry Purcell once, nothing prevents them from doing so again. It is a question of nature's caprice, of talent, and of opportunity, combined, not a question of national temperament, just as our national temperament does not hinder us from turning out in almost unlimited numbers opera-singers who have conquered first the Old World and

[1] Later, in conversation with a friend, I expressed this as my opinion of an ideal solution of the whole knotty problem: opera to be performed as a rule and everywhere in our country (New York included) in English *except* at the Metropolitan Opera House, which should continue to aim (and still more earnestly than now) at unsurpassable model performances of master-operas new and old in the original language and with as little subserviency to the changing taste of the public as would be compatible with the financial security of the institution.

then the New, and who can hold their own against the best of foreign artists.

With this fervent appeal to nature for a second Henry Purcell, and with an earnest appeal to the powers that be to persist in their enlightened encouragement of the American opera-composer until *succès d'estime* or failure are superseded by emphatic success, I bring to an end these, at best, long-distance impressions of music in America by a firm believer in its future who happens to hail from Washington, unfortunately as yet the musically most provincial capital of present world-powers.

ANTON BEER-WALBRUNN

ANTON BEER-WALBRUNN

(*New Music Review*, 1909)

Presumably not one in a thousand of the readers of "The New Music Review" knows whether this hyphenated German is a pianist, vocalist, or conductor. Beer-Walbrunn belongs to neither of these fertile tribes. He is a composer, born in Bavaria in the same month of the same year as Richard Strauss. Otherwise these two have nothing in common, either in personal appearance, business instincts, artistic tendencies or type of talent. Beer-Walbrunn does not possess the dare-deviltry of Strauss in igniting heaps of rubbish with immense sparks of genius, nor the consummate skill of that other Bavarian in blending Bach, Brahms and Reger into a Janus-personality that now revels in repulsive, external complications and then speaks from the depths in simple musical truths. Beer-Walbrunn is not a man of violent contrasts, not the fascinating high-priest of a new cult like Debussy; he could never stagger humanity and he has not the sweeping gesture of triumphant genius that overwhelms, offends and breeds rebellion. This is Beer-Walbrunn's misfortune so far as worldly recognition and worldly goods go, but he possesses some rare qualities which have added, to Germany's unfashionable individualities, one who commands respect for fidelity to his own ideals and who is winning one by one firm believers in his uncommon gifts. Beer-Walbrunn has gradually grown into a master who in an international exhibition of fine arts would be accorded a nook all by himself by virtue of unmistakable individuality, though the hanging committee might cordially dislike his style, technique and artistic creed. In music we have not yet attained to this spirit of

professional courtesy. We musicians are possessed of
the vicious craze to squeeze musical art-values into
three or four channels. We are essentially politicians
with the methods of even the ward politician, and we
sacrifice too often the interests of our art to intolerance,
party interests and party prejudice. In our wild rush
for the sensational, we forget that the aggressively new
has its conventional patterns, too, and we allow the
dust from the broad highways to blind our eyes to
beauty, less "modern," less fashionable, less conspicuous,
but just as durable, that is hidden in the byways.

To continue the simile: Paul Moos, the eminent
critic and esthetician, once said that there is a corner to
Beer-Walbrunn's art which one must pass before one
may understand and love him, exactly as was the case
with the novels of Wilhelm Raabe. Moos used the
word "Ecke." This, and still more the adjective "eckig,"
suggest a *nuance* not in the literal translation "corner".
The German word conveys the impression of something
almost stiff and awkward. If this is putting it too
severely, look at any of Dürer's woodcuts, and the
typically German *nuance* of the word "Ecke" will
need no further explanation, as applied to Beer-Walbrunn's art. Nor is this quality, which has so often
stood between him and his critics, of mysterious pro-
venience, if we apply the biographical test.

Let us see what Riemann says:

" . . . *b.* June 29, 1864, at Kohlberg near Weiden (upper Bavaria),
son of a village schoolmaster, visited the preparatory school at
Regensburg and the seminary at Arnberg, became assistant-teacher
there and later at Eichstätt, (also cathedral organist,) gave up
the schoolmaster's career and became with the financial assistance
of Domkapellmeister W. Widmann of Eichstätt a student at the
Royal Conservatory at Munich. . . . "

These data spell Bavarian province where Bavaria is
most provincial. Barren of sentiment, as befits a biographical dictionary, they do not tell the tale of priva-
tion and misery from childhood on, well known to

Beer-Walbrunn's friends; not the tale of tragic conflict
between instinct, ambition on one side and filial duty,
tradition on the other, for, musical as Beer-Walbrunn's
father was and musical as he tried to make his boy, a
schoolmaster he should become like his forebears, and
not a musician. Nor do the data tell us how Beer-
Walbrunn grew up to an intimate knowledge of Palestrina, Bach, the classics, but how Wagner's "Lohengrin"
was about the border-line of his familiarity with modern
music. They do not inform us how he drilled amateur
orchestras, mastered half a dozen instruments, besides
the organ, became a routinier in young years and poured
forth works large and small with a strong leaning towards
program music, for which in later years he has shown
very little sympathy. And the Musiklexikon, as if
Beer-Walbrunn had resorted to feminine reticence on
the question of age, omits the most important point:
he remained a routined but esthetically underfed auto-
didact until he entered the conservatory at Munich in
1889, leaving it with the official trade-mark of the
musical profession in 1891.

Here then was a would-be composer, country-bred
and province-fed, who at the age of twenty-five is
subjected to a polishing process by a conservative
master like Rheinberger, and who at the same time is
suddenly thrown into a hotbed of conflicting artistic
tendencies like Munich. Obviously, such a man will
begin life anew in a different direction from him who,
though perhaps born on the farm, breathes the air of
a musical metropolis at the age when men are like wax
in the hands of their teachers and models. This climatic
influence during the period of germination will persist,
and no transportation or inoculation of the maturing
mind will fully efface the influence. Some of its characteristic qualities may be detrimental, others invigorating, and since many roads lead to Rome, it merely
depends on a reserve fund of talent and individuality

to become what Lachner called "Auch Einer." The finished product may not at all fit into the current order of things, but that does not necessarily detract from its intrinsic art value. Nor is it at all just to impeach an outsider and not the favorites for defects which are the results of early surroundings.

In Beer-Walbrunn's art one is struck first of all by the fact that Wagner's "Lohengrin" appears to have been the *ultima Thule* of his formative period, barring some reminiscences of later visions that flow into every composer's pen. He apparently drew no real nourishment from Brahms. Even the last Beethoven appears to have sown few seeds. Mozart, more than any other master, seems to have stood godfather to his ideals, and there can be little doubt that he enjoyed Mendelssohn immensely in the formative period of his life and that he came under the lasting spell of Schubert and Schumann. A provincial Bavarian, he did not escape Lachner and later Rheinberger. Therefore, the basic foundation of his style is far removed from the "New-Germans" of the Weimar fraternity and cannot appeal to those who fail to see in a man like Rheinberger more than a mere conservative or even reactionary schoolmaster. But Rheinberger is really underestimated nowadays. He impresses me, at least, as a kind of German Saint-Saëns. At any rate, he was an excellent model for acquiring mastery of form, solidity of workmanship and a delicate ear against unnecessary contrapuntal noise and melodic harshness. Oddly enough, Beer-Walbrunn does not figure among his favorite pupils. This is not surprising, since he, though working on the same basis, reached out for harmonic and orchestral combinations which Rheinberger instinctively felt to be beyond his own time and horizon.

Thus Beer-Walbrunn, below a somewhat archaic surface, is modern in spirit and quite as progressive as some of his better known contemporaries. He and they are simply incommensurable, the more so because Beer-Walbrunn, not unlike MacDowell, ostensibly cultivates clear-cut melodic curves and believes in "melodies" as against interval-speech. In fact, he prides himself on being a "melodischer Moderner," and this melodic gift and tendency gives even his declamatory passages a peculiar twist; but it also explains his willingness to repeat words not so much for a subtle *nuance* of expression as for the sake of melodic form. Furthermore, his music is not at all polyrhythmic, and therein he differs in principle from MacDowell. Indeed, it is difficult to become accustomed to his rhythmic regularity. There is something *carré*, undeniably old-fashioned and monotonous about his rhythm. One hears, as it were, the bar-line altogether too often. This is all the more noticeable, since his style is inherently homophonic except when the organist elopes with his better half, and then his familiarity with Bach leads him into a curious conflict between early eighteenth-century counterpoint, early nineteenth-century homophony and late nineteenth-century heterophony.

Beer-Walbrunn's harmonies are close and compact. He rarely mirrors overtones as do Chopin, Debussy, or (in a less prismatic manner) Strauss. His harmonies are rather of velvety smoothness, not infrequently remarkable for sheer beauty, and occasionally Beer-Walbrunn takes one quite unawares by the bold blending of tints that in their fullness are quite his own. It would be well for his reputation if one could say the same of his treatment of the pianoforte. Unfortunately, though pianistic and well sounding, it cannot interest the modern pianist, because Beer-Walbrunn has given Chopin and Liszt a wide berth. Mozart, Hummel— some have said Hünten, Kuhlau—have led him into a blind alley. Decidedly provincial and antiquated are his untrimmed scales and arpeggios. Thus, modern fingers do not take kindly to the intricacies of a pianistic style whose individuality and occasional brilliancy are due merely to an inbred development of old-fashioned methods and formulas. Worse than this is the uneven level of Beer-Walbrunn's ideas. He can be exasperatingly conventional. This defect he shares, of course, with many other contemporaries, but their conventionality does not jar so because it still possesses a degree of freshness, whereas Beer-Walbrunn's dates from our grandfathers, and conventionalities certainly do not improve with age. Between the conventional and the commonplace there is a fine line of distinction, and exceedingly few composers do not overstep this line at the critical moment. To these few Beer-Walbrunn does not belong. He can be downright commonplace in the midst of his most splendid flights of fancy, and when the commonplace and the conventional meet in his music, the jar is sudden and paralyzing. But justice demands the statement that of late years he has gained almost complete control over his self-critical faculties and now rarely succumbs to bad taste in the selection of his ideas. While they still at times do not rise above old-fashioned patterns, they seldom give the rabble the welcome hand.

If Beer-Walbrunn were merely a musical hayseed, a German Yankee Doodle come to town, he could pass muster only as an anachronistic curiosity. But behind the provincial mannerisms there are brain, heart and personality. As he cannot bluff by appearances, he must, more than the city-bred composer faultlessly dressed after the latest fashion plates, stand on real merit. Nor is it at all certain that his provincialism is a mere tower of weakness. At any rate, he brought with him from the backwoods the precious gift of *naïveté* and the equally precious gift of unstudied simplicity. Absolutely sincere in his utterances, he would never deliberately commit a musical falsehood or advertise himself by a cheap *jeu d'esprit*. He abhors artificial brilliancy and scorns the present tendency to drag virtuosity for virtuosity's sake into the composer's art. Of the *poseur* there is no trace in him. He derides the fallacy that bigness is synonymous with greatness and that a musical idea, to be profound and beautiful, must be complicated and spicy. Neither does he seek complications, nor does he avoid them. He merely holds that they must come about naturally and not be a matter of musical upholstery. He avoids violent contrasts and everything that smacks of the intemperate, morbid, sensational. Bumptious bathos and maudlin sentimentality are equally foreign to his nature. Thus, old-fashioned and provincial Beer-Walbrunn may be in some respects, but he is not decadent. Virility is the keynote of his art, that virility which combines robustness with delicacy of sentiment and refinement of expression. Firmly convinced that an artist of his type, too, has a right of existence, he is not a man of opportunistic compromise. Quietly and undisturbed by praise or sneers, he bides his time in the belief that sooner or later the pendulum of taste will swing back to the most conspicuous quality of his art, that for which the Germans have the untranslatable word "volkstümlich." Add to this a masterly technique, enviable contrapuntal resourcefulness, a genuinely South German jovial humor and gracefulness, spontaneity, cerebral and emotional depth, and it is not surprising that Beer-Walbrunn is looked upon by many as a musical hermit to be reckoned with in the future.

The peculiar physiology and psychology of Beer-Walbrunn's art could not but have a counterpart in the peculiar reception it has found at the hands of the critics and the public. Beer-Walbrunn has reached his opus 40 since 1889, after discarding entirely his numerous earlier works. Nor are opera 2-7 of much account, since they comprise merely his more serious efforts under Rheinberger, such as the regulation symphony, string quartets, etc. Opus 1 covers two really fine choruses selected judiciously for publication from among a number of similar works, and it is very characteristic that they surpass in originality most things he composed after it had become Rheinberger's right and duty to wield the blue pencil. With his opus 8, a Quartet for pianoforte and strings, composed in 1892, Beer-Walbrunn entered the public arena. One or two excepted, all his later works have been performed, and it is purely a matter of statistics to state that the public seldom failed to side with him vigorously, whereas professional criticism of his works has always ranged between condemnation and unreserved praise. I possess a goodly collection of these reviews. They would make very curious comparative reading, the more so because certain dreaded German critics who formerly sneered at Anton Beer-Walbrunn have completely changed front and now give him his due. Indeed, since Beer-Walbrunn's path was strewn with thorns, since between the time of Count Schack's generous patronage shortly before the death of this esteemed scholar and connoisseur and Beer-Walbrunn's appointment in 1901 to a not very lucrative professorship at his alma mater at Munich, his life was filled with bitter disappointments, it must be said that Beer-Walbrunn has been treated shabbily and ungentlemanly by more than one critic. This opposition has not even stopped at untruths, and more than one case is on record where a critic deliberately suppressed or reversed the fact that the audience was most decidedly for and not against Beer-Walbrunn. Not that I hold that a critic should always take notice of the audience's applause or silence, but if he does he should at least adhere to the plain facts and not confuse the *vox populi* with the *vox critici*.

Surely, a composer who compels the attention and applause of trained audiences on the rare occasions that performers have accorded his works a public hearing, who divides his critics into two camps, and who has gathered around himself a small but faithful army of admirers, must have qualities far above mediocrity. Unfortunately, Beer-Walbrunn's music is not of the kind to create a wild rush of competition between publishers. On the contrary, its commercial possibilities are limited because, though "volkstümlich" in tone, it will never become popular. So it happens that more than half of Beer-Walbrunn's by no means torrential *bagage* remains unpublished, and sadly enough most of his later and maturer works. His manuscript music includes a Symphonic Phantasy, Op. 11; a choral work, "Mahomets Gesang," Op. 16 (Nuremberg, 1896); a Quintet for pianoforte and strings, Op. 17; his fourth String Quartet, Op. 19; an Organ Sonata, Op. 32; a Sonata for violin and piano, Op. 30; a Symphony in E major, Op. 36; a Symphonic Poem; three Preludes to Josef Rüderer's paraphrase of Aristophanes' "Birds," Op. 40; the opera "Don Quijote," many songs, etc. Most of these works have been performed at Munich, Berlin, Leipzig and elsewhere with the typical result stated above. No less a man than Karl Straube, Reger's champion, characterized the organ sonata as "colossal," but its difficulties and fantastic combination of realistic and mystic moods have deterred publishers. Still more astonishing is their timidity towards the splendid violin sonata. Since Berber and Stavenhagen went on a tournée with it early in 1906, the work has reappeared with increasing appreciation every season on the chamber-music programs of Munich. Extraordinary has also been the fate of the opera "Don Quijote," composed to the verses of Georg Fuchs, whose verse-drama, "Till Eulenspiegel," and other works, have stamped him one of the real poets of young Germany, but one who also unfortunately undermines the effectiveness of his dramatic works—and "Don Quijote" is not an exception—by undramatic "knots" and episodes. Two acts were practically completed as early as 1896, but the composer rewrote and revised much of the opera time and again before he felt satisfied with what he craved to make his masterwork. What happened? Finished at last after almost ten years of incessant polishing, the score made the customary round of the principal opera houses with the result that none of the conductors cared to risk his reputation on an unquestionably inspired work which boldly disregarded the superstition of theatrical folk against Cervantes' immortal Don as the hero of an opera. No Don Quijote opera had yet succeeded; why should this one, which purported to be not a comic opera but a musical tragi-comedy and one with music rooted firmly in German soil, without the slightest attempt at local Spanish color?[1] Finally, Beer-Walbrunn pinned his faith on Mottl, who had taken charge of the slightly dilapidated opera at Munich. Mottl condescended to look into the score, but stumbled at Beer-Walbrunn's "corner." This being no new experience, Beer-Walbrunn merely requested, as a favor, to play the work for Mottl. The great Felix consented, immediately saw his mistake, and henceforth became convinced that here at last two congenial artists had conquered (even though in a Teutonic spirit) the "Don Quijote" theme for the stage. But even during the rehearsals of the opera, which calls for not less than twelve *dramatis personæ*, Beer-Walbrunn's ill-luck pursued him. The proverbially perfidious climate of Munich played havoc with the vocal cords of Munich's

---

[1] For the benefit of dabblers and dabsters in local color I interject here this episode. To ridicule those German composers who, in imitation of Humperdinck, interlarded their scores with folk-songs, Beer-Walbrunn utilized the folk-song "Über Stock und über Stein" for the brilliant orchestral interlude "The Ride of Don Quijote and Sancho Pansa through the Black Mountains." Promptly he was taken to task for this aberration from Spanish local color by pedants who did not see the point of the joke. Yet, when the Spanish conductor Cortolezis was touring Spain a few years ago with one of the Munich orchestras, this very piece in its concert version excited Spanish audiences to enthusiastic applause. Music as German as Dinkelsbühl! Had it been dipped in "local color," presumably Spanish audiences would not have recognized it and would have remained profoundly unmoved by Spanish music made in Germany.

stars and the first performance had to be postponed so often that it became a joke in Isar-Athens. At last, on January 1, 1908, Mottl performed "Don Quijote" to an enthusiastic, crowded house, which agreed that Feinhals in the title-part had perhaps reached the climax of his career. Everything looked favorable for a long run of the opera, but the weather gods had taken a violent dislike to Beer-Walbrunn and put one singer after the other out of commission—with the result that "Don Quijote" was heard barely three times at long intervals, though each time scoring a complete success. As usual, critical opinion was divided. The veteran Wagnerian, Otto Lessmann, for instance, who never did care for Beer-Walbrunn's music, condemned the work. How could he help it, since this "Don Quijote" is a deliberate attempt to break away from the post-Wagnerian formula and to be, as it were, for Germany what Bizet's "Carmen" was for France? It may even be doubted that Lessmann would have backed water as did other critics who frankly admitted that "Don Quijote" gains remarkably on a second hearing! A revolutionary work in the sense of "Pelléas et Mélisande," Beer-Walbrunn's "Don Quijote" certainly is not, but it has proved that there still is talent in Germany for a natural flow of winsome or stately melody, for skillful ensembles (*e. g.*, the superbly beautiful finale of the last act) and subdued orchestration, beside the stilted post-Wagnerian "Sprechgesang," long-winded, contorted mythological, medieval or biblical monologues and orchestral earthquakes.[1] The immediate result of Beer-Walbrunn's victory, a local

[1] Felix Mottl remained faithful to "Don Quijote." At his suggestion Georg Fuchs remedied certain dramaturgic defects in the libretto and in this improved version (which is also that of the published vocal score) Mottl rehearsed a revival of the opera in 1910—when he died. Again the opera had to be shelved. Then on October 14, 1911, it scored a success recorded by the critics as deservedly still more pronounced than in 1908. At last Beer-Walbrunn's bad luck seemed to have left him, but—his "Sancho Pansa" became sick before the second performance and could not be replaced. Again the opera was shelved and it has remained shelved, for those in power since Mottl's death are not in sympathy with Beer-Walbrunn's musical ideals. I believe Mottl's estimate of the opera to have been correct and theirs wrong.

victory as the North Germans would have it, was his engagement to compose the preludes to Rüderer's paraphrase of Aristophanes' "Birds" under the queer title of "Wolkenkuckucksheim." This work was performed twelve times last summer at that fascinating experiment in dramaturgics, the "Münchener Künstlertheater," and every time Beer-Walbrunn's preludes came in for a special round of applause. It is not surprising, therefore, that the preludes have been accepted by several conductors for performance this winter in the form of a suite.

The fact that all these works and others, though repeatedly performed, are not available in print, puts those at a disadvantage whom curiosity might tempt to become acquainted with Beer-Walbrunn. On the other hand, the works published put me and others at a disadvantage who wish to call attention to a composer unduly underestimated in favor of more "up-to-date" composers of fewer years and lesser talent.[1] The pub-

---

[1] Since this was written, several of Beer-Walbrunn's mature works, as the appended list of his compositions shows, have been published. I am unable to recommend the melodious but otherwise uninteresting "Frühlings-Einzug," Op. 42, or the, at least in my opinion, monotonous chorus "Trost der Nacht," Op. 48. The three organ fugues, Op. 28, are full-blooded and scholarly but also somewhat scholastic. On the other hand, I do not hesitate to recommend to brainy violinists the Violin sonata, Op. 30, the one work of Beer-Walbrunn's which even his opponents have conceded to be a powerful and remarkable addition to sonata literature.

The "Drei Burlesken," Op. 40, for orchestra will always suffer from their misleading title. The music is not at all burlesque in the accepted sense of the word. Hence, the public does not get what it expects and is disappointed unless warned beforehand. I suspect that the composer chose the misleading title because he did not know what else to call these witty pieces. Witty in a strictly musical or technical sense, for one has to study the score with its many funny contrapuntal tricks analytically to appreciate how "geistreich" is Beer-Walbrunn's *tour de force*, his *jeu d'esprit* in showing off his technique of "thematic unity." When I asked him if he had intended to slyly satirize or to have sport with the professional adherents of that principle of composition, Beer-Walbrunn merely smiled a jovial smile and then pleaded guilty to his self-indictment. As for the orchestration, the pieces have a flavor of individuality, refinement and subtlety which is said to have elicited praise even from Richard Strauss, not exactly a friend of Beer-Walbrunn's music otherwise.

Of the unpublished, later works the one-act opera "Das Ungeheuer" (Karlsruhe, 1914) is a shining illustration of how a composer will waste a lot of attractive ideas on an impossible book. That Beer-Walbrunn ever conceived the suicidal notion to compose Tschechow's for operatic purposes impossible dramatic prose trifle, is a mystery to me. So it was to a prominent critic who, apparently not familiar with Tschechow's play, accused the composer of having altered it clumsily beyond recognition—though Beer-Walbrunn in fact set the play to music practically word for word! With his incidental music for Reinhardt's production of "Hamlet" and the Munich Künstlertheater production (1914) of "The Tempest" Beer-Walbrunn convincingly proved his talent for just such delicate tasks which require taste and tact.

lished works mostly belong to his earlier period, when
he had not yet quite found himself, or are below Beer-
Walbrunn's own normal level. To the latter class must
be reckoned the very mediocre "Reisebilder," Op. 21,
for pianoforte. A "Kleine Phantasie" for violin and
pianoforte, Op. 3, is pretty, but need not be taken very
seriously. The same is true of an Ode for 'Cello, Op.
20. The 'Cello Sonata, Op. 15, has a beautiful second
movement, but otherwise will be effective in the home
circle rather than before a chamber-music audience
used to more pretentious things. An orchestral "Deutsche Suite," Op. 22, of which a four-hand arrangement
has also been published, has proved fairly interesting
and attractive as *entremet* between musical dishes of
heavier conception. The six "Einstimmige Lieder,"
Op. 11, published separately at Count Schack's expense,
and the six "Lieder" of Op. 13, published in two groups,
are unequal in value and uneven in style. Beer-Walbrunn's models, especially Schubert, were looking over
his shoulders when he penned the former cycle, and it
cannot be said that his methods of song-composition
were then always above severe criticism. This is a
pity, because there is an outburst of inspiration in
these songs, quite beyond ordinary mortals. What an
irresistible hymnus "Des Knaben Berglied" would be
without its only too obvious defects! Paul Moos has
called "Allein mit der Natur" one of the most powerful
of German songs. I agree with him, but think that
the "Lied der Trauer" is fully as good. Of the songs in
Op. 13 the three published by Peters, "Bitte," "Traum-
land" and "Triumphlied," are eminently characteristic
of Beer-Walbrunn's methods and moods, and of those
subtle shadings that surprisingly often escape those
uninitiated in his style.

This last remark brings me to his third String Quartet,
Op. 14, and the Quartet for pianoforte and strings, Op. 8.
Except for a tendency towards homophonic treatment

and a personal note, unmistakable in all of Beer-Walbrunn's music, whether good or poor, influenced by
other masters or not, these two works have little in
common. There is enough life and sentiment in the
String Quartet to make it a fairly valuable contribution
to chamber music, but one notices throughout a certain
restraint, even in the grinding dissonances of the first
movement. This restraint is absent from the Piano
Quartet with which, in 1892, the propaganda for Beer-
Walbrunn began, though his champions have never
denied that the third movement is Schumannesque,
and that from the first two movements the egg-shells
of the conservatory have not been wholly removed.
These defects aside, I know of no other work so typical
of the unsophisticated Bavarian with his boisterous
joviality, his intensely deep emotions, his robust love
of sonority and of the *volkstümlich* beautiful, all frankly
and yet gracefully expressed. Exactly herein lies the
difficulty for performers who are not in sympathy with
this type of Bavarian or do not understand it. They
are liable to mistake the recklessly easy-going frankness
for vulgarity, and indeed I have known good musicians
to turn Beer-Walbrunn's Piano Quartet into an un-
recognizable jumble of sounds for which the word
vulgarity was still too select. But those who have
heard Bavarians play this exuberant work of their soil
with the true Bavarian touch of refinement and gracefulness, know how it has electrified and deeply moved
Bavarian audiences. That it would ever strongly
appeal, let us say, to Frenchmen or even Americans,
I sincerely doubt.

The most ambitious work of Beer-Walbrunn's "first
period" was his tragic opera in two acts, "Sühne,"
composed 1893 for the Coburg competition and since
published in vocal score. Based on a drama by Körner
and originally called "Liebe," the opera was performed
by a hopelessly inadequate cast at Lübeck on February

16, 1894. The composer withdrew the opera rather than hear it butchered a second time. The one performance, however, had suggested improvements, and so he immediately subjected the work to a revision and reorchestration, but no manager has since mustered courage to give the opera in its present form a second trial. Nor is this difficult to understand. Though "Sühne" is unquestionably the most talented German by-product of the "Cavalleria Rusticana" episode, serious objections must be raised against it from every aspect. The book was too clumsily constructed by Beer-Walbrunn himself, and was not much improved by his friend Georg Fuchs, and the form of the opera is too antediluvian, that is, too ante-Wagnerian. If then, on the whole, the work does not commend itself nowadays for performance, it cannot be denied that it contains scenes full of musical beauty, dramatic power and lapidaric intensity such as would reflect credit on any composer. Barring some Wagnerian reminiscences, more noticeable in "Sühne" than in other recent works, because in style and spirit it is so far removed from Wagner, Beer-Walbrunn has sounded his personal note from beginning to end. This same personal note reappears in all his later works whenever he rises above his average level, and it is so conspicuous in his best published work and one of the best he will ever compose that the dullest ear, without further clue, would identify the composer of "Sühne" and this work. I mean his "Cyklus lyrisch-dramatischer Gesänge nach Shakespeare's Sonetten," Op. 34, composed and first sung at Munich in 1906. These ten songs have been condemned by some critics for the naïve reason that the composer dared compose Shakespeare's sonnets at all, because in their opinion the glorious sonnets do not lend themselves to musical treatment. Others frankly admitted their inability to follow Beer-Walbrunn; and of course those who never did care for him have not been won over.

However, these sonnets made such a profound impression on other critics of standing that they declared them to be every bit as good as anything Hugo Wolf ever did. I, too, am firmly convinced that this song-cycle belongs to the landmarks in German song-literature. I do not know of any living composer in Germany who could have penetrated deeper, with simple means, into the psychology of Shakespeare's sonnets and given them more adequate musical expression. Those who cannot get around the "corner" of Beer-Walbrunn's style, of which this cycle is typical without flaws, will surely not side with us; but to those whom the "corner" does not deter, the study of these master-songs will present a fascinating and thankful task of interpretation. They will then fully understand my allusion to Dürer, and will agree that a composer of Beer-Walbrunn's unbending individuality, of his cerebral and emotional depth, is bound to make his way, not towards remunerative popularity perhaps, but towards the circle of those who are capable of welcoming a master from whatever direction he comes.

Compositions by Anton Beer-Walbrunn

Op.
1   Zwei Chorlieder (1889-90), Munich, A. Schmid Nchf., 1897; Munich, Wunderhorn Verlag, 1912.
2   Concert-Ouvertüre (1890).
3   Kleine Phantasie in G moll for violin and piano (1891-94). Munich, A. Schmid Nchf., 1897; Leipzig, Peters, 1899.
4   Streich-Quartett in C dur (1891).
5   Symphonie in F dur (1891-92).
6   Streich-Quartett, No. 2, in C moll (1892).
7   Der Polenflüchtling, Ballade (first version; 1892).
8   Klavier-Quartett in F dur (1892), Munich, A. Schmid Nchf., 1897; Leipzig, Peters, 1899.
9   Concert-Allegro für Klavier (1892).
10 Sühne. Tragische Oper in 2 Akten (1893), Lübeck, Feb. 16, 1894; Berlin, Stern und Ollendorf, 1896; Munich, A. Schmid Nchf., 1897.
11 Symphonische Phantasie (1894).
12 (Sechs) Einstimmige Lieder (1893), Leipzig, Breitkopf & Härtel.
13a Drei Lieder (1895), Leipzig, Peters, 1900.
13b Drei Lieder (1893-94), Munich, A. Schmid Nchf., 1897.
14 Streich-Quartett No. 3, G dur (1893-97), Munich, A. Schmid Nchf., 1897; Leipzig, Peters, 1899.

15 Sonate in G dur für Violoncello und Klavier (1895), Munich, A. Schmid Nchf., 1897.
16 Mahomets Gesang von Goethe für Soli, Chor, Orchester, Orgel (1895. Nuremberg, March 16, 1896).
17 Klavier-Quintett (1895, 1901).
18 Don Quijote, der sinnreiche Junker von der Mancha. Musikalische Tragikomödie in 3 Aufzügen (1896-1905), Munich, January 1, 1908. Munich, Drei Masken Verlag, 1911.
19 Streich-Quartett No. 4, E moll (1898).
20 Ode für Violoncello und Pianoforte (1899), Leipzig, Peters, 1899.
21 Reisebilder. Cyclus von 6 Klavierstücken (1899), Leipzig, Peters, 1900.
22 Deutsche Suite für grosses Orchester (1900). Leipzig, Peters, 1901 (Score and 4-hands arrangement).
23 Marsch, Tanz and Fantasie für Orchester (1900).
24 Zwei Lieder (1900).
25 Humoreske für Streich-Quartett und Klavier (1901).
26 Streich-Quartett No. 5, D moll (1901).
27 Zwei Lieder. (No. 1, "Mutter, süsser klingt kein Ton," Munich, A. Schmid Nchf., 1901).
28 Drei Fugen für die Orgel, Leipzig, Rob. Forberg, 1906.
29 Drei kleine Fugen für die Orgel (Nos. 1 and 2 in O. Gauss' collection, "Orgel-Kompositionen aus alter und neuer Zeit," Ratisbon, A. Coppenrath, 1909).
30 Sonate für Violine und Klavier (1905). Munich, Wunderhorn Verlag, 1911.
31 Der Polenflüchtling, Ballade. (Second, orchestral version, 1905).
32 Sonate für Orgel, G moll (1906).
33 Bearbeitung von 6 Volinsonaten von Dall'Abaco (1906) (Denkmaler d. Tonkunst in Bayern, ix, 1, 1908).
34 Ein Cyclus lyrisch-dramatischer Gesänge nach Shakespeares Sonetten (1906), Munich, Heinrich Lewy, 1907.
35 Zwei Chöre. (No. 1, "Heimweh," Munich, Wunderhorn Verlag, 1912; No. 2, "Vesperhymne" in Liederbuch für bayerische Gymnasien, 1906.)
36 Sinfonie in E dur (1906).
37 Vier Lieder nach A. Droste-Hülshoff (1906); ("Letzte Worte," said to have been published by Vobach, Berlin).
38 Gavotte von Schlemüller für 'Cello und Klavier, bearbeitet für Orchester (1907).
39 Zwei Lieder (1907). (No. 2, "Ständchen," said to have been published by Vobach, Berlin [1908].)
40 Wolkenkuckucksheim (1908), Drei Burlesken für Orchester, Munich, Wunderhorn Verlag, 1912.
41 Revised version of "Die Sühne" as "Volksoper."
42 No. 1. Frühlings-Einzug. Tonstück für Klavier zu 2 Händen. Munich, Wunderhorn Verlag, 1910.
    No. 2. 4 Variationen über den Choral, "Wie schön leucht't uns der Morgenstern" (1915).
    No. 3. 6 deutsche Volkslieder für Geige und Klavier in leichter Bearbeitung (1915).
43 Bühnenmusik zu "Hamlet" (Berlin, 1909).
44 Bearbeitungen:
    No. 1. Siziliano von W. Fr. Bach für Oboe, Fagott und Klavier (1909). Munich, Wunderhorn Verlag, 1910.

No. 2. Aria, "Zerbrecht, zerreisst," für Sopran, Horn, Klavier oder Orgel (1911). Munich, Wunderhorn Verlag, 1912.

45 Kleine Stücke für Orgel (1910).
46 Bearbeitung der Violinsonate in H dur von W. Fr. Bach. Munich, Wunderhorn Verlag, 1910.
47 Bearbeitung der "Drei Töchter des Cecrops," Oper in 5 Akten von Strungk (1910, for the Denkm. d. Tonkunst).
48 Trost der Nacht, für gemischten Chor (1911). Munich, Wunderhorn Verlag, 1912.
49 Bearbeitung von Teilen zweier alter italienischer Opern: "Antigona" und "Iphigenia" (1912, for the Denkm. d. Tonk.).
50 Das Ungeheuer. Musikalisches Lustspiel in einem Akt nach Tschechow (1912-13). Karlsruhe, April 25, 1914.
51 Bearbeitung der "Sofonisbe," Oper in 3 Akten von Trajeta (1913, for the Denkm. d. Tonk., published 1914).
52 Konzertstück für Geige und Orchester (1913-14).
53 Männerchöre nach Möricke:
      No. 1. Der Maria Geburt.
      No. 2. Wanderlied.
54 Schauspielmusik zu Shakespeares "Sturm" in 2 Akten. (1914. Munich, Künstlertheater, 1914.)
55 Vaterländische Lieder und Chöre (1914).
56 Drei Stücke für Klavier (1915).
57 In memoriam. Adagio in Sonatenform für Klavier (1915).
58 Fantasie-Sonate in Fis moll für Klavier (1915).
59 Fünf geistliche Lieder mit Klavierbegleitung nach Eichendorff (1915-16).
60 Neue Lieder mit Klavierbegleitung nach Eichendorff (1916).

In addition, a considerable number of early, unpublished works without opus-number: Songs, choruses, Pianoforte music, a Violin sonata, a Symphony, etc., etc.

WAS RICHARD WAGNER A JEW?

WAS RICHARD WAGNER A JEW?

(Proceedings of the Music Teachers' National Association for 1911)

Under the pseudonym of "K. Freigedank" Richard Wagner, in 1850, contributed to Brendel's *Neue Zeitschrift für Musik* the famous essay "Das Judenthum in der Musik." With an antisemitism truly Saxonian in its ferocity, he deprecated the Jew's influence in music. The attack was promptly and quite properly resented by the Jews, who really could not be expected to swallow such an insult to their race. Whatsoever the merits of Wagner's condemnation of Jewish influence in music may be, he did not reap the full fruit of his antisemitic art-philosophy until after the republication of the essay with additions and over his own signature in 1869. Therewith he exploded a bomb which had been lying half-buried, and for years he remained a marked man in powerful Jewish journalistic circles, until Wagner the genius triumphed over the enemies of Wagner the pamphleteer. To-day all sensible Jews have forgotten and forgiven what, from their standpoint, they justly considered an unfair and ill-tempered attack on the idealism of their race; but the animosity against the antisemite Wagner has by no means completely died out amongst Jews.

The tables could not possibly be turned on Wagner more revengefully than by proving that this arch-antisemite was himself a Jew. If a Jew, then naturally all his arguments against the art-value of Jewish influences would apply to his own influence with brutal force, and he would stand, self-convicted, an undesirable citizen in the realm of art, unless the other alternative be accepted—a complete vindication of the Jewish influence in music by the Jewish composer Wagner against the antisemitic theorist Wagner.

Exactly here enters the question, "*Was* Richard Wagner a Jew?" It has been going the rounds for many a year, and more than once an affirmative answer has been given. To make such an assertion, which clearly involves the conjugal fidelity of a great man's mother, without proof is certainly objectionable. A mere systematic repetition of an unproved and therefore objectionable assertion would not, of course, make it any more acceptable to decent-minded people, Jews or Christians. If, then, for instance, the *Musical Courier* of late consistently and persistently calls Richard Wagner a Jew, we are forced to the assumption that the editor really believes Wagner's Jewish origin to be above doubt. Just to what lengths some persons will go, cannot be better illustrated than by the article "Inovowrazlov— the Topography of Genius," by one Semmy Carpeles in the *Musical Courier*, 1911, Vol. 63, No. 6, p. 14. The writer of this article refers to Wagner's origin thus:

> Geyer, the father of Richard Wagner, no doubt changed his name from the Hebrew Adler to Geyer, because, as a Jew, he could not secure an engagement at that time on any German stage. Fräulein Jachmann, who was the mother of the illegitimate Richard, was probably not a Jewess; had she been a Jewess, Geyer would have married her and Richard would have been born regularly.

One stands aghast at the audacity of "Semmy Carpeles" to impose such raw stuff on the editor of the *Musical Courier*, and blushes with shame for the credulity of Semmy Carpeles when one sees him nonchalantly basing these words on the following idiotic tissue of inaccuracies and untruths in a communication which he quotes from the *New York Sun*, July 3, 1911:

> You may find men in New York who have heard Wagner himself say that his father was Geyer. But he never knew him, he said. Geyer was an actor in a theatre in Leipsic, together with Wagner's mother, Fräulein Jachmann. They were never married. When Fräulein Jachmann married Police Actuary Wagner, he adopted Richard; so he changed his name to Richard Wagner. Many illegitimate children used, formerly at least, to take the name of their father, although their legal name would have been that of the mother. I have known several such men. So Richard Wagner's

legal name would have been not Richard Geyer, but Richard Jachmann, if not, perhaps, in his time, children adopted generally the father's name. Anyhow, his father was Geyer, not Wagner.

Now, it is not a daily newspaper's business to prevent anybody from making an ass of himself, but it is a sad state of affairs if a contributor to a musical newspaper falls so low as to operate with such a disgusting exudation of ignorance in an article which was bound to be read by many guileless, because historically untrained, musicians in America.

At the root of the controversy lie these simple facts. Richard Wagner was born on May 22, 1813. On Nov. 22, 1813, his father, Carl *Friedrich* Wilhelm Wagner, died, and the widow, Johanna Rosine Wagner, *née* Pätz (Sept. 19, 1774), on Aug. 28, 1814, married Ludwig Geyer, who became acquainted with the two in 1801.

I now marshal as collateral "facts" the arguments which in conversation or in print one finds advanced in support of the theory of Wagner's Jewish origin.

(1) Geyer was an actor, playwright, portrait-painter, in brief, a man of artistic versatility, whereas Friedrich Wagner was a Polizei-Amts-Actuarius (Police Actuary); (2) Richard was not entered in the records of the Kreuzschule at Dresden as Richard Wagner, but as Richard Geyer; (3) At "Wahnfried" there may be seen portraits of Wagner's mother and Geyer, but pictures of Wagner's father are conspicuous by their absence; (4) Richard Wagner resembled Geyer; (5) Richard Wagner in his writings, letters, and conversation repeatedly referred to Geyer as "father Geyer" or "our father Geyer"; (6) Geyer, until his premature death on Sept. 30, 1821, showed a very marked preference for Richard; (7) Wagner himself repeatedly expressed the possibility of his being a son of Geyer and not of Friedrich Wagner; (8) Geyer was a Jew.

These beads of inference appear to be strung on a rather slender thread. Still, they have compelled recent biographers to take notice of the theory. Even professors of musical history at German universities to-day consider it their duty at least to call attention to the claim of Wagner's descent from Geyer. Of course, they do so in a purely scientific spirit, not in a spirit of racial revenge or slander, and to my knowledge none of these methodically trained historians identifies Wagner as of the Jewish race. However, this much is clear: the Jewish claim collapses pitifully unless it be proved beyond a reasonable doubt, first, that Richard Wagner was the illegitimate son of Geyer, second, that Geyer was a Jew.

It would be strange indeed for a genius like Wagner to have been born of parents totally indifferent to art. As a matter of fact, both Wagner's mother (most assuredly *not* a Jewess) and his father Friedrich were very fond of the theatre. Indeed, his father's passion for the stage and stage-folk was such that he neglected his wife, as Wagner tells us in his autobiography. So successful had Friedrich Wagner been as an amateur actor that he reluctantly took up the legal profession. It was he who induced Geyer to decide on the stage as his main profession, and he had a stage-career in mind for several of his children. Of these nine children—two of them dying at an early age—five actually devoted themselves to the theatre (Albert, Luise, Rosalie, Clara, Richard), and of these at least the oldest, Albert (whom we all know as a singer and actor at Würzburg and later as stage-manager at Berlin), cannot by the wildest stretch of a morbid imagination be connected with Geyer, since he was born in 1799. Thus, if heredity is brought into this matter, Geyer is not needed at all to explain the source of Wagner's artistic instincts, some of whose forebears, indeed, on the father's side, were musicians.

Upon entering the Kreuzschule at Dresden in 1822, Wagner was actually inscribed as Richard Geyer and not as Richard Wagner. This fact was well known to the great composer, who in his autobiography, when speaking of Geyer, had this to say on the subject (I quote from the authorized, but not wholly satisfactory translation):

This excellent man, under whose care our family moved to Dresden when I was two years old, and by whom my mother had another daughter, Cecilia, now also took my education in hand with the greatest care and affection. He wished to adopt me altogether [the authorized translation drops here the words 'als eigenen Sohn'] and accordingly, when I was sent to my first school, he gave me his own name, so that till the age of fourteen I was known to my Dresden schoolfellows as Richard Geyer; and it was not until some years after my stepfather's death, and on my family's return to Leipsic, the home of my own kith and kin, that I resumed the name of Wagner.

This he did at the latest on Jan. 21, 1828, when he was inscribed in the books of the Nikolaischule of Leipsic as "Wilhelm Richard Wagner," his father being entered as "verstorb. Actuarius." The "first school" Wagner mentions above was the Kreuzschule of Dresden, in the records of which he actually appears as "Wilhelm Richard Geyer, Sohn des verstorbenen Hofschauspielers Geyer." Both records appear in facsimile in the most sumptuous and (for his early years) in some respects most important book, "Richard Wagner: His Life and Works from 1813 to 1834.—Compiled from original letters, manuscript, and other documents by the Honourable Mrs. Burrell, *née* Banks, and illustrated with portraits and facsimiles, 1898."[1]

Students of this unwieldy volume know that Mrs. Burrell secured in some manner an uncut and unbound copy of the original, privately printed edition of Wagner's "Mein Leben," which was distributed only among the most intimate and confidential friends of the composer. Mrs. Burrell was then struck, as we all are, now that

[1] The book is merely the torso of a documentary biography contemplated by Mrs. Burrell, who died in 1898. The volume was printed in one hundred copies only, of which one is at the Library of Congress. It is engraved throughout on specially prepared paper with Wagner's name as watermark and so profusely illustrated that the cost of production must have been enormous.

the autobiography has become public, by Wagner's statement quoted above. She investigated the matter, and she was informed by leading Saxon ecclesiastics and schoolmen, among them the director of the school in question, whose testimony she reproduces, that quite frequently in Saxon schools of that period stepchildren were registered, for purely administrative purposes, *not* under the name of the real father, but under that of the stepfather! Hence, such an entry might easily have been made without even an expressed desire on Geyer's part to adopt Richard Wagner as his own son. Nor is it at all necessary to infer from such a desire that he therewith implied Richard to be really *his* son, since many a stepfather before and after has done the same thing without the possibility of any such inferences. Finally, if any argumentative weight is attached to the entry of Richard Wilhelm *Geyer* in the records of the Kreuzschule, equal weight attaches to the entry of Richard Wilhelm *Wagner* in the records of the Niko- laischule of Leipsic. In other words, the Kreuzschule entry loses, if not all of its inferential force, at least enough to effect a draw in the contest between the rightful names Wagner and Geyer.

Mrs. Burrell's book plays havoc with still another of the singular inferences supporting the theory of Wagner's descent from Geyer. It is the picture-argument based on the fact that from the end of 1858 Wagner gave a place of prominence and honor to a photograph of the Geyer self-portrait in the possession of the Brockhaus family, into which his sister Luise had married. Wagner's first words in the matter are contained in a letter to his sister Cecilia from Venice, Jan. 28, 1859 (see the "Familienbriefe"): "Father Geyer's picture now always lies before me on my writing-desk."

That Wagner later adorned his home "Wahnfried" at Bayreuth with this and other pictures of his step- father, but not of his father, may set those thinking who do not appreciate the psychological consequences of the fact that Wagner was but half a year old when his father died. It would have been perfectly natural under the circumstances for Wagner to give to a portrait of his stepfather a place of even greater honor than to a picture of his father. If there be such who do not concede this, then we may ask, How, in the name of common sense, Wagner could pay the proper filial respect to a picture of his father, if no such picture exists? Mrs. Burrell's patient hunt for a portrait of Friedrich Wagner ended with the information given her by Wagner's stepsister Cecilia that the family knew of no extant picture of Friedrich Wagner, and that she remembered only a very dusty, old pastel which must be long since smudged out.

Of course, this simple explanation of a so frightfully suspicious looking circumstance would not remove the other collateral argument that Wagner resembled Richard Geyer. Here, again, Mrs. Burrell's book plays havoc with hasty inferences. Not finding a picture of Wagner's father, she accomplished the next best thing and found a bust of Richard's uncle, the æsthetician and playwright Adolf Wagner. She presents photographs of this bust in three different positions, and the likeness between Richard Wagner and his uncle, particularly the mouth, "so extremely like Richard's," is at least as great as that between Geyer and Richard Wagner—which, in my humble opinion, is not at all pronounced. Mrs. Burrell, in order further to clinch the argument against "a stupid confusion," as she calls it in one place, submits an authentic photograph of Richard Wagner's oldest brother Albert, born in 1799, and therefore beyond reach of Geyer-inferences. Chamberlain, in his splendid work on Wagner, reproduces another picture of Albert, and no unbiased person can fail to observe that the resemblance between the brothers Albert and Richard is so striking as to be beyond denial.

Commenting upon the fact that neither brother shows a marked likeness to their mother, Mrs. Burrell concludes: "These facts make it probable that both eldest and youngest sons, with fourteen years between them, took after their father."

This striking family likeness between the two brothers on one hand, and between them and their uncle Adolf on the other, has been accepted by such recent Wagner biographers as Julius Kapp and Max Koch as sufficient evidence against the soundness of the Geyer theory. To save the situation, Dr. Edgar Istel, one of the best younger writers on music in Germany—a Jew, by the way—in a review of Mrs. Burrell's scarce book in *Die Musik* (1910-11, no. 4, p. 210) takes refuge behind this theory:

> The likeness of Richard Wagner to his uncle Adolf Wagner and his brother Albert would be no proof against the paternity of Geyer (no picture of father Wagner being extant), since it is known that frequently the first child of a second marriage still resembles the first husband; as if the nature of the woman had to gradually become accustomed to producing in new forms.

If the champions of the Geyer theory must seek shelter behind such disputed biological observations, they might just as well surrender. However, admitting for the sake of argument that Istel's remark is based on sound biological facts, what would it help him? If the Wagner family likeness is not a proof of Friedrich Wagner's paternity, it most assuredly, on the other hand, is not a proof of Geyer's paternity. Since the burden of proof in the whole matter rests absolutely on the Geyer champions, they are in any event debarred from using the likeness of Richard Wagner to Geyer as an effective argument.

So far, then, all the "inferences" have been shown to lack solid substance or even circumstantial *evidence*, and the critic of the claim of Wagner's descent from Geyer has had plain sailing. His task becomes more complicated as soon as he reaches the strongest argument of his opponents, namely, the fact that Wagner himself is known to have admitted the possibility of his descent from Geyer. But immediately the question arises, To whom did he say this, when, and in what manner or form?

Glasenapp (1905, 4th ed., 1st vol., p. 78) writes:

That the deceased [*i. e.*, his stepfather Geyer] might even have been his real father, this idea he has repeatedly expressed as a possibility in conversation with intimate friends, of whom we could name several.

Notice how carefully this is worded, "as a possibility," and "in conversation with intimate friends." Suffice it to say that any statement, wherever found, that Wagner positively called Geyer his real father is a fabrication. That there are living, for instance, in New York, as claimed in the *New York Sun* of July 3, 1911, men who heard Wagner himself say that Geyer was his real father, is, to put it mildly, improbable. In all fairness, we demand affidavits of these residents of New York who were on such terms of intimacy with Wagner that he could entrust them with such a delicate secret and confession.

At Munich, the story goes that Peter Cornelius was one of the intimate friends to whom Wagner hinted at the possibility of his descent from Geyer, but Cornelius seems to have avoided any reference to such a conversation in his writings. Nietzsche acted differently, and it is primarily due to a seductive phrase of his that the story of Wagner's illegitimate (and incidentally) Jewish origin gained such circulation, first in Germany and then in other countries. Said Nietzsche in 1888, in a foot-note to the postscript to "The Case of Wagner," that famous vitriolic and regrettable attack on his former idol:

Was Wagner German at all? We have some reason for asking this. It is difficult to discover in him any German trait whatsoever. Being a great learner, he has learned to imitate much that is German—that is all. His character itself is *in opposition* to what has hitherto been regarded as German—not to speak of the German musician! His father was a stage-player named Geyer. A Geyer is almost an Adler.

It is this phrase which to my own knowledge went the rounds of all cafés where literary and artistic people meet in Germany, and it has remained with us in the most twisted forms, one being, that Geyer's name was not Geyer at all but Adler—the veriest nonsense, of course, but exceedingly convenient for certain purposes.

Nietzsche, bent on denying to Wagner all dramatic genius, and seeing in him (in 1888) a mere actor, a wizard, one might almost say a charlatan, of stage-craft, continues:

> What has hitherto been put in circulation as the "Life of Wagner" is *fable convenue*, if not worse. I confess my distrust of every point which rests solely on the testimony of Wagner himself.

Very well, then, let us draw the conclusions of this distrust. After the death of her second husband, Wagner's mother remained the only person who could possibly have given binding testimony on the paternal parentage of her son Richard. Now, Glasenapp, whose devotion to Wagner is such that his critical enemies would not be surprised at Glasenapp's acceptance even of a Chinese origin of Wagner, and his discovery of the Lord's reasons therefor in the interest of the Germanic *Gesamtkunstwerk*, if Wagner himself had implicitly believed in such a Chinese origin, ends his delicately brief discussion of the problem thus:

> And yet, *if* a secret was to be preserved here, then his mother took it with her into her grave and has never confided it either to him [Richard Wagner] or any of the grown children.

At any rate, she did not confide such a secret to Wagner, for otherwise he could never have written what he wrote to his sister Cecilia on Jan. 14, 1870, from Triebschen after the receipt of transcripts of letters written by Geyer:

> The contents of these letters has not only moved me, but verily shaken me to the depths. The example of complete self-sacrifice

for a noble purpose in private life has hardly ever presented itself so clearly as in this case. . . . Especially the delicate, fine, and highly cultured tone of these letters, particularly of those to our mother, moves me. . . . At the same time, it was possible for me to gain a deep insight out of these letters to Mother into the relations of the two in difficult times. I believe I see now with absolute clearness, though I must consider it extremely difficult to express myself on these relations, as I see them. It impresses me, as if our father Geyer, with his self-sacrifice for the whole family, believed to atone for a guilt (eine Schuld zu verbüssen).

The letter has become accessible since 1907 through the publication of the "Familienbriefe von Richard Wagner 1832-1874." It is to my knowledge the only instance that Wagner in his writings ever permitted himself to use words concerning the relations between Geyer and his mother which might be construed by others to mean that he had conclusive doubts as to his paternal parentage. These doubts he would seem to have entertained even before reading those letters on Christmas Day, 1869, for the first time. Wagner does not specify the dates or the contents of the letters. It is therefore impossible to say whether or not these letters were in part identical with those from Geyer to Wagner's mother that are available in print. Until Geyer's letters are given to the public, it is equally impossible to know whether or not Wagner really could have hinted at a clandestine love-affair between Geyer and his mother, of which he was the fruit, previous to their marriage. Possibly his words have a hidden meaning quite different from the now current interpretation, but let us accept, for the sake of argument, as probable that he really desired to convey to his step-sister that interpretation and no other. Who can say that this interpretation would be acceptable to other readers of the same letters? Is it not possible that Wagner, for real or fancied reasons, having had previous doubts as to his origin, too willingly and too hastily saw in these letters a corroboration of his doubts, and that other, more unbiased readers, would decline to share his views? Nor will a cautious historian stop here. He will demand proof that Wagner continued to put the above—at best, probable—construction on the letters. How if Wagner in later years relinquished his first interpretation? How if it should turn out that this first interpretation was but temporary and not permanent with him? Would not then Wagner's supposedly implied testimony have lost most of, if not all, its force?

In this connection, I think, the facsimile in Mrs. Burrell's book of a letter written by Wagner to Friedrich Feustel of Bayreuth on Oct. 23, 1872, should not be overlooked. Feustel had asked for Wagner's baptismal record. Wagner sent it with a humorously-worded note, and signed it, "Richard Wagner, Polizeiamts-Actuarius-Sohn." Now, what I mean is this. If, in 1872, Wagner still adhered to his original (by some, implied) interpretation of Geyer's letters, would it not be rather queer that he, even in jest, should sign himself deliberately in this way, after hinting in conversation with intimate friends,—who, it appears, repeated the conversation to their intimate friends, etc.—at the possibility of his descent from Geyer? Would not ninety-nine out of a hundred men, under the circumstances, have simply signed "Richard Wagner," and avoided any allusion to the matter of paternity?

In other words, Wagner's letter to his sister Cecilia opens up a line of questions to which neither one side nor the other has as yet attempted to give answers satisfactory to those who see in history something more serious than the record of sensational gossip, vindictive slander, or personal impressions. Again, if it is important to know whether or not Wagner until his death entertained doubts about his origin, it is equally important to know when he first expressed such doubts to intimate friends. Important, for this reason. Should no authenticated date previous to

January, 1870, be established, the surmise would become
plausible that Wagner made such a confession only *after*
the study of Geyer's letters to his mother on Christmas
Day, 1869. Therewith we should be led back in a circle
to the same line of questions as just pointed out, and
Wagner's own inferences would not have helped us
much towards a satisfactory solution of the problem.
And here enters his much abused "Autobiography,"
recently published.[1]

The first volume went to press about June 17, 1870.
Consequently, Wagner had ample time between January,
1870, and June, 1870, to embody in the manuscript
by way of corrections any and all conclusions or inferences drawn from his study of Geyer's letters or
other matter, documentary or not, which would throw
additional light on his origin. His autobiography pulls
early skeletons out of their closets with an unreserve
which is shocking to Anglo-Saxons, and to people who
despise Wagner the man, since they can no longer
afford to hate Wagner the artist. If Wagner was a
creature of such low character, of such caddishness, as
some critics picture him, he, presumably, would not
have hesitated to parade the skeleton of his illegiti-
macy by inserting words wrought with unmistakable
meaning. On the other hand, if Wagner strictly adhered
to his object, as he says in the prefatory note, to give
"the unadorned truth," then again he would not have

[1] This was struck off originally in about eighteen copies for Wagner's most
intimate friends. This was well known, but just when it was written, and when
it was printed, perhaps not even the recipients of these strictly confidential copies
fully knew. Mrs. Burrell did not belong to these friends. Nevertheless, she
succeeded in procuring a copy, and she did not hesitate to express her indignation
at this "unmentionable book" when reproducing part of it in facsimile in her
work on Wagner. She furthermore proves from marginal dates in her copy and
by letters from Wagner to G. A. Bonfantini of Basle, who printed the limited
original edition of "Mein Leben," that the autobiography was dictated from
1865 to 1869, and that the first volume was printed from about June 17, 1870,
to June 29, 1874. We also know from Wagner's letter to his sister Luise, dated
Geneva, January 3, 1866, that he was just then busy dictating his autobiography,
and that he had arrived at his twenty-first birthday in the narrative. Finally,
a comparison of the extracts in Burrell's book with the corresponding parts in
the German version of "My Life" must lead to an acceptance of Siegfried Wagner's
reported word as a gentleman that the original version has not been doctored,
and that all irresponsible suspicions to the contrary should be discounted until
somebody proves such a surgical operation by a page-by-page comparison of the
original private and the recent public edition.

hesitated to rewrite those portions of his autobiography which refer to his origin in accordance with his remarks to his sister Cecilia—that is, to repeat it, provided these remarks really have that meaning and no other! *The autobiography, as a matter of fact, contains no statement which would compel us to see in it a corroboration of the Geyer theory.*

At the very beginning of the autobiography, he speaks of "my father Friedrich Wagner" and repeats the use of "my father" as applied to Friedrich Wagner repeatedly. As to Geyer, Wagner now speaks of him as "my step-father," and again as "my father," there being no consistent differentiation between his father Friedrich Wagner and his stepfather Geyer in this respect, though on p. 15 (of the German version) the word "Wagner," which he put in parenthesis, may have a pointed though latent meaning:

After one year [following the death of Geyer] I was taken . . . to Leipsic, where I was delivered for a few days into the care of the relatives of my father (Wagner).

Writing of Geyer, the most incriminating passage in the autobiography is this (p. 2, English translation):

Even when the police official [Friedrich Wagner] was spending his evenings at the theatre, the worthy actor generally filled his place in the family circle, and it seems had frequently to appease my mother, who, rightly or wrongly, complained of the frivolity of her husband.[1] How deeply the homeless (*heimathlos*) artist, hard pressed by life and tossed to and fro, longed to feel himself at home in a sympathetic family circle, was proved by the fact that a year after his friend's death he married his widow, and from that time forward became a most loving father to the seven children that had been left behind. . . .

Of his mother he says (p. 11 of the English translation):

Her chief characteristics seem to have been a keen sense of humor and an amiable temper, so we need not suppose that it was merely a sense of duty towards the family of a departed comrade that afterwards induced the admirable Ludwig Geyer to enter into

---

[1] In this translation, the word "frivolity" is not an equivalent of the German "Flatterhaftigkeit," which implies, or any rate may imply, something worse than frivolity, namely, infidelity.

matrimony with her when she was no longer youthful, but rather that he was impelled to that step by a sincere and warm regard for the widow of his friend.

It would be jumping at dangerous conclusions if we were to interpret Wagner's remark about the neglect of his mother by his father in such a manner as to deduce therefrom a neglect which would have made it physically impossible for Friedrich Wagner to have been the father of Richard. On the other hand, Ludwig Geyer would not be the first, nor the last, man to thus take a husband's place in the family circle without committing adultery. The world is not yet so rotten that there cannot exist daily and intimate intercourse between man and woman, affectionate and intimate friendship of a Platonic kind. It is not for us to prove that the intercourse between this pair was Platonic, it is for the other side to prove, beyond a reasonable doubt, that the intercourse was *not* Platonic.

As to Wagner's calling Geyer in his autobiography, in his letters, and elsewhere "father," "our father," even "my father," it was, as it is to-day in thousands of similar cases, the most natural appellation. Why, then, should just Wagner be expected to have called Geyer consistently "stepfather"? At any rate, it was at least as natural for him to call his stepfather simply father, as it was for Geyer to address Richard's brother Albert (born in 1799) in a letter of Sept. 14, 1821, as "Mein Sohn," or to sign himself in that of Sept. 13, 1820, as "Dein redlicher Vater L. Geyer," or in that of June 5, 1821, as "Dein liebevoller Vater" (all these in Mrs. Burrell's book). And to draw any inference from the fact that the "Cossack" Richard, as Geyer sometimes called him, was the pet of both his mother and his stepfather would be equally silly, vicious, and preposterous. It would have been unnatural not to watch the progress of the youngest boy, a delicate and sickly, yet lively and almost wild child of such peculiar whims and propensities as Richard, with particular care and affection. Especially, as Richard was to both of them more or less a mystery, a boy, during Geyer's lifetime, of no clearly outlined talents. Characteristic in this connection, after Richard had failed to show more than normal talent for the fine arts, is Geyer's often quoted death-bed utterance, pathetic in its hopeful doubt: "Sollte er vielleicht Talent zur Musik haben?" ("Does he perhaps have talent for music?") Nor can I really find that Geyer's preference for Richard was such as to overshadow his affection for the other children. Albert, on account of age and difference of character, should have been the least acceptable to Geyer, and yet his letters to Albert breathe a tender, fatherly spirit than which that of his real father could not have been more tender and fatherly.

The originals of the letters from Geyer to Frau Wagner on which Richard Wagner commented to his sister Cecilia are not preserved at "Wahnfried," but in the archives of the Avenarius family into which Cecilia had married. Now, Glasenapp in his preface of 1904 explicitly thanks the "House Wahnfried, whose archive-treasures at all times stood at my [his] disposal without reservation," and he pays the same tribute of thanks to Ferdinand Avenarius. Glasenapp's second chapter shows, as comparison with Geyer's letters quoted by Mrs. Burrell proves, that he must have had access to the letters written by Geyer to the widow Wagner, in other words, letters read also by Wagner on Christmas Day, 1869, and now preserved in transcript at Wahnfried. Glasenapp, moreover, quotes the letter written by Wagner to Cecilia. Yet Glasenapp, beyond reference to Wagner's confidential hints to intimate friends of a possibility of his descent from Geyer, and beyond the statement that Wagner's mother carried the secret, if there was any such secret, unrevealed to her grave, does not give his own interpretation of these letters.

As if stunned by Wagner's comment, he clings to his idol's word "Schuld" (guilt), and asks in desperation:

Guilt? What guilt? The guilt of having given to the world a Richard Wagner? We do not proceed in our surmise ("Vermutungen") farther than do the words in this letter.

Clearly, either Glasenapp from his reading of the letters failed to understand why Wagner should put exactly that interpretation on those letters, and was baffled, just as much as we are, by the meaning of Wagner's words, or else Wagner had letters before him not submitted to Glasenapp and which were more clearly amenable to such an interpretation, if that was really Wagner's hidden inference, and a correct one at that.

Let us suppose that the latter alternative must be preferred, though in my opinion that is not at all necessary. A dilemma of an extraordinary nature then presents itself. Mrs. Burrell, who also had access to the Avenarius archives—to forestall confusion I interject the remark that Mrs. Burrell does not occupy herself with the theme of my address at all—quotes in her book four letters written by Geyer from Dresden to the widow Wagner at the time he came to the rescue of the family and before his marriage to the widow. The first, dated Dec. 22, 1813, and mainly reporting on the health of the children now under his personal care, begins:

Friend: Heartfelt thanks for your kind letter, which drew me out of a very uncomfortable mood and gave me new strength, since I found you more composed and with fortitude resigned to fate, which surely will treat you with loving consideration.

The second, dated Jan. 14, 1814, begins:

Dear friend: From the depths of my heart I thank Heaven for the reconvalescence of Albert and for the return of quietude into your heart with these glad tidings. Poor, good woman! Heaven has made of you such a sufferer, but has given you also the strength to bear your misfortunes, and your joy over the Lord's fulfilment of your prayers for the preservation of Albert's life, must be truly strengthening and elevating. . . May the Lord protect you! To all friends and to my Albert *Gruss und Kuss* from your for ever faithful friend Geyer.

The third letter, dated January 28, 1814, reads in part:

Beloved friend: . . . You have promised me, to be in future very good, brave, and full of confidence towards me, and I hope that my good and very dear [*herzensliebe*] friend will keep her word. Perhaps I may seem to you to have somewhat changed, but, by the Lord, I am a better man and I hope for an opportunity to prove it to you. Heaven just at present means well with me, having given me the beautiful mission to be your friend; and, by keeping this goal steadily in view, I now find myself rewarded in my art, which I cultivate with strictest care and with remarkable progress, as my Madonna [he refers to one of his best pictures] will bear testimony. If my art favors me so, will it ever be possible for you, who, together with my art, are the only joys [*Freuden*] of my life, to stop being my friend? But my demands on both are probably too great that I may ever flatter myself of reaching the goal of my wishes! . . . In eternity yours, Geyer.

The fourth letter, dated Feb 11, 1814, begins:

Beloved friend: My anxiety for you had reached a high degree when I at last received your letter, and saw that you are well and also now and then think of me with your good wishes. Though under the present sad circumstances you will have little pleasure in Dresden, you must not forget that it would afford us, and particularly me, great joy to see you again after all this sorrowful suffering and to press you to our hearts. . . . Unchangingly [*unwandelbar*] yours, Geyer.

These translations lay no claim to merit of style, but they are fairly literal. Yet, one important point disappears entirely in the translation: Geyer throughout addresses the widow with the formal "Sie," not with the intimate "Du." The tone of these letters is one of deep sympathy, refinement, sincere affection, intimate friendship, chaste and knightly. But why proceed? In the name of common sense, I ask, are these letters in address, signature, form, contents and tone the utterances of a man who has possessed a woman, soul and body, for several years? Such an opinion would be possible only on the rather far-fetched assumption that Geyer was cleverly and deliberately concealing the real state of affairs. I do not believe that the parties to a clandestine love-affair would go to that unnecessary trouble in confidential letters after the death

of the husband. But, supposing this, for a moment,
to be true, what would follow? That Richard Wagner
must have seen less harmless and more incriminating
letters which compelled him to infer, what we, if we
are so inclined, may in turn infer from *his* letter to
his sister Cecilia. These really incriminating letters
would have been written during the lifetime of the
husband, that is, when, as surmised above for the sake
of argument, such extreme caution and concealment of
the real status of affairs would actually have been
necessary! Few will be willing to follow anybody into
such an abyss of absurdity as that into which the
dilemma would then force us. Most of us, I trust,
will refuse to believe that the Avenarius archives contain
two such diametrically opposed kinds of letters. But
this forces us immediately to a further conclusion,
namely, that Wagner had only such letters as quoted
above before him, perhaps, indeed, these four letters
only and no others. If that be the case, and unless the
Avenarius archives have been tampered with, then two
conclusions are inevitable. Either Wagner was not
justified in drawing from these letters the inference of
an illicit love-affair between his mother and Geyer of
which he was the offspring, *or* we are not justified in
reading this inference into his letter to his sister Cecilia.
Confronted by this dilemma, it may be profitable to
read his words again:

At the same time it was possible for me, to gain exactly from
these letters to Mother a sharp insight into the relations of the
two in difficult times. I believe now I see with absolute clearness,
though I must consider it extremely difficult to express myself on
my view of these relations. It impresses me, as if our father Geyer
believed to atone for a guilt with his self-sacrifice for the whole family.

May not the "difficult times" be reasonably interpreted to refer to the time between his father's death
and her so unconventionally, though in her desperate
situation quite pardonably, rapid marriage to Geyer,

which took place ten months after the father's death, the shortest period permissible under Saxony's laws? And Geyer's guilt (Schuld)? May there not be hidden here an allusion to something in Geyer's life quite different from adultery, some guilt of which the inquisitive world as yet knows nothing and may never know anything, a guilt of which, however, Friedrich Wagner had known and from the consequences of which he had rescued his friend Geyer, thereby earning the latter's undying gratitude? And if Richard Wagner uses the words "eine Schuld abbüssen," why give to the German word "Schuld," with its many shades of color from mere "indebtedness" to "crime," just one of the very darkest? Finally, it cannot have been so extremely difficult, after all, for Wagner to tell his sister in a confidential letter, in language delicate but *unmistakably* clear, that he considered himself her real brother, not her step-brother.[1]

Such objections to the usual interpretation of Wagner's words are at least permissible, and, taken together with the innocent, chaste tenor and tone of Geyer's accessible letters to the widow Wagner, they again force the Geyer party on the defensive in a matter which to an analytical mind is very much more complicated than they seem to think. We must, in other words, deny them the moral right to use Wagner himself as a witness for their claims, until they have proved beyond a reasonable doubt that Wagner meant in his letter to Cecilia what they, the Geyer champions, mean.

They may now say: Agreed, that Wagner's letter to Cecilia does not necessarily imply our inference; agreed, that we cannot use Geyer's letters for our purpose; agreed, further, that it yet remains to be proved that Wagner entertained doubts as to his paternal

---

[1] Since writing the above pages I have come across Richard Batka's article "Richard Wagner oder Richard Geyer? Eine Vaterschaftsfrage" in the "Merker," 1909. He there states that Mr. Wolfgang Schumann, the stepson of Avenarius, after reading the letters, informed him that no romantic conclusions are to be drawn therefrom. Batka shares my opinion of the Geyer legend.

parentage before Christmas Day, 1869, and after January, 1870, until his death—still, we have the fact on our side that Wagner expressed to intimate friends in confidential conversation the possibility of his being Geyer's son and not the son of Friedrich Wagner. A son who, notwithstanding his undisputed and touching love for his mother, thus impeaches her fidelity as a wife, must have had his reasons.—Most assuredly, but that does not prove his reasons to have been correct, or to have been based on facts which allow no other interpretation; and until Wagner's real reasons are forthcoming, no historian, no critic, no journalist is justified in advancing one inch beyond Wagner himself. In other words, Wagner's descent from Geyer remains at its very best a *hypothetical possibility*. Even then the arguments against a hasty acceptance of this hypothetical possibility are not exhausted.

Geyer can possibly have been Wagner's father only if he is proved to have been in Leipsic from six months, at the very latest, to nine months before Wagner's birth on May 22, 1813. I know very well that the Seconda theatrical company usually played at Leipsic from the Oster-Messe until the Michaelis-Messe (that is, from spring to fall), but it must be proved, if the Geyer claim is to be operated in that orderly, methodical fashion which has been sadly lacking so far and which alone makes history sound, that this was true also of the year 1812. After that is done, then it must be proved, regardless of Wagner's own reasons for the hypothetical possibility of his descent from Geyer, that Friedrich Wagner neglected his wife at exactly the same time in such a manner as to have made it physically impossible for him to have been Richard Wagner's real father. Finally, unless this physical impossibility is established, not even a statement from the lips or pen of Wagner's own mother that she believed Richard, under the circumstances, to have been Geyer's rather than her husband's son, would be acceptable as circumstantial evidence.

To conclude the analysis of this phase of the matter, it is of course possible that Wagner was not Friedrich Wagner's son, just as it is possible that none of us is the child of the man whose name we bear, but among decent-minded, level-headed, and unprejudiced folk such theoretical possibilities do not count for practical purposes. The probability that we are the sons of our legal fathers amounts for us to a certainty, unless absolute proof to the contrary be produced. This axiom should apply with equal force to Wagner, no matter what our grievances against him as a man and pamphleteer may be. Until he is absolutely proved *not* to have been the son of Friedrich Wagner, we are in decency bound to believe that he justly bears the name of Wilhelm Richard Wagner. We are equally in decency bound to refer, if we do so at all, to the theory of his descent from Geyer, as a mere hypothetical possibility derived from arguments, either flimsy, or contradictory, or non-conclusive, or unscrupulous.

If Wagner was not Geyer's son, then the answer to the question "Was Richard Wagner a Jew?" lacks the *sine qua non* on which the question rests. If Wagner was not Geyer's son, then, of course, all speculation as to his Jewish blood is futile and a sheer waste of time. However, we must always take into consideration a remote possibility that the hypothesis of his descent from Geyer can be proved. But, even in that case, it would still remain to be shown that Geyer himself was a Jew, before the claim of Jewish blood in Wagner could be accepted as a fact.

Before this side of the matter is taken up, it must be emphatically denied that Wagner is known to have coupled a suspicion of Jewish descent with a suspicion of his descent from Geyer. He merely gave expression to intimate friends of the latter possibility. But, supposing that this possibility occupied his mind before 1870, and, further, supposing that he believed or knew Geyer to have been a Jew, is it conceivable that Wagner in that case would have had the audacity to launch on the public, over his own signature, an enlarged and, in its additional matter, equally antisemitic edition of "Das Judenthum in der Musik" in 1869? To such lengths not even those will dare to go who, not content with recognizing palpable weakness of character in Wagner, assail practically every action of Wagner the mere man with sweeping condemnation. However, such speculations, too, would be a sheer waste of time in view of the fact that Wagner is not known to have ever entertained the slightest doubt of his Christian, or rather, Germanic origin.

On what is the often repeated assertion based, that Geyer was a Jew? On nothing, except on his supposedly Jewish name and on his supposedly Jewish features! This seems incredible, yet it is true. Not the slightest attempt has ever been made by those who juggle with historical truth, to investigate Geyer's origin. And as to his Jewish name and features, they are such dangerous arguments that they should have been handled with more care.

To accept every Jew who looks somewhat like a Christian therefore as a Christian, and every Christian who looks somewhat like a Jew therefore as a Jew, without further investigation, would be the height of uncritical folly. To illustrate this, just cast a glance at the picture of Wagner's mother made in 1839 and reproduced by Chamberlain in his work on Wagner. Many a Jewess has looked much less Jewish than Wagner's mother, yet, as Kekulé von Stradonitz proved in an article based on church and other records, "Ueber die mütterlichen Ahnen Richard Wagners" in the Wagner Jahrbuch, 1907, Johanna Rosina Pätz (this is the correct maiden name of Wagner's mother) descended on both sides from families of pure German blood. But how about the supposedly Jewish type of Geyer's features? Two portraits, both self-portraits, are accessible to the public; one (the scarcer) in Mrs. Burrell's book, for instance; the other often reproduced (for instance, by Chamberlain). This is the well-known portrait with the old German cap, and in this portrait, one may, if so inclined, detect slight traces of a Jewish type. The other portrait, however, shows not the slightest indication of such a type. Of course, this is my personal opinion, and others, perhaps Jews, might disagree with me. Only an impartial test, made by a number of competent judges who have no inkling of the purpose of the inquiry, could settle this point beyond dispute. Still, the Jewish type is so far from unmistakable in Geyer's portraits, that the most that possibly could be admitted is that he looks just as much like a Jew as he looks like a Christian. Hence, the honors would be evenly divided on this score, which means that Geyer's supposedly Jewish features cannot be advanced as an effective argument *for* his Jewish origin.

As to his Jewish name, it is indeed a fact that many Jews received zoölogical names in Germany at the hands of the police and census authorities. Hence the anecdote of the German boy who innocently asked his father why so many animals have Jewish names. This is the historical basis, too, of Nietzsche's famous, but cheap and superficial, witticism, "Ein Geyer ist beinahe ein Adler." The translator, Mr. Common, added for his English readers the explanatory foot-note: "Geyer (vulture) and Adler (eagle) are both names of Jewish families." Even Mrs. Burrell, otherwise so careful to verify her impressions by documents, fell into this trap, for it is a trap, and of clumsy workmanship at that. She enumerates a few such zoölogical names, and on p. lxxvi says:

His [Geyer's] name points to a Jewish origin, and I believe he possessed Jewish versatility rather than genius.

On p. xxviii, too, she says:

Vulture is a distinctly Jewish name, one of those taken when in Germany the Jews were forced to adopt surnames.

And yet, just a few words before, Mrs. Burrell writes, "Ludwig Geyer's forebears were Lutheran village-folk."

Well, if Nietzsche says, "A Geyer is almost an Adler," his "almost" makes all the difference in the world, and just enough to undermine his inference. True, Adler is almost exclusively a Jewish name, but other animal names like Fuchs (fox,) Wolf (wolf) and Strauss (ostrich) are not, and the name Geyer is not at all a Jewish name of such frequency that any valuable deductions could be made therefrom as to the probable Jewish origin of its bearer. Indeed, the name Geyer is much more a Christian German name than a Jewish German name. At any rate, those who, without misgivings, see a Jewish name in Geyer, must admit, if they are capable of admitting anything, that Geyer is not so typically a Jewish name in Germany as to permit their off-hand inferences. Again the honors, at the very worst, are evenly divided, and the theory of a possible Jewish origin of Wagner, even if he was Geyer's son, has not gained in substance.

And now comes an argument against Geyer's membership in the Jewish race, which turns the scales in our favor. To my knowledge, nobody has yet taken the trouble to stop and consider that Ludwig Geyer was not his full name. It was *Ludwig Heinrich Christian Geyer!* I venture to assert that no Semitic symptoms appear in what we call his Christian names. Imagine a Jewish father, at a time when the Jewish emancipation was just beginning (Geyer was born in 1770), giving his son the name *Christian!* Somewhere in the "fore-names," as the Germans aptly call them, a Jewish ingredient would more likely appear than not. Hence, even if the currently abbreviated name Ludwig Geyer

is to be deemed neutral, the full name Ludwig Heinrich
Christian Geyer is decidedly a genuine Christian, and
not a Jewish, name.

Now, combine this with the fact, that, as we know
from Geyer's letters to the widow Wagner quoted by
Mrs. Burrell, Geyer's brother was a Premier-Lieutenant
(first lieutenant) in the German army, and things begin
to look exceedingly dark for the Jewish claim. Undoubtedly, there have been non-baptized Jewish officers
(and good ones) in the German army, especially in
former decades, but the probabilities in any given,
doubtful case are entirely against the supposition.
Unless an officer's name is unmistakably Jewish, like
Mendelssohn, for instance, or Adler, it is fairly safe to
assume that he was not a Jew. But maybe Geyer's
brother was baptized, which would have made it then,
as now, fairly easy for him to enter the officers' corps
in Germany; and perhaps Geyer himself was baptized,
while his father and his forebears were Jews! Though
baptized, Geyer would then still be of Jewish blood and
through him Wagner, if he was Geyer's son. I am
afraid that this last and rather narrow alley of escape
ends in a *cul-de-sac*, and that the enemy will have to
surrender.

Ere this it might have aroused suspicion as to Ludwig
Heinrich Christian Geyer's Jewish origin, that his father
(compare Glasenapp) was "Aktuarius beim Oberaufseher-
amte" in Eisleben, and soon after Ludwig's birth was
transferred as "Justizamtmann nach Artern." In other
words, he was a judiciary official. Now, it has always
been equally difficult for a Jew to enter the judiciary
career in Germany as the military career, unless he
was a baptized Jew. Consequently, the probabilities
are again entirely against the assumption that Geyer's
father was a Jew, unless he be found to have relinquished
the Jewish faith. This, then, would take us back to
Geyer's grandfather, who might have been a Jew. But

why prolong the agony?   When Edgar Istel wrote his review of Mrs. Burrell's book and made the extraordinary biological observation quoted above, the editor of *Die Musik* simply remarked in a foot-note:

This assumption is contradicted by the findings of the Geyer specialist, Otto Bournot, who, as appears from Julius Kapp's new Wagner biography, proves that Geyer cannot have been Wagner's father.

One naturally hastens to refer to Kapp's statement. Though it is very brief, it is useful:

Also it may be mentioned in passing that the *recently found church records prove the forebears of Geyer all to have been Protestant church musicians.*

Unfortunately, Bournot's book has not yet left the press, and it is therefore impossible to say whether or not his reasons for rejecting even the possibility of Wagner's descent from Geyer must be accepted as conclusive.   On the other hand, the statement about the ancestry of Geyer is easily verified by a study of Glasenapp's "Tabellarisch geordneter Ueberblick über die Familiengeschichte des Hauses Wagner" in the Wagner Jahrbuch, 1908.   There we find that Geyer's mother, Christiane Wilhelmine Elisabeth Fredy, was of strictly Protestant lineage, and that Geyer's father, Christian Gottlieb Benjamin (born 1744), was an Aktuarius; his grandfather, Gottlieb Benjamin (born 1710), a Protestant cantor in Eisleben; his great-grandfather, Benjamin (born in 1682), an organist; his great-great-grandfather, Benjamin (born c. 1640), a Stadtmusikus—in brief, also a purely Protestant lineage, so far as it can be traced.

This settles the matter.   The question "Was Richard Wagner a Jew?" must be answered with an emphatic *No!* regardless of whether he was the son of Ludwig Geyer[1] or not.   Furthermore, if Otto Bournot has

---

[1] But this does not satisfy Hans Belart, of whom more anon. He contends that instead of four generations at least ten or twelve must be traced in order to settle Geyer's racial descent. Practically this amounts to the argument that Wagner had Jewish blood in his veins *because* we cannot prove that he had not. That is worse than a woman's reason. Moreover it works both ways, and so I

produced equally conclusive proof that (perhaps for chronological reasons) Wagner not only *was* not, but *can* not have been Geyer's son, then this whole sensational canard should promptly be dropped from books, magazines and newspapers, be they Jewish or not. Indeed, it would be in the best interests of those Jews who have, maybe as firm believers in it, circulated this myth, frankly to step forward and say, *Pater peccavimus.* The Jews have so many geniuses to their credit, in theology, philosophy, ethics, science, literature, music, philanthropy, even warfare, that they really do not need a Wagner to swell their ranks.   Moreover, the road of the Jewish race is thorny and hard enough. Antisemitism will not be downed, and those of us who number Jews among their best and most trusted friends can only regret if other Jews help to kindle the flames of antisemitism by printing without proof and in an objectionable tone stories that are offensive to decent-minded folk, Christians and Jews alike.

Epilogue

In his book of essays, "The Pathos of Distance" (Scribner, 1913), Mr. James Huneker pictures Wagner as "a mean, tricky, lofty soul, one that wavered along the scale from Caliban to Prospero," with emphasis on the Caliban notches in the scale—which continues to be the fashion.   And, harking back to Nietzsche's *mauvais*

---

declare without fear of possible proof to the contrary that Meyerbeer, Mendelssohn, Rubinstein, Goldmark, Mahler, were not Jews, but one-sided Gentiles! Indeed, if said scribifax had made out Wagner's ancestors as Jews on both sides, we should be justified in claiming him as at least a one-sided Gentile on the strength of that very argument.   It enables us, furthermore, if we are so inclined, to call Palestrina, Gluck, Haydn, Mozart, Beethoven, Berlioz, Debussy, Bruckner, Verdi, MacDowell, *e tutti quanti*, Jews!

The title of Otto Bournot's careful biography of his ancestor speaks for itself: "Ludwig Heinrich Christian Geyer, der Stiefvater Richard Wagners" (Leipzig, 1913). Bournot *inter alia* reached the important conclusion that Geyer's "Schuld" (see page 187) was in the nature of a pecuniary indebtedness to Wagner's father, as I had suspected.   At this conclusion Belart merely sneers.   He also has the effrontery to take improper relations between Geyer and Wagner's mother for granted simply because Bournot narrates that Geyer visited the Wagner family at Leipzig in the summer of 1912.

mot, Mr. Huneker has this to say on the problem here discussed:

"His father was a stage-player named Geyer!" Coming from Nietzsche, this statement is not surprising, for he had read these memoirs ["My Life"] while at Villa Triebschen. Why then, it will be asked, does this fact not appear in the first page of the autobiography? Despite asseverations to the contrary, we suspect that Bayreuth edited not wisely but too well. Others beside Nietzsche had seen the opening line of the work: "I am the son of Ludwig Geyer!" The late Felix Mottl, in the presence of several well-known music critics of New York City, declared in 1904 that he had read the above statement. He also told the same story to German journalists. . . .

I am afraid that Mr. Huneker (whom I admire and enjoy) has been rubbing elbows too closely with firms of scribblers *à la* Belart & Co., Ltd. I am also afraid that Mr. Huneker, too early in life, cast overboard the traditional suspicion that musicians are incorrigible gossips and auto-anecdotists.

However, I turn to a book by another distinguished critic, whom I admire and enjoy: Mr. Ernest Newman's "Wagner as Man and Artist" (Dent & Sons, 1914). It contains a chapter on "The Racial Origin of Wagner." Apparently written without cognizance of my essay of 1911, it reaches practically the same conclusions—a comforting coincidence. The chapter disposes of sundry matters not discussed by me (*e. g.*, the Mottl-Huneker report) as follows:

Wagner did not like Brahms, and so he accused [where?] poor Johannes of being a Jew. It was therefore natural that the out-and-out Brahms partisans should hail with glee any opportunity of making a retort in kind upon Wagner. This is attempted by Sir Charles Stanford in a preface to a volume of Brahms compositions recently issued by Messrs. T. C. & E. C. Jack. He affirms afresh—what we all know quite well—that Brahms was of the purest Teutonic blood. . . So confident. . . is this statement of the Hebraic origin of Wagner that any plain man, unversed in these matters, who happens to read Sir Charles Stanford's preface, will naturally assume that Wagner's Hebraism is as universally admitted as the death of Queen Anne. Yet Sir Charles offers no evidence as to Wagner being a Jew; he simply tells us that the fact has been "discovered."

Where and when, we may ask, was this "discovery" made? . . . The root of the legend is a notorious remark of Nietzsche's. That philosopher had seen one of the privately printed copies of the Autobiography about 1870, and his query in the postscript to *Der Fall Wagner*, "was Wagner a German at all?" and his point-blank statement that "his father was an actor of the name of Geyer," were supposed to have their justification in the autobiography. It was confidently asserted that when *that* appeared the truth would be made known to all the world in Wagner's own confession. Well, the Autobiography *has* appeared, and what Wagner says there is that Friedrich Wagner was his father. There is not the shadow of a hint in the book that Geyer was anything more than a friend of the family. (Mr. James Huneker, who discusses the subject in an essay in his book *The Pathos of Distance* (1913), thinks he sees such a hint, and a pretty broad one, in one passage that he quotes [the one in which Wagner says that "the worthy actor, . . . it seems, had frequently to appease my mother, who, rightly or wrongly, complained of the *Flatterhaftigkeit* of her husband"]; but the wish, I imagine, is father to the thought: few. people would care to put the construction upon it that he does.) Mr. Huneker as good as asserts that the commencement of the Autobiography has been tampered with. The reputation of the Villa Wahnfried in editorial matters is certainly not of the best; but after the express assurance that has been given the world that the Autobiography has been printed just as Wagner left it, something more than mere suspicion is required to bolster up a charge of such atrocious bad faith. Mr. Huneker tells us that "the late Felix Mottl [etc." follows the passage quoted above]. That is a little staggering; but again one prefers to think that Mottl or someone else was mistaken rather than that Cosima and Siegfried Wagner have been guilty of an incredible piece of literary dishonesty. . . .

Sir Charles Stanford attempts to support his very dubious thesis [of a Jewish origin of Wagner] by some show of musical argument. He alleges that the most marked characteristic in such little Jewish music as still exists is the continual repetition of short phrases—a method, he says, which Mendelssohn "uses to the verge of monotony" in his later works, and which is visible again in Wagner's employment of leading motives. Note, to begin with, the restriction of the use of this method to Mendelssohn's *later* works. Being a Jew, Mendelssohn surely would have betrayed this characteristic in the work of his whole life, if it really be a characteristic rooted in the Hebrew nature. It looks as though the ingenuous argument were that there is no Jew like an old Jew. But it is of even less applicability to Wagner than to Mendelssohn. . . .

Mr. Newman then proceeds to demolish Sir Charles' "surely very flimsy foundations on which to erect a theory that Wagner was a Jew," and asks this deliciously sarcastic question:

Will some one provide us with a sort of inch-rule and table of measurements, by the application of which we shall be able to. say precisely where musical Judaism ends and Gentilism begins?

So far, I should be perfectly willing to rest my case with Mr. Newman. But, in my opinion, he weakens his own case without any necessity whatsoever by the two quotations here following and briefly discussed:

Yet some suspicion clusters around a fact that cannot be discovered from the ordinary biographies of Wagner. The date of marriage of Johanna Wagner and Geyer is . . . now known to have taken place in August, 1814—on the 14th according to Otto Bournot; on the 28th, according to Mrs. Burrell;—and a daughter, Cäcilie, was born to them on the 26th of February, 1815, *i. e.*, six months later. This fact must necessarily count somewhat in our estimate of the nature of the earlier relations between Geyer and Frau Wagner.

Somewhat? Perhaps! Necessarily? No! "Estimate" of the nature of the earlier relations? It is not a question of estimate—that it is a matter of taste and inclination—it is a question of facts; and once Mr. Newman permits such estimates to enter the structure of his arguments, he will be an easy prey for all who argue "entertainingly" but unmethodically. The date of birth of Cecilia permits us to draw inferences only as to the relations between Geyer and Frau Wagner from one to three months earlier than the marriage. On this they had decided in the spring of the terrible year 1814, in their own mutual interest and out of consideration for the welfare of Frau Wagner's children. And, as Mrs. Burrell (p. 39) phrases her allusion to subsequent relations, "everybody will admit that it was not an occasion for adhering to the letter of the law and going through the ceremony of waiting for a year or even ten months." What must have happened in the summer of 1814, however, never will justify anybody without absolute proof to "estimate" the nature of *previous* relations between the two, more especially not the nature of their relations in the autumn preceding the birth of Richard Wagner on May 22, 1813. And Mr. Newman himself is satisfied that those letters written by Geyer in December, 1813, and January and February, 1814, to the widow Wagner are not those of a man who had wronged his dead friend and benefactor!

The other passage in Mr. Newman's book to which exception must be taken as not in keeping with an otherwise methodical argument, and as showing an ear slightly open to Mr. Huneker's seductive phrases, is this:

> The point with which we are most closely concerned here is not how *Mein Leben* came to be written, but what it contains on the first page. The copies that Nietzsche and Mottl saw belonged to the same imprint as Mrs. Burrell's copy. This last must be in existence somewhere. If the possessor would allow an inspection of it, it could be settled once for all whether the first page opens with the words "I am the son of Ludwig Geyer," or "My father, Friedrich Wagner. . . ". If Mottl was speaking the truth, there is an end of the matter—except that our last remaining shred of respect for the editorial probity of Wahnfried will be gone. If Mottl was deceiving himself and others, we can only fall back on a balance of the evidence I have tried to marshal in the preceding pages.

Let us turn for a moment to Wagner's "Mein Leben," as accessible to all of us. It begins:

> Am 22. Mai, 1813 in Leipzig auf dem Brühl im "roth und weissen Löwen," zwei Treppen hoch, geboren, wurde ich zwei Tage darauf in der Thomaskirche mit dem Namen Wilhelm Richard getauft. Mein Vater, Friedrich Wagner, zur Zeit meiner Geburt Polizei-actuarius in Leipzig. . . starb im October des Jahres meiner Geburt. . .

Two precise, easy-flowing sentences with all the data that a lover of autobiographies would desire. But I forget; originally, in the privately printed edition of the seventies, according to Nietzsche, Mottl and others— "who saw it"—the opening line had been: "I am the son of Ludwig Geyer"! Does even Mr. Huneker believe that Cosima and Siegfried deliberately faked six or seven lines—and of course kept a watchful eye on the rest of the bulky volumes with the object of destroying all traces of their forgery—in order to remove that "opening" line? For such a line obviously does not coincide at any point with the quoted sentences, so that by merely suppressing it and changing a few words Wagner's autobiography as we know it would begin as it does begin.

It is, of course, clear that Felix Mottl made his declaration in 1904, but I, for one, do not believe that he ever in his life saw a line "I am the son of Ludwig Geyer" in a book prepared and revised by Richard Wagner for future publication. Not that Felix Mottl deliberately lied, but I believe that his memory played him a trick and that he remembered as an experience of his own one attributed to Nietzsche. As to Mr. Huneker's "and others," they do not count until their names are produced together with convincing details as to when and where they saw such a line. As to Nietzsche, will those who operate with his name in this connection kindly step forward with a reference to when and where Nietzsche stated that Wagner's autobiography, which (we know) had passed through his hands, opened with or contained the line "I am the son of Ludwig Geyer"? In 1888 he merely averred that Richard Wagner's "father was a stage-player named Geyer";—not a syllable to the effect of having seen this stated in Wagner's autobiography. Had he seen it there, he hardly would have hesitated to say so. Ah! but perhaps Nietzsche was just as much of a Caliban as Wagner, and he refrained from such a reference to Wagner's autobiography because he feared that the tables would then be turned against him because of his *confessed distrust* "of every point which rests solely on the testimony of Wagner himself"!

Happily, there enters into this maze of gossip one who was not given to gossip—Mrs. Burrell. Mr. Newman pins his hopes for a settlement of the Geyer problem on an inspection of Mrs. Burrell's copy of the original issue of "Mein Leben." This is a rather unkind, though unintentional, slur on Mrs. Burrell's willingness to report and ability to notice, *if it were there*, an important and startling biographical line like "I am the son of Ludwig Geyer" in a book which she had studied and which she despised. Now, Mrs.

Burrell, who is *generally right in her facts*—the italicized words are those of Mr. Newman—and who almost made a sport of reproducing biographical documents in photographic facsimile, reproduces the title-page and the preface of her copy of "Mein Leben," but not the opening page. Mrs. Burrell would not, could not in the interest of her own reputation as a biographer, have hesitated to quote or photograph or discuss, or mention, the opening (or any other) page if it had contained such startling biographical information as "I am the son of Ludwig Geyer." The very fact that Mrs. Burrell did not call our attention to such a line or a line of the same content is practically conclusive evidence in itself that it does not occur in her copy of the original issue of "Mein Leben." Hence, a further belated inspection thereof is unnecessary. But more telling than this negative argument are the facts, first, that Mrs. Burrell, as I have shown, alluded to the whole Geyer story as a "stupid confusion," and secondly, that *she never in her volume shows the slightest doubt that Richard Wagner was the son of Friedrich Wagner.*

As long as writers with the mental attitude of Thersites, Aretino, Belart, etc., are born, the Ludwig Geyer yarn will thrive. If critics must find fault with the character of Richard Wagner, must they also drag into their moral abattoir his mother and stepfather? From all accounts, Ludwig Geyer behaved nobly toward the widow and children of his friend and benefactor. Yet some writers obviously prefer to tarnish the character of such a man without much ado, instead of giving him the benefit of doubt as long as available evidence and methodical reasoning permit. As to Richard Wagner, it has become the fashion to picture him as a Caliban peopling his island of life with Calibans. The thing has been overdone; Wagner as a man was really rather better than most of his detractors. The time will come when they will have carved out of their unfair abuse of Wagner a boomerang to smash the skull of their own reputation.

*

*   *

Interruption of the mail-service between America and Germany since the outbreak of the war has prevented me from incorporating in this epilogue an analysis of two books bearing on the problem under discussion. The one is Hans Belart's "Richard Wagner's Beziehungen zu François und Eliza Wille....Ludwig Geyer, der Schauspieler und Maler als leiblicher Vater Rich. Wagners" (Dresden, C. Reissner, 1914). At the time of publication a German magazine reviewed Belart's arguments. Their flimsiness was so apparent that I had no desire to read the book, the less so because I did not then contemplate republishing my own article. Now that I have read and examined the Geyer chapter in Belart's pamphlet, I am even less inclined to waste time on a confutation of his pseudo-scientific arguments based on phrenology, heredity, "Komödiantengebräuche und kulturelle Sitten," etc., and stitched together with the disorderly logic of the sensation-seeker who maltreats his sources and jumps at conclusions in order to reach an erotic goal. And when one has read what Belart's pen in the first chapter of his pamphlet makes of the relations between Eliza Wille and Wagner, one almost suspects that there is not only madness in his methods, but method in his madness. With a logic such as his, one can prove everything—or nothing.

The other book alluded to is Elizabeth Foerster-Nietzsche's "Wagner und Nietzsche zur Zeit ihrer Freundschaft" (München, G. Müller, 1915). I have been told that in this book Nietzsche's conversation with Wagner about the Geyer-problem is recorded. I was not told exactly in what manner. Yet everything depends on what Wagner said, when and why he said it—and on whether or no Nietzsche reported Wagner's words correctly without flavouring them with his own interpretation. As for Wagner himself, did he merely express an opinion to Nietzsche, or did he produce unequivocal evidence to back up his opinion? His mere opinion or belief counts for very little, and is not binding on others. Or did Wagner, perhaps—he naturally loved Geyer more than Friedrich Wagner—simply prefer to consider himself the son of Geyer rather than of Wagner? In that case, subtle psychologists may also see Wagner's great love for Cosima, the daughter of Franz Liszt, reflected in his preferential belief (with everything implied); but biographers cannot rear an edifice on such motives of psychological adjustment.

SIGNS OF A NEW UPLIFT IN ITALY'S MUSICAL LIFE

SIGNS OF A NEW UPLIFT IN ITALY'S MUSICAL LIFE

(From the "Sammelbände" of the I.M.G., 1900)

A "new uplift" naturally presupposes a degradation. In fact, Italy, in point of musical culture, no longer marches in the van among enlightened nations, but ranks after Germany, Austria-Hungary, Belgium, France, England, the United States, Norway, Russia, and other civilized states. I do not now propose to survey the cause of this degradation along broad historical lines; but some few side-lights must be thrown upon it, the better to illuminate the contrast between past and present.

The decline in Italy's musical standing antedates the beginning of the nineteenth century. Grotesque as it may sound, its symptoms appeared and multiplied precisely during the period of the Italian hegemony, as a phenomenon attendant on the mighty development of the Opera in the seicento, and yet more in the settecento; more especially from the time in which the opera no longer served exclusively as a pastime for gentlefolk, but began—in 1637, at Venice—to become a popular spectacle. True, at that same time both the song and instrumental chamber-music in all their varieties shared in the general upward movement; but in the course of time they found it increasingly difficult to compete in popularity with the opera. No wonder; for they were more intimate in their effects and too engrossing in their demands on the hearer. At least, in comparison with the opera, which gradually degenerated into a "show" for ear and eye. The ever-growing host of Musical Academies, of which every hamlet could finally boast two or three, could do little to mend matters. Although toward the end of the sixteenth century they were really promotive of musical progress—let me recall, for instance, the "invention" of opera at Florence—at the close of the seventeenth century, and throughout the eighteenth, they not infrequently led an equivocal existence. Music was often an incidental affair, quite subordinate to social or Society interests, or less innocent things. The singing-teacher Angelo Bertalotti[1] (1661–1747) narrates the following delightful episode in the early history of the Accademia Filarmonica of Bologna, founded in 1666:

They played good music every Thursday, and Signor Vincenzo Carrati, a distinguished citizen in whose house the meetings took place, derived so great pleasure from it, that he had an abundance of refreshments handed around to keep the company alert. But the Academicians, and still oftener certain non-Academicians who attended the practice-evenings, appropriated even the refreshments reserved for the players, thus causing disturbances and quarrels. In consequence, the refreshments were done away with. This radical remedy had a bad after-effect. The young people absented themselves, being no longer attracted by these adventitious trifles, and the evenings had to be carried on by the elderly gentlemen, who were really unequal to the task. So they frequently found themselves in difficulties. And, because of the suppression of refreshments, or for some other reason, thenceforward the practice-evenings were not regularly held every week.

We shall not go far wrong in assuming that the "other reason" hinted at referred to the growing interest in the opera. For, in fact, this latter gradually absorbed public interest so completely, that at last (and down to the present time) the Italian populace took the term "music" to mean nothing more nor less than "opera-music." And far into the nineteenth century, even their writers on music, when striving to check the decline of Italian art by dint of pamphleteering, usually had in mind only the opera (or church music too, possibly), without one word of mention for other varieties of music. Of this there are instances by the score. As a striking confirmation, Article 5 in El. Pantologo, "La Musica italiana nel secolo XIX" (Florence, 1828),

[1] *Cf.* Annibale Bertocchi, "Notizie sulla R. Accademia Filarmonica in Bologna." Lecture in the Aula of the Academy, April 30, 1897.

may suffice. Here we read, after an ecstatic eulogy of the composers of opera, the sentence, "Corelli, Veracini, Boccherini, tutti abili professori di violino e direttori d'orchestra." That is, merely skilled virtuosi! Not a syllable about their works! In fine, the entire classical instrumental music of the Italians had fairly sunk into oblivion, even among the educated classes. And the vocal treasures of the sixteenth century fared yet worse. Andrea Maier, then a highly esteemed critic, strayed in 1819 thus far afield: "Palestrina and Peri . . . were like fleeting flashes that only for instants pierced the long night (*nota bene*, between Guido d'Arezzo and Jommelli!), without leaving the slightest trace of their splendor behind."

Naturally, men of the calibre of a Padre Martini or Mattei held themselves and their pupils aloof from such an idiotic standpoint. Similarly, in the Conservatories, in the salons of certain aristocrats, in the Academies, and here and there in artistic circles, as well, ensemble music was still zealously cultivated at the beginning of the nineteenth century. In these same circles, too, German music excited a lively interest, and they did their best to keep abreast of the times. Otherwise one would fail to understand why the publisher Lorenzo Manini should advertise, in 1787, the following works in the *Gazzetta Cremonese*:[1] (1) Trio . . . del celebre Hoffmeister. . . (3) Quartetto . . . di Haydn. (4) Suonata da cembalo con accomp. di violino . . . di Sterkel. (6) Quartetti . . . di Stabhinger. All in all, from the very beginning of the eighteenth century[2] one can trace German influences on form-development among the Italians, which in time increased rather than diminished. To be sure, the opposing influence was far stronger, as we know. It is significant enough, how-

[1] *Cf.* L. Lucchini, "Cenni Storici sui più celebri Musicisti Cremonesi." Casalmaggiore, 1887.

[2] *Cf.* Scheibe, "Kritischer Musikus."

ever, that Rossini, the idol of the Italians, who (according to the current national notion) owed his style solely to his own and the national genius, was jocularly called "il tedeschino" by his teacher Mattei because he persistently studied and copied Haydn and Mozart, and played them with his friends. As for that, we know that Spontini, Cherubini, and Rossini's rival Pacini (witness his Autobiography), were similarly inclined.

To what avail? Opera none the less flooded the whole land, and it was Rossini himself who dragged Italy into this perilous vortex. "Egli nacque per la beata tranquillità"—thus he was characterized in 1823 by one of the most famous *virtuose* of his music, namely, Marie Giorgi Righetti. And the great Vitiator of Taste inoculated his entire people and period with this *beata tranquillità* — beatific contemplativeness. During his Italian period he performed the feat of definitively forcing Italian opera aside from Monteverdi. That is to say, not from the inventor, but assuredly from the founder of a genuine music-drama, who wrought with undeveloped resources, indeed, yet purposefully, along the same lines as Richard Wagner—with the leading-motive, with the orchestra as a psychological background of the dramatic picture, and with the program-overture. Thus Italian opera—after many veerings in the right direction—took on the shape wherein its mongrel nature stands confessed: the concert-opera, or (to modify the phrase) the virtuoso concert with scenery, orchestral accompaniment, and connecting text. What need was there now of church music, choral song, and concert music? All three could readily supply their needs from the opera. It was like a wholesale warehouse, crammed full of solo and ensemble numbers, to wit, bravura arias, duets, terzets, quartets, etc., Ave Marias, drinking-songs, and lastly even symphonies, namely, the *Vorspiele* or preludes (formally often rightly so named), which after all frequently had nothing in common with the following opera as regards either character or motives. "Ma chi prescrisse mai l'indole delle sinfonie delle opere in musica?" naïvely exclaimed the Righetti. In one word, church, concert and salon became a welcome repository for the opera.

Every house was ravaged by the operatic plague. The arrangements of *opere teatrali* for low music-hall orchestras all the way down to the transcriptions of entire operas for violin solo—violin scores, as it were[1]— multiplied like rabbits. Whatever still remained of taste and artistic feeling was swept away by the well-nigh immeasurable flood of sentimental rubbish and salon literature. So much for the household music.

But what were they playing and singing around 1850 in the Italian churches? Arias and galops by Rossini, Verdi, and others, provided with liturgical texts. When they wished to be in style, they chose religious numbers from the most popular operas. For example, there may be found in the Ricordi catalogue, under the heading *Sonate, Versetti, Messe, ecc., per organo*, "La Ceciliana, Collezione di pezzi originali e sopra motivi d'opere teatrali"; and further on, under *Guida per l'organista*, "La Traviata, La Favorita, Simon Boccanegra," etc. So one easily gains an understanding of the musical soirées which Capocci[2] arranged with the approbation of the priesthood in the Oratory of San Filippo, the time-honored birthplace of the oratorio! Favorite operas were frequently put on the program, rearranged for men's voices alone. This delectable modus operandi was undertaken *inter alia* in the case of Rossini's *Semiramide*, different words being adapted to the two parts of Semiramide and Arsace; and in this form they were blithely sung by two singers of the Sixtine Chapel.

This makes the opulent section devoted to *Musica sacra* in Ricordi's catalogue all the more bewildering.

[1] See Ricordi's catalogue.
[2] See the admirable work by G. P. Zuliani, "Roma musicale. Appunti—Osservazioni—Notizie." Rome, Botta, 1878.

But let us not yield to bewilderment. Even to this
day, music in the Italian churches retains a predomi-
natingly secular character. Now, considering that since
that time a decided improvement has taken place, the
masses and motets then composed must infallibly,
despite their devotional titles, have smelt of the street
and the side-scenes for miles away. So much for the
church music.

And what were they playing and singing in concerts?
I intentionally avoid writing "in concert-halls." For
these latter are extremely scarce in Italy. Most concerts were then given, as they are now, in the theatre;
this being, by the way, another factor which imper-
ceptibly but surely was bound to promote the blending
of the art-styles and to wipe out the distinctions between
them. Programs like that of Giuseppe Grassi's Accademia Vocale ed Istrumentale, of May 2, 1844,[1] were
not at all rare: (1) Ouverture a grande orchestra nel
Cavallo di Bronzo del Maestro Auber. (Usually only
"Ouverture" is printed, without mention of the opera
or the author.) (2) Variazioni per violino sopra un
tema del "Pirata," . . . Coro a Introduzione nel Roberto
il Diavolo del M° Meyerbeer. (4)Cavatina nella Pia da
Tolomei del M° Donizetti. (5) Fantasia per Violino
sopra una Romanza francese e la Muta di Portici. (6)
Ouverture a Grande Orchestra del M° Mercadante.
(7) Capriccio di Bériot sopra un Tema di Beethoven.
(8) Coro nel Voto di Jefte del M° Genesali. (9) Cava-
tina nell' opera il Sesostri del M° Baccilieri. (10)
Variazioni sopra dei Temi della Sonnambula. — But as
late as 1880 the following enormity was possible in
Bologna.[2] On May 28th, at a charity concert, after
orchestral works by Nicolai, Liszt and Saint-Saëns, the
audience was treated to a Minuet by Boccherini and

[1] Luigi Bignami, "Cronologia di tutti gli spettacoli rappresentati nel gran
Teatro Comunale di Bologna 1763-1880."

[2] Cf. Bignami, op. cit.

Liszt's Second Rhapsodie played by twenty-four ladies on twelve pianos. At the foot of the program, all the countesses and other ladies who lent their pianos are mentioned by name. And this at Bologna on May the 28th, in the year of grace 1880!

A brief statistical survey of the *Catalogo generale* issued by the mammoth publishing-house of Ricordi & Co. will show more clearly than any amount of historical consideration to what an extent the whole interest in and production of music in Italy—in other words, supply and demand—have been absorbed by the opera. In this catalogue of about 100,000 published numbers, whose three volumes contain 1,525 pages, folios 822 to 824 are devoted to international string-quartets. On these three pages are found 34 composers with 85 works (among which, for evident reasons, I do not count "Romanzas" as string-quartets). Of the above, 24 composers with 47 works are Italian. By contrast we find in the section for *Opere teatrali* for piano solo some 110 Italians with 400 operas. This disproportion grows to be monstrous, however, when we reach the fearsomely swollen section of the *Spartiti manoscritti, Opere teatrali, farsi, oratorii, cantate.* Here I have counted over 1,420 works by some 400 composers. Of these works the oratorios and cantatas number hardly more than 70. So there remain, still in round numbers, some 1,350 *opere teatrali.* Of the 400 composers, about 80, with 185 works, were found to be foreigners. Subtracting these, there are left 320 Italians with 1,165 works.

Thus we have for the string-quartet 24 composers with 47 works; for the opera 320 composers with 1,165 works. Neither of these calculations can be appreciably affected by the inconsiderable infusion of works belonging to the eighteenth century.

The objection may be raised, that only string-quartets in the Ricordi catalogue have been taken into account, and that many more than these have been produced in

Italy.   True enough; I might even support this contention with names of unrepresented composers.   But
Ricordi has, in the first place, bought out a number of
important publishing houses (among them those of
Fr. Lucca, and G. Guidi of Florence, the latter being
almost the sole firm worthy of note in connection with
Italian string-quartets), and, in the second place, more
operas have also been written than those published by
Ricordi.

Publishers, as a rule, are not so altruistic as to purchase every manuscript opera offered them.   On the
contrary, because of the heavy expense involved, they
pick and choose.   And so the effect of this argument
would be, at most, to shift the ratio of $24/47 : 320/1165$
to the advantage (or disadvantage) of the opera.

If only all these composers had been masters like
Rossini, Donizetti, Bellini, Verdi, Mercadante, Pacini,
Ponchielli, Petrella!—men able to create, within a
decadent form, music which was original, charmful, of
real significance and, now and again, unsurpassed in
beauty.

If only the dramatic vocal art of Italy had saved its
brilliancy and its purity from out this operatic deluge!
But various observations of Rossini's, Verdi's and
Pacini's, and a flood of polemic literature on the subject,
prove how the decline of vocal art kept pace with the
increase in operatic productions.   Besides, the last great
artists of the Italian school were frequently not Italians
at all, but Frenchmen, Germans, or Spaniards:—Mali-
bran, Hungher, Stolz, Waldmann, Krauss, Duprez,
Garcia, etc.   Then, consider the number of those who
Italianized their good French or German names!   The
mischievous notion began to spread, that vocal art was
of small account, and sheer vocal display everything.
"But, my dear man, even a donkey has a voice!" was
Simon Mayr's fitting retort to Donizetti when the latter
attempted to defend the new fashion.   Unhappily,

Donizetti knew his compatriots better than did the semi-Italian Mayr. For the chief cause of the indescribable deterioration of Italian vocal art was, and still is, that the people go wild over any mere amateur who happens to possess a ringing voice and a stout pair of lungs. Bravura finally triumphed over everything else, including common sense.

In proof, read what follows:[1] In a certain duet between soprano and baritone, the former begged her partner to sing a transposed version of the duet, as her weak voice would be overpowered by his at the original pitch. The baritone refused. And the sequel? He jauntily sang his part *solo*, at the original pitch. The audience, instead of protesting, listened with delight to this remarkable solo. When the baritone had finished, came a higgledy-piggledy modulation by the orchestra, after which the soprano sang *her* part at a pitch convenient for her voice, likewise with overwhelming applause. And the whole piece figured as a duet!

If only the public of that period had attended the opera merely for the gratification of their ears in suchlike musical revels! But often—very often—not musical emotion was sought, but political agitation. It was a time of political ebullition. The police, working with decent and indecent expedients, kept watch over every step, every word, every assemblage. By violent means they sought to suppress the entire movement which was inevitably leading to the final unification of Italy. So they, of course, controlled the musical associations, dissolved them at will, and carried everything with a high hand. The Roman police, for example,[2] when Cav. Venanza (whom they found troublesome) suggested to the Accademia Filarmonica that Spontini's *Fernando Cortes* should be produced, made no bones of

---

[1] See the work "Riflessioni sulla causa della Decadenza della scuola di canto in Italia" (Paris, Dupont, 1881), by the great singing-master Delle Sedie.

[2] Zuliani, *op. cit.*

throwing him into prison for a term of eight years as guilty of political intrigue. Thus the opera became a ready instrumentality for outwitting the police. However they might have the book censored, or mutilated, or revised, passages were sure to be left which the public might, could and would interpret to fit current political conditions. In this way the opera grew to be a political meeting in which the singers assumed, as it were, the rôles of popular orators. Without previous conferences, there was a common understanding, and this sufficed to keep the fires of liberty continually ablaze. Now wed the words to a passionate, inflammatory music like that in *I Lombardi* or *La Battaglia di Legnano* by Verdi—who was explicitly called *il maestro della rivoluzione italiana*,[2] whose name became a battle-cry:

Viva Vittorio Emmanuele Re D'Italia

and whose successes at that time depended in great part on political, rather than æsthetic, elements—and the opera became a soul-stirring scene for the fanatics of freedom, but a disgusting spectacle for such as came to hear opera as opera.

This extrinsic peculiarity of the moribund Italian opera was also not calculated to promote the taste and decorum of the public. And it was precisely this Italian opera-going public, even now the most unmannerly and obstreperous in Europe, which so sadly needed to acquire a modicum of good behavior. It had always stood in ill-repute. Thus Riccoboni, in his "Réflexions historiques et critiques sur les différents théâtres de l'Europe" (1740), speaks of the Italian theatre as follows:

In almost all the Italian towns the audiences are very restless, being in an uproar even before the piece begins. The Italians are violent and boisterous in expressing their applause; "Viva!"—"Va

[2] *Cf.* Monaldi's Biography of Verdi.

dentro!'' (chase yourself!) . . . and often overwhelm the artists with insults, to show their exasperation more plainly, and throw rotten apples on the stage. . . . Ladies and gentlemen having seats in the Parquet take care not to put on good clothes, said seats being rendered very uncomfortable by the habit of spitting anywhere and everywhere, more especially from the boxes into the Parterre, and the tossing down of unconsumed fragments of luncheon.

We have similar reports from an Anonymus,[1] from De Brosses in his "Letters of Travel," Grétry, F. Filippi, the *Gazzetta Musicale di Milano* (1858, No. 28), etc. As for myself, I have had similar, and in great part precisely the same experiences in Padua, Verona, Bologna, in the year of our Lord 1899!!

So matters stood about 1850, when a reform movement set in. It originated, of course, among social elements to whom musical conditions in the nation at large were uncongenial—first of all in those circles which, despite the operatic deluge, contrived to apportion their musical requirements equally between opera, concert music, and chamber-music. Next in order came the *Gazzetta Musicale di Milano*, founded in 1842. The chief purpose of this organ of Ricordi's was, and still is, to further the interests of that firm. But the *Gazzetta*, being cleverly edited, has managed from the outset to combine these interests with those of its readers, the useful with the agreeable. It carefully recorded, in particular, every triumph of Italian opera, it published a vast deal of correspondence from all quarters of the globe (that concerning Germany, to be sure, frequently at second or third hand), and sought to satisfy the curiosity of its clientèle in all other ways. Now, whether or no G. Ricordi actually intended it, these international reports, small talk and gossip, together with sundry original articles (*e. g.*, Simon Mayr's "Stato e Coltura della Musica in Germania," 1844-45), set forth beyond all question that in Germany, especially, great things

[1] "Voyage historique et politique de Suisse, d'Italie et d'Allemagne." Frankfort, 1736.

were preparing; that the Germans had broken away from the Italian leading-strings, and that a German opera was already in existence. Nor was this all; choral singing, symphony and quartet were cultivated there on a par with the opera. "Germany is sweating music from every pore!" wrote a reporter to his astounded readers at home; and the echo of quite unfamiliar names came from over the Alps. With the names of Haydn, Mozart, and Beethoven, which were known by hearsay, at least, a number of others appeared to be conjoined in an irresistible onward sweep of German musical activities.

Now the more lucid minds of Italy began to feel a certain uneasiness. Scattered individuals aroused themselves and called loudly for progress and reform; soon the movement swelled into a veritable tidal wave of books, pamphlets, essays, articles—a swing toward reform which had by no means spent its force at the turn of our century. Six distinctive demands were made:

1.   That the government should bestow greater attention on public musical instruction, music being unquestionably to be recognized as an important educational factor.

2.   The same with regard to choral singing, already firmly rooted in other countries. In Italy, the organization of choral societies should be taken in hand systematically and vigorously.

3.   That church music should be purified.

4.   That instrumental music should be revivified in Italy.

5.   "Vinte le puerili suggestioni della vanità" (Biaggi), that Italian opera should be subjected to a searching examination as to its vitality, and (if needful) be rejuvenated by an infusion of foreign blood.

6.   That the Italian public should not be left in ignorance of Richard Wagner.

The justifiability of the first three points was quite generally admitted. But just these three were the latest to be taken in hand, the first one for the special reason that the authorities did not have the necessary means at their disposal to carry out such reforms. True, school-singing has been fostered, but thus far the ·harvest has been meagre. The methods seem to be at fault; at least, van Elewyck and L. Torchi find little in them to commend.

The reorganization of the Conservatories, too, did not get fairly under way until after 1870. There was too long a contention over questions of management, *e. g.*, whether day-school or boarding-school (*Liceo* or *Convitto*) were preferable. Matters were changed when Verdi, Casamorata, Serrao and Mazzucato wrote their celebrated Report "On the Reform of the Institutes of Music" to the Ministry of Public Instruction. This list of shortcomings made an impression, and a general polishing and patching began.

The revival was first in evidence in the Royal Institute of Music at Florence (under Casamorata), which laid less stress upon the training of virtuosi than on controlling and promoting musical instruction throughout the city. The institution (since about 1860) has been admirably managed, and up to 1874 had already given some 4000 students, free of expense, a sound training in music.[1]

In Turin, the reform in instruction is bound up with the name of Carlo Pedrotti. This master was not only a notable composer and conductor, but a born director of a musical institute. He first displayed this talent at the Liceo Musicale in Turin (from about 1870), and later (from 1882 onward) at the Liceo Rossini in Pesaro. After his death in 1893, Mascagni had therefore the very exacting, though most enviable,

---

[1] Van Elewyck, "De l'État actuel de la musique en Italie. Rapport officiel adressé à Monsieur le Ministre de l'intérieur du royaume de Belgique," 1875.

task of proving himself not unworthy of his predecessor.

The Milan Conservatory, already noteworthy under Lauro Rossi, was further elevated by the united efforts of Bazzini and Mazzucato (from 1873) into a place of unquestioned superiority. For Bazzini, the great store of experience gained in Leipzig and Paris was of prime importance.

The Liceo Musicale in Rome, dependent on the Royal Accademia di Santa Cecilia, has likewise developed rapidly since 1868 to an assured prosperity, thanks to the devoted labors of Commendatore Em. Broglio, Sgambati, Pinelli and Petturi, seconded after 1870 by De Sanctis, Orsini, Rommacciotti, Terziani, and other famous musicians.[1] Of a truth, there were plenty of obstacles in their path. Sgambati and Pinelli at first gave lessons gratis, until the city authorities contributed a (yearly) subvention of 30,000 lire, while the Province and the central government gave 10,000 lire each. Thereby at least the continuance of a practically managed music-school in the Eternal City was assured.

But why write a history of the Italian Conservatories? The Instituti musicali del Regno d'Italia at Bologna (Martucci, L. Torchi, Sarti), *Florence*, Genoa, *Milan*, *Naples* (Platania), Novara, Padua (Pollini), *Palermo*, *Parma* (Tebaldini), Pesaro, *Rome*, Turin, Venice (Liceo Benedetto Marcello, since 1877 under Enrico Bossi), besides others,[2] are estimable, in part excellent, institutions, managed quite like similar ones in Germany. The one in Parma may, however, be confidently held up as a model institute, since Giovanni Tebaldini took over its management in 1897. His attention has been chiefly directed to the branches of ensemble music, so sadly neglected in Italy.[3]   Whereas at Bologna and

[1] *Cf.* Zuliani.

[2] Those in italics are Royal institutions, the others municipal; private schools are not mentioned.

[3] "Annuario del R. Cons. di Parma, 1897-98" (Parma, L. Battei, 1899). Report to the President of the Conservatory.

elsewhere there exists, for example, neither chorus class nor orchestra class, such classes are organized at Parma just as methodically as in Cologne or Vienna.[1] But not this alone. In Parma there are even classes in Gregorian chant and vocal polyphony. The programs for the practice-evenings also make an excellent impression. For one thing, the balance between Italian and non-Italian classics is maintained with artistic taste. And as just the Italian instrumental classics are, in great part, unknown quantities in Italy, Tebaldini designedly devotes entire evenings to them. (June 2, 1898.) Still further to enhance the utility of these "history classes," as one is tempted to call them, Tebaldini introduced the program with an explanatory lecture, closing with these words: "To produce the works of masters of earlier times, not on formal historical grounds, but to give them new life, is a requirement which nowadays may logically be imposed on every Conservatory . . . . above all, for purely didactic reasons!"

My remarks on choral singing in the Conservatories illustrate, better than aught else, the slender interest taken in Italy, even at this late day, in choral singing. Innumerable suggestions for promoting this important factor in music have already been made. For why should just Italy be deprived of the rich resources of oratorio and chorus music? As a matter of fact, a multitude of choral societies have been brought into being, but very few of them survive their infancy. And I fancy that some decades will pass before choral singing receives half the attention it deserves in Italy.

[1] At Bologna one point impressed me unpleasantly. I attended the annual examination concert, and found that nearly all the students, excepting those of Sarti (the leader of the Bolognese Quartet), played pieces far beyond their capacity. This is the more to be regretted, because some of the pupils are doubtless very talented. I might have ascribed the bungling to excitement and the frightful heat (mid-June), had the vocal classes not shown the same deficiency. Students in their second or third year sang excerpts from *Don Giovanni, Don Carlos, Re di Lahore*, etc.; the effect may easily be guessed. The auditors, of course, applauded frantically, and the newspapers treated these raw efforts of mere scholars—all these *saggi finali*, in fact—as if they were artistic events of the first rank. This certainly does not do those young people any good. On the contrary, they lose all sense of proportion with respect to their own performances and the work of their teachers.

The Italian character and social prejudices are formidable obstacles in the path of the good cause.

First of all, the Italian does not like a long preparation of months for a final triumph—the triumph on the concert evening! For it is vanity, rather than delight in a common artistic endeavor, that urges him to join a choral society. He wearies of the regular hours of rehearsal and of painstaking, thorough study. Neither does he care to let his wife and daughter display themselves and sing in a chorus of both sexes; that is improper, according to Italian views, and besides, the very idea of a "chorus" connotes, for him, something of an inferior, despicable and mercenary nature. An Italian finds it difficult to discriminate between a theatre chorus (which is, in fact, frequently a motley crew of poor beggars and unfortunate girls), and a choral society whose members are brought together by a love of good music, desiring artistic enjoyment for themselves and to impart it to others, without thought of flirtation. He is unable to conceive the meeting together of young folks of both sexes as due to anything but a more or less disguised sex-impulse. Besides, why should one take so much trouble, when choruses are ready to hand?—namely, theatre choruses, which (in his opinion) can sing all the amusing, nice, celebrated, northern (brr!) music exactly as well. It remains to be seen whether this petty opposition to a species of music from which other nations derive, year after year, many hours of the purest enjoyment, will die out.

Still another social factor operates unfavorably. There are in Italy scores of choral and other musical societies which are not supported by regular contributions from their members, and do not try to cover their expenses by the sale of concert-tickets, but form private associations under the presidency of some patron. This patron (usually a conte, marchese, or principe) bears all expenses, opens his palace-halls for rehearsals, interests himself in every other way for the prosperity of the society, but considers it withal as a personal diversion, has a word to say even in artistic matters, and lets the whole thing drop whenever he finds it too expensive or otherwise inconvenient. The directorate, weary of continual personal friction, has by that time generally lost all desire to reorganize the society, and one fine day it is dissolved, one can hardly say how, when, or where.

All these things, as aforesaid, are most unfavorable for the development of Italian choral singing. Nevertheless, the latter half of the nineteenth century witnessed a slight improvement.

Florence must again be mentioned in first place. Here Prof. Jefte Sbolci founded, previous to 1840, his *Società per lo studio della musica classica*, which by 1858 already had the goodly number of two hundred and forty concerts to its credit. Then, in 1860, the *Società Cherubini* began its career under M. Laussot, whose successor (in 1873) was the highly distinguished pianist Buonamici, a pupil of Bülow and Rheinberger.

Milan owed its first really systematically trained choral society to the exertions of Martin Roeder—one can see how German influences filter through at all points. Roeder,[1] who in many ways did much for the improvement of Italian taste, founded at the beginning of the 'seventies the *Società del Quartetto Corale* as a subdivision of the *Società del Quartetto di Milano*. The Milanese owe it to his well-planned, unswervable advance from the easy to the more difficult that they have become acquainted, step by step, with the entire classic and romantic choral literature. The fact that Roeder's enterprise has succeeded is, in my opinion, to be ascribed in part to the *Gazzetta Musicale di Milano*, whose fulminant articles shook the citizens and musicians of the better class out of the lethargy of prejudice, and

[1] Martin Roeder, "Ueber den Stand der öffentlichen Musikpflege in Italien." Breitkopf & Härtel, 1881; Waldersee-Vorträge.

almost put them under moral obligation to support Roeder. Another association, the *Società Corale Leoni*, must be mentioned for completeness' sake and also because it was only the cordial coöperation of these two societies which made possible the Milanese première of the Ninth Symphony in April, 1878.

In Turin, since the organization of the *Società Corale Stefano Tempia* (in 1875, if I mistake not), choral music has been aroused from its trance, so that concert-goers are no longer forced (as in 1855) to accept *Il Trovatore* as a "concerto di musica classica vocale e strumentale." On the contrary, the programs —with historical notes—of the Società Tempia display a really exemplary cultivation of serious choral music.

Rome deserves mention in the same breath with Florence, Milan and Turin. The superabundance of robust and mellow voices in the Romagna is almost a challenge to the founding of choral societies. And yet, some fifty years ago, secular choruses were unheard-of organizations, the Philharmonic Academy alone excepted. But the history of even this society consists, in the nineteenth century, in a perpetual alternation between dissolution by the police and reorganization. How keen the police were on the scent of treason, has been mentioned above. When the Academy took on the predicate of "Royal" in 1870, it might doubtless have led a peaceful, contemplative and profitable existence, had personal bickerings not brought about the resignation of numerous members. These secessionists founded, under the presidency of Prince Alfieri and maestro Mustafà (a favorite of the Pope's), the *Società Musicale Romana*, which soon had a membership of 120 singers, performing within a short time the operas *La Vestale* and *Cortez*, by Spontini, and Händel's *Messiah*. The *Filarmonica*, having thus become a mother, remained for some time quite exhausted. It then took heart of grace, and proved its vitality (200 voices) by a successful production of Mendelssohn's *St. Paul*,[1] of *The Seasons*, and of a Requiem by Cherubini. All this in the 'seventies.

Since then no great changes have taken place, either in Rome or elsewhere. Most of the above societies still flourish; a number of others were started, had no success, and perished almost before the musical press had a chance to take note of their existence; not until the close of the century did certain choral societies arise, whose disappearance would be regretted. Among these were the *Società Filarmonica Giuseppe Verdi* in Venice, which fosters chiefly modern composers (Perosi, Wolf-Ferrari's sacred cantata *La Sulamite*, 1899), the *Società G. S. Bach* in Rome, under A. Costa (giving a work like the St. Matthew Passion in 1896), the *Accademia di canto classico corale G. P. da Palestrina* in Bologna (founded in 1899, and already giving acceptable performances in 1900 under the steady and thoroughly musical guidance of the young maestro Guido Alberto Fano), and the *Società Corale Internazionale* of Milan, founded by Ermanno Wolf-Ferrari, a pupil of Rheinberger.

This choral movement takes on a more definite form in conjunction with the reform-movement in church music. It has been shown above, in what a morass this latter was floundering prior to 1850. But as late as 1875 von Elewyck writes, in his chapter on Rome, that he had heard church music in thirty Roman churches and found an "absence complète d'unité dans le plainchant, multiplicité d'éditions, accompagnements d'orgue très-divers, mais presque tous fort incorrects," and at Palermo, even in the High Mass, "des fragments d'opéra, alternant avec le chœur de la liturgie et produisant la plus détestable cacophonie."

---

[1] Neither this performance, nor the one by Roeder at Milan, in 1878, was the first in Italy, as is generally assumed. Casamorata (*cf.* the *Gazz. Musicale di Milano*, 1878), shows that there were productions as early as 1841 and 1846 (Florence).

Such a state of affairs could not be greatly affected by either Gaspari (Bologna), Maglione (Florence), Baini (Rome), or a handful of associations like the *Società Piofilarmonica di Torino* (under Luigi Rossi). Not until 1874 did a marked revulsion set in, as Padre Don Guerino Amelli and maestro Salvatore Meluzzi energetically advocated a reform at the Catholic Congress in Venice.[1] This led, a year later, to the foundation of a school for church singing in Venice, and in 1877, at the Catholic Congress in Bergamo, (1) to the founding of the *Generale Associazione Italiana di Santa Cecilia*, (2) to the effective support of the periodical "Musica Sacra," established in May of that year, and (3) to a campaign against the totally inadequate church organs, which were still (according to Elewyck) in part portatives.

Nevertheless, this strife over the organs would probably have been decided in favor of the Preachers of Conservatism, had it not happened that Saint-Saëns, at a concert in the Milan Conservatory in 1879, roundly refused, after various desperate attempts, to continue playing on that squeaky "kist o' whistles." Refusal by such an authority made a tremendous impression. Shame was felt, and the Reform Party got the upper hand. It gradually established schools for church singing, after the pattern of those at Ratisbon and Malines, in Milan, Venice, and elsewhere; it founded a new periodical, "Guido Aretinus," and made new converts daily among the younger generation. But, as things go in Italy, this enthusiasm lasted three or four years, and in 1885 the whole movement seemed likely to be lost in the sands. As Tebaldini dejectedly wrote, only he himself and Prof. Terrabugio were still actively interested in "Musica Sacra." All at once the party was awakened to new life by the intervention of Bishop Caligari in Padua. The diocese of Padua, and others,

[1] *Cf.* Giovanni Tebaldini, "La Musica sacra in Italia." Palma, Milan, 1893.

joined the movement; Enrico Bossi (now Director of
the Liceo Benedetto Marcello in Venice) contributed
his golden gifts as an organist, and Conte Francesco
Lurani added a contribution of gold of more prosaic
stamp; the daily press began to exhibit a warmer sympathy for the devotees of Palestrina (possibly for the
special reason that Verdi referred, in and out of season,
to Palestrina as the greatest of Italian masters); the
most important German and French works on the
Liturgy and Church Music were translated and published; "Musica Sacra" instituted competitions (*concorsi*) for organ music in the strict style; the Pope
became interested, and with the aid of maestro Mustafà
subjected the superannuated Cappella Sistina to an
overhauling; Giovanni Tebaldini gave lectures here,
there and everywhere with his own peculiar forcefulness
and virulence, and finally founded the periodical "La
Scuola Veneta di Musica Sacra";—in a word, at the
beginning of the 'nineties it was no longer possible to
doubt that the mouldy usages of yore were being swept
aside.   Just at this time, fortunately, the Palestrina
celebrations occurred.   Two years later, grand memorial
festivals for Saint Anthony were held in Padua (June
13–17, August 16–18), where Tebaldini, then still
maestro di cappella at S. Antonio (where, after he was
called to the Parma Conservatory, he was succeeded
by Ravanello), carried out programs of a positively
astounding variety and excellence.   Thus the Reform
found, through fortuitous aid, an opportunity to prepare
the way for a final onslaught.   At least, it would now
seem as if nothing further blocked the path of the
movement, more especially since the establishment of
the Società di San Gregorio Magno (Rome, 1897),
which began operations with a *concorso* for a four-part
Mass in the strict style; and since the Congress for
Church Music at Turin in 1898, at which all pertinent
questions were freely discussed.

Finally, mention must be made of Don Lorenzo
Perosi, well known as the pupil of Haberl in Ratisbon.
Whether one over- or undervalues his gifts, he was
undeniably the first to awaken an interest for churchly
music among the generality of the Italian people.[1]
Not "churchly" in our sense, but with that strange
blending of mysticism and worldly pomp which char-
acterizes the Italian churches. Of both these qualities,
his music contains a quite sufficient amount. But just
for this reason, it can form a bond between the champions
of Palestrina—or, rather, of a strict churchly style
taking Palestrina as its pattern—and the faithful
masses;—a bond which is absolutely essential to the
practical efficacy of the Reform Party's endeavors.
For it would be vain to ask that the Italian churchgoer,
hitherto accustomed in divine service to popular, sugary
music with an occasional bit in opera-style, should
suddenly feel himself at home in a Palestrina motet in
the pure style. Besides, Perosi is not the only recent
writer of oratorios in Italy. At Palermo, nine composers
competed at the Concorso Bonerba for oratorio; the
prize-winner was Benedetto Morasco's oratorio, in
four sections, *La Liberazione di Betulia*. This work
having obtained no further publicity, no opinion can
be advanced as to whether it gives proofs of talent
equal (say) to Perosi's *Resurrection of Christ*.

As mentioned at the very beginning of this article,
the reforms in the spheres of instruction, choral singing,
and church music, were confronted by no active opposition; it was, at most, passive. Matters were very
different when the other three points—instrumental
music, opera in general, and Wagner in particular—
began to be pushed.

The question, in point of fact, was this: Whether
the Italians, who to this very day like to consider

---

[1] Verdi's Requiem for Manzoni is intentionally passed over; as a Requiem
by a religious secular composer, I consider it a masterwork.

themselves the lords of creation in matters musical, might or might not be allowed to take lessons of the Germans. There ensued a strife whose imbecility, meanness, fury and shortsightedness have at times been on a par with the contemporaneous conflict over the music of the future in Germany. Since Händel's time the Italian public had occasionally—though seldomer than is usually supposed, as statistics prove—tolerated operas by German composers (Hasse, Gluck, Weigl, Winter, Mayr, Nicolai) in which a piquant dash of German sentiment was overbalanced by the Italian element. Italian audiences rejoiced over the apt pupils of the Maestri, lent them applauding hands, and felt themselves, as proprietors of the sole means of operatic grace, exalted far above time and space. And now, all of a sudden, the Italians were to sit at the feet of the Germans! Precisely at the moment when Italy fancied it had an endless roll of "geniuses" at its disposal, successfully playing a worldwide game of hocus-pocus. The plebeian saying, "Quel che piace, è bello" (what we like, is fine) was sophistically applied to the most plebeian of all art-forms, namely, the opera.—Quel che piace, è bello! Our much-abused opera pleases us a thousand times better than the cold, academic music of a Mozart or a Weber, therefore it is very fine, far finer than German opera, anyhow. But when anything is fine, why reform it? Quod erat demonstrandum. Then what's the meaning of the impudence and ingratitude of the Germans, these "tedeschi nebulosi," beyond the Alps, and of the depravity of the traitorous crew on this side?! "We Italians have no need of study. We draw inspiration from the fair skies above us, and have nothing to learn from foreigners." Brave words, indeed, these of Cav. Lingiardi.[1] But even these are overmatched by G. B. de Lorenzi:[2] "Do let us rather

[1] P. C. Remondini, "Intorno agli Organi Italiani." Genoa, 1879.

[2] S. Lorenzi, "La Musica del nostro secolo e la musica dell' avvenire, ecc." Vicenza, 1871.

engage a German for music, a Russian for sculpture, a
Turk for painting, a Laplander for architecture, a
Patagonian for esthetics, and an Icelander for poetry!"
These elegant extracts might be multiplied at pleasure;
the above absurdities were taken at random from among
my excerpts. But they will suffice. They show how the
average Italian set himself against outside influences, less
because he deemed his opera to be really beyond amend-
ment (i. e., faultless), or from jealousy of competition,
than simply because of wounded vanity. And all the
while he knew German opera only from hearsay—from
press-notices. He had no conception of its nature or
of its opulence, nor has he down to the present day.
Occasional isolated performances[1] of Gluck's *Iphigenie
in Aulis* (Naples, 1812), Mozart's *Figaro* (Naples,
1814, 1870; Milan, 1815), *Don Giovanni* (Naples, 1812;
Milan, 1814, 1815, 1825, 1836, 1871; Parma, 1842),
Così fan tutte (Milan, 1807, 1814; Naples, 1821), *Magic
Flute* (Milan, 1815), Weber's *Der Freischütz* (Florence,
1843; Milan, 1872), Nicolai's *Templer und Jüdin* (Parma,
1843; Milan, 1866), and two or three other operas,
among which those of Simon Mayr, Weigl, Meyerbeer
and Flotow are, of course, not included, could give the
Italians no correct and lasting concept of operas written
by Germans in the German spirit.

Under such conditions, Filippo Filippi did well to
take up the cudgels. Having himself first of all to
labor through prepossession for and overvaluation of
the Italians (he called, for example, the much too
eclectic *Don Carlos* of Verdi an "imposing score"),
and the distorted views of German music, this brilliant
—even if not infallible—musical writer held his ground
in the very midst of the movement from about 1865
until his death in 1885. He speedily joined issue with
the whole of Italy, but showed himself capable of re-

---

[1] Compare the statistical data by Bignami, Cambiasi, Ferrari, Florimo, Lia-
novasani, etc.

repelling every assault. In the periodicals "La Per-
severanza," "Gazzetta Musicale di Milano," and "Il
Mondo Artistico" (he founded this last in 1867), and
in his collected essays "Viaggio *and* Secondo Viaggio
musicale nelle regioni dell' avvenire" (German translation 1876) and "Musica e Musicisti," he strove un-
tiringly, not so much to expose the weak points of
Italian opera as to emphasize the coexistence of German
genius, and to get at the essence of German music.
His chief demand might be briefly stated in the sentence,
Whoever would criticize Wagner, should first know him.

   This sounds like a truism. But none of the howlers
and criticasters knew Wagner even in 1870, not to say
ten or twenty years earlier. What Filippi wrote from
Weimar, in 1870, was quite characteristic: " . . . . .
At home we seize every opportunity to drag Wagner
out in order to defame him, without in the least understanding his character or that of the people for whom
he writes, without familiarity with any of his artistic
aims, or with any of his works, save in fragments. . . .
My admiration for Wagner dates from the day on which
I first heard the soul-stirring harmonies of the Pilgrims'
Chorus from *Tannhäuser*."

   Now, do not forget that on April the 20th, 1868, for
the first time in Italy—to the best of my knowledge—
an excerpt from Wagner's works was publicly performed, namely, an aria from *Tannhäuser* in a concert
by the Società Cherubini at Florence.[1] Then came (at
Milan, in 1868-69), the overtures to *The Flying Dutchman*, *Tannhäuser* and *Rienzi*, and other selections.
In private circles, too—except in Rome (Franz Liszt)
and Florence (Mme. Laussot, etc)—there could have
been little known of the music of the future; for it was
only in 1868 that Francesco Lucca acquired the Wag-

[1] I do not take into consideration transcriptions, like that of the *Tannhäuser*
March by Liszt (pianist Andreoli, Milan, 1866), or Wilhelmj's arrangement of
the *Lohengrin* Prelude for double-quartet (Società Cherubini, Florence, Dec. 30th,
1867).

nerian works and published them bit by bit, commencing with the *Tannhäuser* March and Overture for piano two and four hands. The *Rienzi* vocal score (translated by Arrigo Boito) did not appear till 1869, and the real "music of the future" much later, if we disregard the "Cinque Canti" ("Träume," etc.)! And the theoretical writings, such as "Oper und Drama," were not published by Fratelli Bocca in Turin until some time in the 'nineties, the translator being L. Torchi.

But it can be proved that the fight over Wagner broke out at the beginning of the 'sixties in Italy. This being so, whence did his opponents derive their wisdom?

From the "Gazzetta Musicale di Milano"! Hardly ushered into existence (1842), it showed its lust for a tussle with each and every adversary of Italian music in a skirmish with Fétis. It took him still more roughly to task when he published his noted polemics against Verdi in 1850. But it made a positively brutal attack on the "Neue Berliner Musikzeitung" when this latter, also in 1850, turned a searchlight on musical conditions in Italy. (See No. 48.) "First learn to stand steady on your own legs, dear Sirs. And should you happen to need Italian maestri to hold you up straight, then let your sense of shame move you, at least, to do them honor." For the rest, this same article throws a flood of light on the knowledge then possessed by Italians concerning the nature, abundance and value of German music. Over against Haydn, Mozart and Beethoven are set, as equal in rank, men of the type of Morlacchi, Vaccai, Coccai and Coppola;—Bach and Gluck, for example, being wholly ignored. And, further on: "Should you mention Meyerbeer, gentlemen, we would bow in homage, for we know what is due to the exalted geniuses of all nations."—Meyerbeer's music as typical of German art! And as Verdi, in particular, served an apprenticeship to Meyerbeer during the transition to his last style, what irony of logic! For between the lines we read an admission of the influence of German opera on the Italian.

But these amenities, together with the war of words anent Emil Naumann's Italian "Reisebriefe" (1852) and Hanslick in the years following, sound like a gentle barking beside the infuriated howls and foul abuse which broke loose after 1855 over Wagner and the music of the future. Whereas the Gazzetta had turned a benevolent eye on Wagner's first steps (*Rienzi*), and even reprinted, with flattering commendation, the articles which he wrote in Paris for Schlesinger's "Gazette musicale de Paris" (see No. 5 *et seq.*, 1842), venomous reports on him from Berlin, London, Paris, and other cities, gradually gathered in volume. From these reports the contributors to the Gazzetta later drew the material for their soi-disant arguments. The German Preachers of Conservatism and anti-Wagnerians were quoted with rapture, and the Parisian fiasco of *Tannhäuser* was told and retold with malignant delight. A brief reaction for the better set in when Filippo Filippi assumed the editorship (toward the beginning of the 'sixties). He perceived that the correspondents were often merely pushing the interests of Ricordi the publisher; so now and then he put a curb on the conscienceless chatter. But the Gazzetta ceased publication at the close of 1862, not appearing again until 1866 under the editorship of F. Ghislanzoni (librettist to the Ricordi firm) and later of S. Farina, and then directly hauling round to the old course. Wagner was pilloried as a clown and secondrate inkslinger. And worse was to come when Francesco Lucca was so bold and far-sighted as to purchase his Italian rights. Even before this happened, the defence of Italian opera at all costs being question of life or death for the house of Ricordi, owners of the Gazzetta, there could be no doubt of its attitude where Wagner was concerned. The Gazzetta no longer lent itself to pretendedly serious discussions. It no longer called attention to the popularity of Italian opera abroad. In its regular Review of the Year (Prospetto retrospettivo) it no longer compared Italian opera-production with the parallel German output, stating the matter this wise: We Italians, in 1853, brought 52 operas to market, the Germans only 12; we 61 (!) in 1857, they only 17; consequently, there is no trace of decadence with us.—No, it adopted a far more effective expedient. It laughed and sneered. It made fun of the Germans for continually spelling Italian names incorrectly, and for knowing less about Italian conditions, by and large, than the Italians knew about German. As if they themselves had never put their foot in it! For example, they took Johanna Wagner for Wagner's wife (1847), Peter Cornelius the painter and Peter Cornelius the poet-musician for one and the same person (1858, p. 270), set down Wagner's birthyear as 1815 instead of 1813 (1859, No. 15), etc. Filippi was ridiculed because, under his editorship, the subscription-list of the Gazzetta sank to 32, and publication was suspended (1871, p. 142); and Richard Wagner's name hardly appeared except in the Rubrica amena (the "funny column").

Certain *bon mots* of Rossini's, current in the music-trade, were turned against the *avveniristi* (musicians of the future) for a like purpose. Generally speaking, the cause of a genius, an innovator, is in a bad way when the bourgeois no longer stands in awe of him, but banters him. And yet worse, when a "still greater genius, a still greater innovator," gives the pitch for the laughing chorus. The Philistine then feels quite safe in his course. Now, the Italians, to this very day, do not assign to their idol Rossini a niche among the gifted consummators, but set him in the forefront of intrepid pioneers. Quite aside from this fact, around 1870 there was certainly no Italian who imagined instituting any comparison whatsoever between Wagner's talent and Rossini's. "If even Rossini, that genius of geniuses, permits himself to poke fun at Wagner, there's surely no reason why I shouldn't"—so the Italian Philistine may have thought.

It availed nothing that Rossini, the great musician, gourmet, and wit, denied in a Paris newspaper the authorship of the scurvy jokes about Wagner, complaining bitterly of the "friends" who launched their expectorations under his name, or that, in a letter to Filippi, he vehemently expressed his contempt for all *sputasentenze* (phrasespitters). The witticisms pursued their tranquil course as watchwords, and everybody who, either from conviction or for business reasons, chose to take up arms for Italian opera, still rallied, as before, to Rossini as their standard-bearer. But when the Philistine thinks himself in the right, he grows brutal, and only awaits a favorable opportunity to give free rein to his brutality. Such an opportunity was afforded the Milanese when Arrigo Boito's *Mefistofele* was brought out at La Scala in 1868. Every one knew that Boito possessed talent. But they also knew that the youthful maestro had been in Germany, that he was not only familiar with Germany and the German masters, but revered and studied them, and had learned much from them. They held him for a "Zukunftsmusiker," a follower of Wagner. The time was ripe for a "horrible example." The Italian music of the future should be destroyed root and branch. Had Boito's work engendered tedium and displeasure, because its style was unwonted to the Italians—at that time they had never heard a note of Wagner—it would have been a fiasco like so many other unsuccessful works. But the scandalous tumults which arose in opposition to *Mefistofele* were more than the objection of the audiences to a neophyte's work; they signified more than a failure; they proclaimed the unmistakable intent of the Milanese to take full vengeance on the Reform Party. Not even the open letter addressed by Giulio Ricordi, in the Gazzetta Musicale (1868, No. 11), to his friend Boito, can gloss over this fact. Would Ricordi now—since the success of *Mefistofele*, for which the way was prepared by that of *Lohengrin* and *Tannhäuser* in Italy, has been steadily increasing for twenty years, so that every small town longs to applaud the work—care to repeat his former closing sentence: "I venture the unvarnished assertion that you have a future as a poet, as an admirable writer, but never as a composer of music-dramas"?

After the brutal assault on *Mefistofele* at La Scala, the naturalization of Wagner seemed to be put off for years. To be sure, Milan appeared agreeably surprised when the Società del Quartetto brought out the overtures to *Rienzi*, *The Flying Dutchman*, and *Tannhäuser*. People had expected "scientific," impenetrable, gray, gloomy Northern mist-woven fabrics, and were suddenly confronted with a language of tones whose beauties were manifest even to Italians, without great mental effort. The Gazzetta itself was taken aback. Still, it made shift to turn the scales against Wagner. It said (1869, No. 19) with regard to the overture to *The Flying Dutchman*, "This is realistic music. But . . . . when we compare it with the examples of descriptive and imitative music here quoted ('classico temporale del Barbiere di Siviglia, la tempesta del Rigoletto e la burrasca nell' Africana'), it must be admitted that Rossini, Verdi and Meyerbeer obtained the same effects with simpler means. Wagner has done both good and harm to art. He ought to have been the continuator of the Germanic school, which Meyerbeer popularized with his immortal works. But we find in Wagner, side by side with wonderfully beautiful ideas, a desperate, ineffectual striving. Is this a striving toward the music-drama? No! it is the toil of a destroyer. Such a striving is destructive of idealism, without which Art is but an empty word."

As aforesaid, despite such piecemeal successes the naturalization of the music of the future was endangered. For the Società del Quartetto had a vastly different audience from that of La Scala.

True enough, reports were circulated that *Rienzi*, or *Tannhäuser*, or *Lohengrin*, was to be produced at Florence and in La Scala. But they were dismissed by the Gazzetta to the realm of "fantasticherie" (1869, No. 38); and not until the rumors became persistent did it join, willy-nilly, in the cry, "Dateci del Lohengrin! dateci del Rienzi!" (1870, p. 212). But with this very peculiar and very Italian reason for doing so (in 1868, p. 307): "Il giudizio italiano pronuncierà inappellabilmente per le gemonie o per l'apoteosi!" (The judgment of Italy will pronounce the irrevocable sentence—scaffold or apotheosis!)

Just then (1871) Bologna stepped forward from the subordinate position she had hitherto occupied in the musical life of the nineteenth century. "Bononia docet" the ancient motto runs; and this proud phrase should now be suited with a deed. Rumors arose, at first in French papers, that *Bologna la dotta*, *Bologna la grassa*, proposed to venture a production of Wagner's *Lohengrin*. The mistrust and astonishment awakened by these rumors gave way to an intense excitement when they began to assume substantial form, and reports of the actual commencement of rehearsals were received. Tales were spread abroad of unimagined difficulties, fantastic scenery, wondrous strains as of Paradise, lured from the orchestra by the magic wand of the all-inspiring and enkindling Angelo Mariani;—and so forth. From every nook and corner of Italy the most notable critics announced their attendance at the première. The performance promised to be a congress of all the notables of musical Italy. In a word, a positive *Lohengrin* fever attacked both musicians and dilettanti.

On November the 1st, 1871, *Lohengrin* made his triumphal entry in the Teatro Communale at Bologna. Wagner's victory was complete. The Italians possibly found the second act a trifle tedious, but the first and third roused them to unexampled acclamations. The *Lohengrin* frenzy invaded the very streets. One of the reigning beauties of Bologna appeared in public wearing a hat *à la Lohengrin*, the noted perfumer Bortolotti sold his *Essenza Lohengrin* like hot cakes,[1] and the City Council of Bologna presented Wagner with the freedom of the ·city. Even Hans von Bülow was so swept along with the general enthusiasm,[2] that he came near representing this production of *Lohengrin* as an unequalled and not to be equalled model-performance.[3] The open letter written by Wagner to Arrigo Boito[4] served to throw the good Bolognese quite off their balance. Thenceforward they were Wagnerians "on principle," and took it upon themselves to make their home city the Wagner centre of Italy.

Now, whether this production was really an ideal one—further on, in a detailed and connected description I can and must prove that it was not—or had its weak points, the following facts are beyond question: Angelo Mariani (1822-1873) had finally established his fame as the foremost conductor of Italy, taking rank alongside of men like Bülow; secondly, by an exhibition of superhuman ability and will-power, of discretion and genius, he brought about a really brilliant performance, whatever its shortcomings; thirdly, he made a masterwork, which was foreign in every aspect, easy of comprehension to his compatriots, and thus, fourthly, broke through the "ring" of the Chauvinists (granting that

---

[1] Gazzetta Musicale di Mialano, 1871, No. 50.

[2] See his Collected Writings.

[3] One of the eccentric capers of which he was so fond. As early as 1876 he took occasion to express himself much more coolly.

[4] L'Arpa, Giornale letterario, etc. (Bologna, 1871, No. 12), printed it.

he himself had taken up *Lohengrin* at first less from
enthusiasm—as some say—than to show Filippo Filippi
that even an Italian was capable of interpreting Wagner).
Fifthly, the Wagnerians had at last won a practical
musician as their strategical leader, and Wagner's art
had found, in Bologna, a point of vantage on Italian
territory. Sixthly, the movement for or against Wagner's
influence on Italian opera could finally be led into
practical channels, since people began to know his
works through their actual performance. And so, with
all this, a new force furthering the uplift of Italian
musicmaking in the sphere of opera, too, had been
unloosed.

Of course, no ground was gained without fighting.
The Gazzetta Musicale, in particular, was by no means
disarmed. True, it admitted the success of *Lohengrin*
in various articles, but sought to belittle it, cutting the
strangest capers in the attempt to degrade the work to
the level of mediocrity. And it did gain a point (with
the help of other periodicals, like the Pungolo), after
further successes of *Lohengrin* in Florence under Mariani,
by encompassing the total failure of the work at Milan
in 1873. The riots provoked by *Tannhäuser* in the
Paris Opéra were almost eclipsed by the brutality and
insane fury of the audience at La Scala. However,
Wagner had broken through the dam; he had effected
an entrance and was still advancing, and such mishaps
did not indicate the defeat of his art, but the confounding
of his opponent's judgment. It would take too long
to follow his triumphal progress through all its stages
down to the present; the earliest were these: *Lohengrin*
(Turin, 1877; Rome, 1878, 1880; Venice and Genoa,
1880), *Tannhäuser* (Bologna, 1882), *The Flying Dutchman* (Bologna, 1877), *Rienzi* (Venice, 1874). Wagner's
occasional sojourns in Italy did their part in proving
him not to be the Italianophobe as which he had been
represented for a time. We may also mention Angelo

Neumann's *Nibelung* Cycles in the 'eighties, the *Tristan* performances at Bologna in 1888 under G. Martucci, and the founding of the Società del Wagner (Bayreuther-Zweigverein), which undertook, by means of annual Wagner Concerts, to diffuse and promote a better understanding of the master. Then came the *Meistersinger* fiasco at Milan (1889). No wonder; for since the unhappy *Lohengrin* affair Wagner had been laid on the shelf for good and all. How could a public who protested against *Lohengrin* be expected to enjoy *Die Meistersinger?!* But, early in the 'nineties, Ricordi bought out Lucca's publishing house, including (of course) Wagner's works; and since then they—especially *Lohengrin* and *Tannhäuser*—have spread over all Italy, into every provincial town. In 1898, for instance, *Tannhäuser* was given in cities like Padua and Piacenza, and *Lohengrin* in Mantua, Padua, Pavia and Palermo. Not invariably, we admit, to full houses, and not always with success!

This leads up to the question, Is there, in Italy, a genuine understanding for Wagner? What has been the influence of his works on Italian opera? Can they, and ought they, to have a profound effect on Italian composers? A triad of questions which are intimately related to each other by nature.

Evil tongues[1] have asserted that not even the Bolognese *Lohengrin* had its origin in purely artistic motives. Everybody knows that an approved Italian *stagione* must offer at least one novelty. Now, the assertion is made that it was not so much the Wagner enthusiasm of Mayor Cesarini as far more material considerations which caused the selection of *Lohengrin*. *Aida*, then recently composed, would have been the first choice, but other cities had already seized upon it, and the good Bolognese would hardly have accepted a second-

[1] Hans von Bülow (1876).—E. Panzacchi, "Lettere due a proposito del Tannhäuser" (1872).

hand production. Evil tongues likewise sneeringly allude
to the unheard-of success of Gobatti's *Goths*—a work
which Hans von Bülow called a monstrosity—and add
that Gobatti, precisely like Wagner, was presented
with the freedom of the city. Gobatti—Wagner!! The
skeptics also call attention to the great majority of
cases in which the Italians, at the performance of
Wagner's works, rush frantically into the theatre on
first nights, but on the following evenings, for fear of
ennui, stay at home or go to the café.

Furthermore, it is said that the comprehension of
Wagner by the Bolognese is quite out of proportion to
their self-conceit. They are fond of criticizing Bayreuth,
as if everything done there were the veriest botchery.
Given such conditions, it can readily be seen why the
Società del Wagner—just because it is, so to speak, an
offshoot of Bayreuth—should gradually pine away.
But if the Bolognese public feels (in the depths of its
soul) bored by Wagner, how can the other towns know
what to make of him?

And yet, in Bologna as well as in Rome, Turin,
Venice, Naples, Florence, where Wagner is much
studied and played, there are plenty of people whose
interest in him is not simply a combination of curiosity,
fashion and parochial vanity. One should not, however,
expect of the average Italian a profound understanding
of Wagner; indeed, it is very questionable whether "the
German" in general feels himself at home on the heights,
or in the depths (as you will), of *Tristan* and the *Ring*.
Wagner's Northern world of the sagas allures the Italian
merely as an adventurous excursion. Through it all
he will feel homesick for the *dramma umano*, the stage-
play of every-day life. Least of all will he familiarize
himself with Wagner's notion of making the opera
something more than a work which causes time to
pass agreeably or, in certain cases, excites his enthusiasm.
A plunge, as it were, into a spring of spiritual healing

has no charms for him. Rossini, with striking acumen, sums up the musical ideal of his countrymen in the words, 'Il diletto dev' essere la base e lo scopo di quest' arte. Melodia semplice—Ritmo chiaro." [1]

Some one may adduce *Die Meistersinger* as a veritable *dramma umano*. That it certainly is, but one conceived and created by a German for Germans, itself German to the core. In this very opera the critic is confronted with the gulf set for evermore between Wagner and the people of Italy. But this is no reason for excluding Wagner from the Italian stage.

No art is more national than music. But neither is any other better adapted for international exchange; and with regard to musical art, as in all else, the dictum holds good, "Isolation means stagnation." To this plain assertion of E. Panzacchi,[2] the great orator, poet and critic, but slight objection can be offered. However, he goes on to prove, as the theoretical disputations toward the beginning of the 'seventies had already abundantly established, that Wagner's influence over the Italian opera, the Italian music-drama, would extend only to extrinsic elements of form;—this, despite the fact that Panzacchi is a zealous admirer of Wagner. Even an arch-Wagnerite like Filippi was unable to avoid this conclusion. Neither did such sober-minded anti-Wagnerites as Platania, Rufa, Mazzucato, Biaggi, Fr. d'Arcais, Sassaroli, Florimo, etc., in any way oppose the admittance of Wagner into the musical life of Italy; they rather emphasized the essential difference between his nature and that of the Southlander, thereby repudiating the utility and the possibility of intimately blending the German opera with the Italian. But for the most part they made the mistake of drawing a line of delimitation between the talents of German and

---

[1] *Cf.* his letter to Lauro Rossi, June 21, 1868, published in F. Florimo's "Riccardo Wagner ed i Wagneristi" (1863, Chap. II).

[2] *Op. cit.*

Italian. In the German pigeonhole they bestowed Harmony; in the Italian, Melody. Luigi Torchi—whose brilliant essay "Riccardo Wagner" [1] undeniably towers high above the luxuriant growths of Italian Wagner literature, and occupies a commanding position among publications of any sort concerning Wagner—was the first partially to straighten out the above warped axiom: "La musica italiana e essenzialmente cantante, quella dei tedeschi espressiva." For the rest, his 600-page volume arrives at the same conclusion as the writers mentioned above, namely, that Wagner can influence Italian music only as a rejuvenator, not as a model;— a conclusion founded, in his case, on a refreshing insight into the German character (Torchi studied for several years under Reinecke), on a surprising familiarity with the writings of the German romanticists, and on his biographico-psychological study of Wagner's art as a whole.

Time has already pronounced its verdict. Who are the Italian disciples of Wagner? Disregarding Boito, obstinately silent since his youthful opera *Mefistofele*, and the "bandmaster-music" of Mancinelli and others, only A. Catalani and A. Franchetti can be mentioned as gifted *avveniristi*. But for all that, the latest works of Verdi, and those of Puccini, Mascagni, Leoncavallo, Giordano, and others, discover a method unquestionably different from the ruminant style of the "ever-shallower Italian opera." The construction has gained in unity and conciseness, the orchestra has a more psychological cast, the melody is more modern. And wherefrom is all this? *Not from Wagner, but from the eclectic opera of the French.*

Rossini's *Tell* already confesses this source. The same is writ large on every page of Verdi's works in his transition-period (prior to *Aida*), especially *Don Carlos*. Indeed, his successorship to Meyerbeer was interpreted

[1] Bologna, 1890; Zanichelli.

as in his favor by the Gazzetta Musicale (1867, No. 27).
The 'sixties witnessed the further importation of Gounod.
"Tutti fausteggiarono," writes d'Arcais in the "Nuova
Antologia" (1890, p. 523) of that epoch. After Gounod
came Bizet, and finally Massenet, whom we may confidently term the *accoucheur* of the *veristi*. Not one of
Puccini's or Leoncavallo's operas can delude us into
seeking any other origin; not even Mascagni's *Iris*,
despite suspicious endeavors to "Wagnerize."

And Verdi? To-day he stands quite apart. Having
broken away from his earlier models, to a certain extent,
in *Aida*, he entered upon the years of self-criticism, of
theoretical problems, of a purposeful building-up of the
Italian opera of the future. Verdi, in his last period,
is frequently termed a stylistic follower of Wagner.
That is, I think, quite erroneous. For he could hardly
have had more than a very slight acquaintance with
Wagner's music before finishing *Aida*; and does *Otello*,
or *Falstaff*, really betray a continuation of Wagner's
style? Shall we not come nearer the mark in considering
that these works also bear a distant relationship to the
French opera?

After *Aida*, Verdi unquestionably underwent a transformation. Otherwise, his creative temperament would
not have permitted a silence of fifteen years. Now,
even Verdi could not close his eyes to the fact that a
new era had set in. *Lohengrin*, to which he listened
from the rear of a box on its fourth evening in Bologna,[1]
probably enlightened him completely on that score.
Later he doubtless studied carefully not only this opera,
but the German classics in general.[2] Remember, that
during this time his string-quartet appeared, but no
opera. This is significant. He felt that the music of
his nation needed new paths. But where should they

---

[1] *Cf.* "L'Arpa," 1871, No. 11.

[2] Marie Wieck, visiting him in 1878, found "The Well-Tempered Clavichord"
on his reading-desk. (*Cf.* the "Allgem. Musik-Zeitung.")

start? From Wagner? Most assuredly not. His instinct must have warned him against that. Or can we rate his critical faculty lower than that of dozens of mediocre writers? And read the opinion he pronounces on Wagner:[1]

Wagner belongs among the very greatest ones. In his music—however strange (always excepting *Lohengrin*) it may seem to our susceptibilities—there is life, blood and nerve. In his art he makes love of the fatherland felt in a truly wonderful way. He carried his fetish-worship to such lengths as to invent music according to a program settled in advance. This was hurtful to him. And after all, it was not he who wrought the mischief, but his imitators!

No one could write thus, who beheld his own and his nation's salvation in the stylistic continuation of Wagner. On the other hand, his true meaning is apparent when we compare the above with Verdi's letter of Jan. 5, 1871, to F. Florimo.[2]

The music of the future causes me no alarm. I should have said to the students (I mean, if it had been possible for me to accept the proffered position as Director of the Conservatory at Naples): Practise the Fugue steadily and perseveringly, till you weary of it, till the hand feels quite strong and free and has gained full mastery over the notes. . . . Study Palestrina and a few of his contemporaries. Then skip over to Marcello, and pay special attention to the recitative. Attend but few performances of modern operas, and do not allow yourself to be dazzled by their manifold harmonic and orchestral beauties, or by the diminished seventh-chord, our very last resort—why, we cannot compose four measures without bringing in half a dozen of these sevenths! . . . . In any event, do not increase the host of present-day imitators and decadents, who seek, seek, seek, and (Heaven be praised!) never find anything. In singing, I should like to see the old-time studies combined with modern declamation. . . . Go back to the old ways—that will be progress![3]

For my own part, there is no doubt that Verdi (together with Boito) has actually translated into deeds

[1] Monaldi, "Giuseppe Verdi, 1839-1889" (Turin, Bocca, 1899).

[2] Florimo, "Riccardo Wagner ed i Wagneristi" (Ancona, Morelli, 1883).

[3] Read, besides, his letter to Hans von Bülow of April 14, 1892 (Gazz. Musicale, 1892, 32): "Wagner very rightly asserts that all ought to maintain the peculiarities of their nationality! You are happy indeed to be still the sons of Bach!... And we?... We too, the sons of Palestrina, once had a great School—and our own! To-day it has become a bastard, and threatens collapse! Could we only begin over again!"

these words on his continuation of the Italian classicists. In *Othello* and *Falstaff* are to be seen the lordly foundation-columns of a future purely Italian opera, and in their presence all the vulgar and sickly-sweet spot-cash fabrications of the Frenchified *veristi* are as naught. Yet—what a tragedy! Only at the close of his career, when the thoughts no longer gush forth in superabundant overflow, does the Nestor—and, at the same time, the most youthful—of the *maestri* succeed in crowning his lifework, in taking the momentous step into the future, in attuning his spirit to a novel form, and in becoming for the Italians what Richard Wagner was to the Germans. *Aida*, *Othello* and *Falstaff* are a legacy bequeathed by Giuseppe Verdi to his nation. Will the nation revere it?

Thus the German opera, including Wagner, has not had the influence on the transformation of Italian opera that may have been expected. What musical life in Italy actually owes it is rather an enrichment of the repertory. Quite otherwise with the German chamber-music and symphony; these have effected a revolution from the ground up. They filled a sensible void in Italy's musical activities. The earlier neglect of the German classicists gradually gave way to a thorough study of them, and nowadays Italy would seem to be suffering from an overdose of Germanism. To say the least, the Italians do not favor their own instrumental classics (from about 1650 to 1750) with the attention which is requisite in order to bring about a renascence of a strongly marked Italian style of chamber-music.

The phrase "complete ignorance" must, like all such general assertions, be qualified by an "almost." But isolated performances of the Beethoven symphonies—as a curiosity the "Schlacht bei Vittoria"[1] may be mentioned—or passably well-arranged programs like those of the Società Filarmonica (Milan), the Collegio Filar-

[1] Giorgetti's letter to Pantologo, Florence, 1828.

monico Fiorentino (1847), the violin virtuoso Luigi
Sessa (La Scala, March, 1860), and some others, were
oases in the desert. And what do they signify in comparison with the well-attested fact,[1] that not until 1862
was a string-quartet of Cherubini's publicly performed
for the first time in Italy!—at Florence, Nov. 23, 1862!
But the oases are multiplying, so that to-day one should
rather speak, in the reverse sense, of scattered deserts
in a fruitful land.

Zuliani says, in Chap. III of his above-mentioned
work (i. e., in 1878):

> Twenty years ago, pure instrumental music was a thing un-
> known in Rome; . . . . a few maestri cultivated the German
> classics. . . . The pianists played nothing but opera-music in
> poor arrangements. . . . Tullio Ramacciotti, an excellent vio-
> linist, a highly educated and progressive-minded artist, was the
> first to venture upon the unpopular mission of inviting the public
> to attend quartet-soirées—with slight success; some few foreigners
> came to them; Roman society, even the liberally educated, felt
> a holy horror when anybody so much as mentioned classical
> instrumental music. . . . It was a thankless apostolate.

This was in the year 1851.[2] A change came when
Franz Liszt took hold of the matter, giving advice out
of his abundant experience. And when Sgambati,
together with Pinelli (fresh from his studies with Joachim), threw themselves on the enemy, the breach was
finally made. But at what sacrifices! Sgambati paid
the expenses, out of his own pocket, to give the Romans
their first[3] performance of a Beethoven symphony.
Pinelli, at his initial orchestral concert, took in no less
than—fourteen lire. Out of these fourteen lire, sixty
musicians were to be paid! Here the year 1870 again
had a favorable effect. The Queen attended the chamber

---

[1] *Cf*. Boccherini, "Giornale Musicale per la Società del Quartetto," Florence,
1868, p. 74; "Gazz. Mus. di Milano," 1862, No. 48.

[2] In its twelfth number of that year the Gazz. Mus. published a letter from
Rome dated March 15: . . . "On Saturday, the 15th, the instrumental concerts
are to begin which professors Ramacciotti, Angelini, Costaggini and Orselli will
give in the Teatro Argentina. In each of these concerts, of which there are to
be thirteen, three compositions will be performed, selected from works by Beethoven, Mozart, Haydn, Hummel, Spohr, Onslow, etc."

[3] *Cf*. Zuliani, "Roma Musicale," 1878.

and symphony concerts, and drew after her a large part of the well-to-do and patrician circles. Neither should the valuable influence of the German ambassador, Baron von Keudell, and his spouse, remain unnoticed. But the Società Orchestrale Romana—founded by the brothers Ettore and Decio Pinelli, with the aid of the musicians Turino, Gozi, the two Monachesi, Paolinelli, Jacobacci, De Leva, and others—had a prolonged struggle against the phalanx of those who were actively or passively opposed to instrumental music, or antagonized German music because it was German, before the Society was firmly established. Not to mention all the personal and managerial wranglings which always accompany the inception of such enterprises.

We have noticed Rome first of all. However, Florence once again preceded the Eternal City. Prof. Jefte Sbolci has already been mentioned, in the paragraphs on Choral Music, as the founder and director of the Società per lo Studio della Musica Classica. Now, as this Society, like almost all such associations in Italy, cultivated symphony and chamber-music side by side with choral singing, it is only proper that the names of Sbolci and the Duke of San Clemente, who vigorously supported him, should receive conspicuous notice here. But a genuine revulsion did not set in until the 'sixties. About the year 1860 certain private individuals—for example, Basevi, Prof. Giorgetti, Maglioni, Giovacchini, the maestri Kraus, Ducci, and Mmes. Capoquadri and Sandryk *née* Cattermole—were accustomed to have chamber-music played in their salons before invited guests.[1] Not long thereafter, all these elements combined to form a real Società del Quartetto. The first matinée took place on Oct. 14, 1861. Professors F. Consolo, Bruni, M. Asso and Jefte Sbolci did their best to render the Inaugural Concert, which included

[1] "Boccherini," introductory article, I, 1, 1862; later "Materiali" (On the History of the Soc. del Quartetto, 1868-69).

works by Haydn, Mozart and Beethoven, fully worthy of the occasion.   The Society also had the happy idea to found a periodical for the benefit of its members. On May 1, 1862, appeared the first number of the "Boccherini," which ceased publication in 1883, after a glorious career.   Abraham Basevi, a lawyer, and a musical writer of no mean importance,[1] took hold of matters even more practically, if possible.   He instituted a *concorso* for string-quartets, offering 300 lire as first prize and 100 (later 200) lire as second prize for the best quartet written by an Italian or any composer educated in Italy.   The winners of this *concorso* were the celebrated double-bass player Giovanni Bottesini and F. Anichini, among twenty-two competitors.   Basevi, however, not content with aiding the cause only once, renewed his *concorso* annually until the end of the decade, but made it international.   From the very beginning the aspirants were quite numerous; in 1862, seventeen quartets were handed in; in 1863, twenty-three; in 1864, twenty-nine; etc.   Not all native composers were as fortunate as Giulio Ricordi (better known, as a composer, under the pen-name of Burgmein), to whom the second prize was awarded in 1864.   But precisely the circumstance that foreigners like W. Langhans, Bungert, G. H. Witt, and others, gained the victory, must have acted as a stimulus to the Italians to perfect themselves in the difficult sphere of the string-quartet. —Basevi was, all in all, the moving spirit and the final resort in time of need.   Thus, when the government requisitioned the *Sala del buon umore*, where the matinées were held, for school-purposes, and nobody knew where to find a hall for the concerts, Basevi at once made up his mind to offer the ground floor of his palace for the purpose.   Nor was this all; he had it enlarged and suitably reconstructed at his own expense.   And so, in

[1] *Cf.* "L'Armonia, Organo della riforma musicale in Italia" (1856), founded as a continuation of the "Gazzetta Musicale di Firenze."   Basevi's noted articles on Verdi are found in the second annual issue.

spite of a few juvenile disorders, the Society was certainly favored by fortune. It gained in importance, and its fame was spread far beyond the confines of Italy by the Florentine Quartet (Jean Becker).

Some other associations, such as the Società Filarmonica del Quartetto (under Prince Poniatowski), were less fortunate. I mention its really tasteful program for 1858 in witness to its well-doing before 1860. Later, however, it dragged along only half alive, rebaptized itself the Società d'incoraggiamento dell' arte musicale, and preferred to navigate shallower waters.

The first attempts at domesticating orchestral music were equally abortive until after 1870. The Reale Istituto Musicale vainly sought in 1863 to establish periodical popular concerts of classical instrumental music similar to those of Pasdeloup in Paris. Not before May 17, 1867, could the attempt be renewed— this time with Mabellini at the head of an orchestra of one hundred pieces. But this attempt also failed; not because the people evinced too little interest, but "because some of the most influential professors refused their coöperation." Nevertheless, the Società del Quartetto inaugurated, one year thereafter (on Feb. 28th), a series of symphonic concerts. Their *Concerti conferenze* (lecture-concerts) were particularly liked. Besides, Basevi was again promoting the movement for orchestral music in a practical manner; the Reale Istituto in 1866 opened, in his name, a *concorso* for an overture in classical form, with the result that forty-eight works were submitted.

So it came, that an animated artistic activity developed in Florence from the separate yet kindred action of the Società del Quartetto, the Società Cherubini, the Soc. Filarmonica, the R. Istituto Musicale, and the Società Orchestrale Fiorentina (organized later under Jefte Sbolci). Nor should we forget Hans von Bülow's artistic contribution during his Florentine sojourn.

Florence had no lack of imitators. The quartet
associations, which, as will have been noticed, had a
much wider scope than their titles imply, sprang up
everywhere out of the ground. The Florentine Società
was quickly followed by others in Lucca, Naples (chiefly
owing to E. Krakamp), Modena, Milan, Pisa, Brescia,
Turin, and other towns.

Turin and Milan speedily moved up abreast of
Florence. To be sure, it is not wholly easy to study
the historical development of the Milan Società at the
source. For the Gazzetta Musicale di Milano ceased
to appear during the years 1862-5—because of lack of
readers, as it observed in the last number for 1862.[1]
(Thirty-two subscribers are certainly none too many!)
Whoever may desire to write the history of the musical
conditions then obtaining, must resort to the daily press.
This course presents few difficulties. But for my purpose it would seem idle, as I wish to furnish only a few
historical data in order to demonstrate a growing
tendency in Italian musical life.

Luckily the "Boccherini" likewise took note of the
first stirrings of life in the Milan Società; and this
latter itself established, after the pattern of its Florentine
colleague, a periodical of its own, the Giornale della
Società del Quartetto di Milano, edited by A. Mazzucato.
But there was this difference between the two periodicals:
the "Boccherini" interested itself almost exclusively for
absolute music, whereas the "Giornale" devoted very
nearly half its columns to the contest over Wagner.

On June 29, 1864, the Società made its public début
with its "primo esperimento"—of course, with a classical
program. It also immediately recognized the practical
value of concorsi, and until to-day has kept up the
custom of instituting one or more annual competitions
for prizes; though these competitions do not necessarily
draw out really important works. But when (as in

[1] See page 222 above.

1864) composers of the type of A. Bazzini and F. Faccio, and later G. Martucci (piano quintet!) win the awards, it must be admitted that the Italians displayed keen insight in their selection of the works, and did not allow themselves to be led astray by grandiloquent phrases and academic veneering.

The Milanese Quartet, from the outset, purposefully divided its interest between chamber-music and the symphony. This was not difficult, as Milan had a superfluity of good musicians. Nevertheless, and although this Società[1] numbered, even in 1867, 155 *soci protettori*, 28 *soci ordinari* and 45 *soci corrispondenti*, or 230 in all, it languished for some years; indeed, for a time it lay as in a trance. Otherwise the Gazz. Mus. (1887, p. 123) would not have said: "The Società del Quartetto, dormant for some time, is at present giving signs of renewed life, thanks to the exertions of its meritorious president, Count Giorgio Belgiojoso."

All in all, the Gazzetta generally observed a friendly attitude toward the Society, though once in a while it might grumble about the tendency to favor German instrumental music, and call attention to sundry obscure Italian classicists known to the Gazzetta itself only on paper.

However, the united efforts of the Società and the Conservatorio, which latter did a great deal to elevate the Milanese taste by means of its artistic *saggi* (student-concerts), helped bridge over the period of stagnation. In the middle of the 'seventies Milan was already but little behind most of the northern cities, at least in the quality of the programs. From Haydn down to Raff, Rubinstein and Wagner, the entire literature of the Germans was presented to the public. The Gazzetta Musicale, which as late as 1866 reproached the Florentines with "concertomania" because of their handful of concerts (No. 34), complained in 1875 (No. 15) that

[2] According to the Gazz. Mus. di Milano.

the symphony evenings of the Milan Società were only three or four in number yearly, instead of at least twenty. Finally, with the growing membership and consequent increase in funds, it became possible to engage the most famous artists on either side of the Alps, like Rubinstein, Piatti, von Bülow, Saint-Saëns, Wilhelmj, Joachim, etc.

G. Andreoli, the noted pianist, now (in 1876) entered the arena with his "Popular Concerts"—a series of six, on an average, for chamber music, and as many for symphonic works. He did not allow himself to be disconcerted by the light attendance,[1] nor did he "water" his programs, but endeavored to carry his audiences as far as Brahms (1879, B♭ major symphony). And after the La Scala orchestra and that of Turin had won high renown in Paris in 1878, the local pride of the Milanese attained to such a pitch that Giulio Ricordi ventured next year to organize the Società Orchestrale del Teatro della Scala, giving four (later six) annual orchestral concerts under F. Faccio. Ricordi, as the sworn enemy of the "avveniristi," and (of course) an equally fanatical partisan of Italian music, so arranged the programs of his Society as to contrast with those of the Quartetto. At the outset they were almost exclusively national in character. For example, the second La Scala concert (with the coöperation of M. Roeder), on April 18, 1880, presented the names of Bazzini, Palestrina, Ronchetti, Cherubini, Lotti, Verdi (Paternoster and Ave Maria, as novelties), Stradella, and Rossini. But in the selfsame year German influence broke through this barrier, too, with the *Tannhäuser* overture.

Thus the La Scala concerts might have formed a brilliant complement to those of the Quartetto. But this latter thought best to avoid competition, and thenceforth contented itself with two symphony evenings.

[1] The Gazz. Mus. di Milano (1878, p. 23), said: "As an entrance-fee is charged for these concerts—a mere trifle, but still an entrance-fee—few persons attend them." Tickets for the whole cycle cost from 12 to 20 lire!

Now, one would suppose that the Milanese, in order to enjoy at least some little symphony music, would have fairly besieged the La Scala concerts.   Not a bit of it; for in 1881 the Orchestra Society found itself obliged, for lack of subscribers, to suspend its evening concerts until 1882, when it recommenced with a fair prospect of success.

Turin owes the renascence of absolute music foremostly to Count Marmorito, Count Franchi-Vernay (Ippolito Valetta), and Carlo Pedrotti, the founders (1866) of the Società del Quartetto, and (1870) of the Concerti Popolari.   The Turin Quartet (leader, Augusto Ferni), although doing admirable work from the start, has never been esteemed according to its deserts.   On the other hand, Pedrotti succeeded in training his orchestra so well that in the orchestral competition at the Paris Exposition of 1878 they triumphantly carried off the prize.   The brightest page in the recent musical history of Turin was written in the year 1884.   The Turin Exhibition then assembled six prominent Italian orchestras—those of Turin, under F. Faccio (Pedrotti had assumed the management of the Liceo Rossini at Pesaro in 1882), of Milan, also under Faccio, of Naples, under Martucci, of Bologna, under Mancinelli, of Rome, under Ettore Pinelli, and of Parma, under Cleofonte Campanini.   Since then, musical activity has somewhat subsided in Turin, it is said.

This note on Turin affords a striking proof, I think, of the more active cultivation of absolute music in Italy.   In 1850 a competition between six well-trained orchestras would have been beyond the bounds of possibility.   Any one who, moreover, compares the volumes of the Gazzetta Musicale from 1850-1865 with those from 1865-1880, will hardly be able to deny an advance.   Everywhere the stirring of a fuller musical life.   Even towns from which only operas were formerly reported, are now frequently represented by classical chamber music. Such cities as Siena begin to organize orchestral societies, and the number of concerts continually increases.

While Rome, Turin, Naples (where matters musical revolved about G. Martucci and Beniamino Cesi), Milan and Florence move but slowly, or by fits and starts, along this upstriving path, one city which had been left far in the rear in a short time overtook the majority of the others—the same city which had unexpectedly done pioneer work for Wagnerian art. I mean Bologna.

A Quartet Society was not organized there until 1879. It began its public career with an orchestral concert under Mancinelli on Nov. 24, producing works by Mozart, Weber, Mendelssohn and Liszt. This in itself showed that "the wind blew from another quarter" in Bologna, as Corrado Ricci rightly observed with pride.[1]

On Jan. 11, 1880, followed the first chamber-music concert of the celebrated "Bolognese Quartet" with the same eminent personnel of which it is still constituted to-day—the professors Sarti, Massarenti, Consolini, and Serato (father of the violin-virtuoso). In 1886 Mancinelli made way for Martucci as director of the Society, and this consummate artist and sound musician (born in Capua, 1856) was yet more adroit than his predecessor in initiating his audiences, by cautious progress through simpler works, into the mysteries of even Brahms' symphonies. One adventitious circumstance also helped to overcome the indifference of the higher circles; as at Rome, in 1870, the Queen brought about a more numerous and fashionable attendance at these concerts by displaying her strong interest in them during the Bolognese Exhibition of 1888.

Martucci's chief concern is divided between Beethoven, Schumann and Wagner. It is significant that the one-

<hr/>

[1] Introductory remarks on "Società del Quartetto in Bologna. I primi cento concerti (1879-1896)"; Azzoguidi, Bologna, 1897.

hundredth concert was wholly devoted to works by the
Master of Bonn. As for that, he has better success
with Beethoven than with Schumann and Wagner;
indeed, as a Beethoven conductor he need fear no rival.
More especially the Ninth Symphony, which has fas-
cinated him, and through him the Bolognese, can hardly
receive a more thoughtful, thrilling and Beethovenish
interpretation than at Martucci's hands.

And still, I find fault with one thing, namely, the
arrangement of the programs. True, considering the
limited average number of seven (4 : 3) concerts, not
everything can be included; and 337 works by 68 composers during the period from 1879 to 1886 is a comparatively acceptable record. But these programs bear
witness to a questionable Teutomania; and but little
is done for the younger Italian generation. There may
be good reasons for passing over the younger Germans.[1]
The public could scarcely be expected to relish them.
But it should be the duty of the Society to aid the rising
talent of the country. Possibly the Directorate asks,
Where are they? Well, that would soon be seen if an
opportunity were presented them of having their works
performed by the Società del Quartetto—an opportunity
roundly denied them, by the way, in §18 of its by-laws:
*Nei concerti si eseguisce soltanto musica di maestri antichi
e moderni saliti in fama.* (In the concerts shall be performed only works by early and modern masters who
have won renown.) But even Italian masters who have
won recognition, like Cherubini, Sgambati, Bazzini,
Martucci, appear only semi-occasionally, while Enrico
Bossi, Sinigaglia and Zuelli are conspicuous by their
absence. And where are the Italian classicists from
1650 to 1750?! A few names such as L. Leo, Corelli,
Marcello, Scarlatti, Sacchini, Sammartini, Stradella,

---

[1] Even Richard Strauss did not get a hearing at the "Four-Nations' Concerts"
(which were intentionally arranged *modernissime*) of 1898, among Italians, Eng-
lishmen, French-Belgians, and Germans—as which last Franz Liszt and Dvořák
figured, instead!

Veracini—these can certainly afford no adequate presentation of this great epoch, which has a significance, for Italy, on a par with the period from 1750 to 1850 for Germany;—an epoch, a general familiarity with which would assuredly be worth more to Italians than dozens of concerts producing works by German masters exclusively.

Let us see how chamber and orchestral music fared, outside of Bologna, toward the turn of the century. The following details will tend to show that the upward trend has not yet come to a standstill.

In 1893 the Royal Institute of Music in Florence,[1] recognizing the necessity of neutralizing the prevalent Teutomania by an exhibition of specifically Tuscan classic compositions, arranged three historical concerts. From the fourteenth to the eighteenth century were selected works by Landino, Corteccia, Malvezzi, Animuccia, Bottegari, Peri, Gagliano, Vitali, Cesti, Lulli, Pasquini, Clari, Veracini, Rutini, Nardini, Boccherini and Cherubini; nineteenth-century compositions by Pacini, Gordigiani and Mabellini were performed. A similar series was brought out two years later by the Accademia di S. Cecilia at Rome. Needless to say that, besides this, the regular series of from eight to ten annual concerts were given as usual, not even shrinking from the expense of engaging, in 1896, the Halir and Rosé Quartets. The Società del Quartetto di Milano has likewise maintained its high level; the Società Orchestrale, in particular, presents model programs there,[2] for instance, that of 1896, bearing the names of Haydn, Tschaikowsky, Wagner, Beethoven, Grieg, Brahms, Schubert, Mancinelli, Girard, Saint-Saëns, Trucio, Ponchielli, Verdi.

---

[1] The "Atti" of this Institute, by the way, decidedly deserve more attention from historians of music, than these important publications have hitherto received.

[2] It should be mentioned, however, that Campanari had to make up a deficit of 10,000 lire after his Beethoven Cycle of 1899; which shows that sufficient support can be found for one such enterprise, but not for two.

In Naples, to be sure, the excellent Ferni Quartet ceased to exist, but maestro Rossomandi, far from being discouraged, organized the Neapolitan Orchestra in 1866, and thus hitched Naples again to the star of reform.

In the same year Rome records the foundation of the Gulli Quintet, which has rapidly attained to favorable recognition, and now probably has few superiors among ensemble associations. Certainly not with regard to its programs, on which one finds, for instance in the first two concerts in 1898, the names of Beethoven, Verdi, Brahms, Franck, Rubinstein and Sinding.

The Tiepoli Festivals in Venice in 1886 afforded Enrico Bossi an opportunity of displaying his "Trio," and the concerts of the Società Benedetto Marcello which he conducts, in a favorable light. The next year, maestri C. Boezio, L. E. Ferrari and E. Gilardini established a *Scuola di Pianoforte* for the purpose of giving model historical piano-recitals. In 1899 the Società Orchestrale Romana celebrated its twenty-fifth anniversary in brilliant style, which would hardly seem to indicate senility. Among other cities we may mention Palermo, where a Società del Quintetto was started in 1893; Brescia, which for almost thirty years—since Bazzini went to work there—has maintained a commanding position in the general uplift; Padua, whose "Trio," under the purposeful, refined and skillful leadership of C. Pollini, is winning new friends every year; Pesaro, where Mascagni energetically promotes the cause of modern music; and various other towns. In fine, any one who takes the trouble to run through the recent volumes of the Gazzetta Musicale, will be astonished at the remarkable increase in concerts of all kinds.

What a contrast between 1868 and 1898! At the former date the Roman and Florentine correspondents of the Gazzetta Musicale only now and then thought it necessary to chronicle a concert. To-day they admit their impotence to make head against the tidal wave of concerts, and find themselves obliged, by considerations of space, to neglect those of minor importance.

Furthermore, the *concorsi*, from the Piano-Étude (Florence, 1893; Golinelli) to the Requiem (Rome, R. Acc. Filarmonica, 1898), have multiplied rather than diminished. The Società del Quartetto di Milano, in particular, has faithfully clung to its old custom, having held its twenty-fifth *concorso* in 1894.[1] Equally faithful to its principles is the Cecilia Academy at Rome. Its *concorso* in 1894 called, *inter alia*, for an Overture in classic form; in 1895, for a Trio, and an Organ Sonata in three movements; in 1896-97, for an Overture (or Prelude for orchestra), a String-Quartet, and again an Organ Sonata, the exacting jury on awards not having been satisfied the year previous. Florestan Rossomandi, founder of the orchestra named after him in Naples, instituted two *concorsi* together in 1896, the one for an orchestral piece in one movement, the other for a symphony in classic form. Now, have not the *concorsi* met a genuine need? did not supply and demand stand in proper proportion to each other? had not serious chamber and symphony music even yet enlisted the interest of Italian composers?—If not, how can we explain the fact that in Turin, at the *concorso* of 1898 for a "Sinfonia o Suite," sixty-two scores were handed in, twenty-five of them being symphonies? or, at the *concorso* of the Società Orchestrale del Teatro alla Scala in 1895, that 223 works by 102 competitors were received?

But not all the manifestations of revival have yet been enumerated. I will barely refer to the congresses of Italian musicians in 1864 and 1881—something unheard-of in Italy; dwell for a moment on the organizing of Musicians' Associations, such as the Società Nazionale Italiana di mutuo soccorso per gli Artisti di Teatro

---

[1] Prizes of 1000 and 500 lire for a Sonata for violin and piano in four movements. We make special mention of the victory of Guido Alberto Fano (of Bologna) in 1897, with a 'Cello Sonata, because this gifted composer will often call for notice in the future.

(Milanese Rules and Regulations of 1860, '75, '81), Società Italiana di mutuo soccorso fra i Professori d'Orchestra (Milan, 1885), Società Italiana di mutuo soccorso fra i Coristi (1885), etc.; and make special mention of the founding of the "Rivista Musicale Italiana" (Turin, Fratelli Bocca, 1894), and the Ricordi publication, "L'Arte Musicale in Italia." The guiding spirit of both is Luigi Torchi of Bologna. Remember, that since the discontinuance of the "Vierteljahrs-Schrift für Musikwissenschaft" not even Germany has possessed a musico-historical and musico-critical organ rivalling this Italian Rivista in importance. Consider that the other publication, no less vast in scope than the "Denkmäler deutscher Tonkunst" and the "Denkmäler der Tonkunst in Österreich," pursues the aim of revitalizing the musical art of Italy from the fifteenth century down to the present. Would such enterprises be possible in a country which was still grovelling in feeble, stolid self-complacency, instead of standing vigorously erect?

No! The revival in Italy's musical life can hardly be called in question after what precedes. Nevertheless, it has been done, notably by J. Valetta in an ingenious but, in my opinion, all too pessimistic essay, "La Musica Strumentale in Italia,"[1] and again in his article "Il basso livello del presente musicale, ecc.;"[2] also by E. di San Martino with his "Saggio sopra alcune cause di decadenza della musica italiana alla fine del secolo XIX" (Rome, Palma); and, finally, by G. Ferrero in his essay "Crisi Teatrali" (in the Rivista Mus. Ital., 1898, p. 604 et seq.). The last-named author voices this pessimism with peculiar vigor (on p. 606):

It induces a most melancholy mood to find oneself committed to the writing of an article on present conditions in Italian musical life. When we meditate upon it, we really do not know whether

[1] "Nuova Antologia," 1894, LIII.
[2] *Ibid.*, 1895, p. 772 et seq.

we ought to believe in an artistic future for this nation, once so abounding in men of genius, and hereafter probably not to be entirely sterile. But how can the genuine artist develop his abilities as matters stand at present? Italy's musical activities are concentrated almost exclusively on the theatre. The people love music only in the theatre and nowhere else. Church and instrumental music form the sole exceptions; exotic growths in a hothouse. The general public feels no keen desire for them, and accepts them quite passively and in small doses, just as if some painful sacrifice were involved.

A gloomier picture could scarce be drawn. But beneath it all one sees too clearly a comparison with Germany and other countries. No sensible person would ever think of putting Italy's musical status on a level with that of the other civilized lands. Such a comparison is not only unwarranted, but (as the quotation shows) is too inducive of melancholy. Thus one forfeits the joyous and daring spirit of a confident outlook on the future. If these skeptics, instead, had chosen to compare the musical life of Italy prior to 1850 with the period after that date, they could not have failed to perceive that many, very many improvements had taken place. And for all that they would not be obliged to swell the ridiculous chorus in which nearly all the Italian musical periodicals join: "We Italians were formerly the pioneers in music, as we again shall be in the future." A cheap expedient for disguising their decadence! But even the pessimists may, and should, feel a justifiable pride in what has been achieved. Then they would coöperate in the continuing uplift with a more cheerful and effective sense of power. The delight in music, the taste and talent for the interpretation of music, have not perished in Italy. Every one knows this, who has lived among the Italians. And if their manner of music-making differs materially from that of the Northerner, that in itself proves nothing to the disadvantage of either side. But have the Italians, in point of fact, lost their creative power? When, according to the statistical showing vouched for by G. Albinati, a nation

two-thirds the size of Germany produces 74 operas
and (as noted above) composes 223 symphonic works
for a single competition, all in one year (1897), it must
surely still be credited with an abundantly prolific vein.
Whether the blood pulsing in this vein is of fine quality,
is quite another question!

With regard to the operas, this question is readily
answered, for we know them. Who would venture to
deny that Mascagni, Leoncavallo and Puccini possess
talent?   But, having this "pretty talent," they are
unfortunately infected with the "French disease," as
Carducci wittily observed of Ferrari, the dramatist.
And the symphonists, the chamber-music writers? Well,
these we do not know. But it certainly would be strange
if the revival in Italian concert-life should not serve to
mature the germinal ideas, so to speak, for a new harvest.
Talents do not die out, unless the nation itself perish.
Matters depend on the more or less favorable conditions
of existence and the opportunities for self-expression.
And just these latter are not given the youth of Italy,
despite the numerous *concorsi!* I myself have dwelt
on the high value of these *concorsi* for Italy's musical
activities, so now I do not take exception to the institution itself, but to the manner of its application. The
sad fact is, that prize-compositions are played only
once or twice by the Società in question, thereafter
being laid at rest in the archives of said Società or some
drawer of the hapless-happy composer's. So it comes
that such works have neither the power nor the opportunity to win a wider hearing.

It were well if the quartet associations should decide
to abandon, first of all, their character as private clubs,
and then to moderate their Teutomania, so that more
Italian manuscripts might see the light. By such means
the interest in concert music might be carried down
among the people; for the upper ten thousand are not
invariably the real banner-bearers of progress. Above

all, however, it would soon be evident that plenty of symphonies and quartets are composed. In these spheres an unexpected increase in production would be seen. And it is more than probable that from among the mass of insignificant works destined for the dust-heap a certain number would emerge, worthy to be set alongside of those by Sgambati, Martucci and Bossi.

Who can say that the artistic revival of Italy would then not go hand in hand with her material progress? Who can say that Italy would not again become, even in music, one of the Great Powers?!

(Translated by Theodore Baker.)